# LiGHT on LiGHT

# LIGHT on LIGHT

Illuminations of the Gospel of Jesus Christ
from the Mystical Visions of the Venerable
Anne Catherine Emmerich

by HURD BARUCH

MAXKOL

Published by MaxKol Communications, Inc.
©2004 Hurd Baruch

ISBN: 0-9634307-2-6

Published in the United States of America

Copies of this book may be obtained by contacting:

MaxKol Communications
PO Box 606
Herndon, VA 20172
Telephone: (703) 421-1300, Fax: (703) 421-1133

website: www.MaxKol.org
e-mail: MaxKol@msn.com

With great care she opened the crown of thorns in the back and, with the assistance of others, removed it from Jesus' head. Some of the thorns had penetrated deeply, and that the removal of the crown might not by disturbing them enlarge the wounds, they had first to be cut off. The crown was deposited near the nails. Then with a pair of round, yellow pincers, Mary drew from the wounds the long splinters and sharp thorns still sunken in the Lord's head, and showed them sadly to the compassionate friends standing around.

—*The Life of Jesus Christ and Biblical Revelations*

Immersed in contemplation, she beheld the tabernacle door open and her Divine Betrothed issue from it under the form of a radiant youth. In His left hand, he held a garland, in His right a Crown of Thorns, which He graciously presented to her choice. She chose the Crown of Thorns. Then Jesus laid it lightly on her brow; and also, putting up both hands, pressed it firmly down. From that instant, she experienced inexpressible pains in her head.

—*The Life of Anne Catherine Emmerich*

To M.E.K.B.,
whose faith became mine

# CONTENTS

# INTRODUCTION

While the Gospels teach us all that is necessary about Jesus for our salvation, they don't begin to satisfy our curiosity about Jesus Himself—what He looked like, how He sounded, who His "brothers and sisters" were, what He said in private to His Mother, what He knew about Himself and His mission. And, they don't come close to relating all of what He said or did—facts which might help us to better understand and appreciate His Passion and death. As John, the Beloved Disciple, wrote at the end of his own Gospel:

> *There are, however, many other things that Jesus did; but if every one of these should be written, not even the world itself, I think, could hold the books that would have to be written. (John 21:25)*

Fortunately, there is a source for the reader who wants to know more about Jesus, but is not satisfied with works of fiction. That source is the mystical visions of persons entitled to veneration for their lives of demonstrated sanctity. One such person was Anna Katherina Emmerick (rendered in English as Anne Catherine Emmerich), a nun who lived in Germany two hundred years ago.

From her earliest childhood she had immense spiritual gifts which, for most of her life, were neither recognized nor admired. These included repeated visions of the entire history of Salvation beginning with the fall of the bad angels, the creation of the earth, and the original sin of Adam and Eve. Following that were visions of certain key events and people of the Old Testament, leading up to the Essene ancestors of St. Anne, the mother of the Blessed Virgin Mary. The closer the time to that of Jesus, the more extensive were her visions, and she was able to describe the three years of His public ministry almost day-by-day— everything from where He was, to who was with Him, what topics He preached on, what types of healings or other miracles He performed, how He was received, and what His enemies were doing to thwart Him.

Anne Catherine Emmerich grew up a peasant girl, almost without education, working on the farm and as a seamstress until, at age 28, she finally was allowed to enter an Augustinian convent in Dülmen. Her sisters in religion looked down on her for her poverty, extreme piety, and ill-health. By the time the convent was forcibly shut nine years later by the anti-clerical civil authorities, she was so physically ill that she was thereafter confined to a sick bed in spartan rented lodgings.

If she had neither seen nor related anything extraordinary, Sister Emmerich's life would still have been notable, for she was a stigmatic—a person marked supernaturally with the five wounds of Christ (hands, feet and side). In addition to these, she bore visible wounds in the form of a Crown of Thorns and two crosses on her body, and an invisible wound on her right shoulder (recalling the abrasion Christ had from carrying His cross). Bleeding from the visible marks was very pronounced during Lent and the penitential days on the Church's calendar.

She was observed to subsist for months at a time on no food at all, other than an occasional consecrated Host and teaspoon of beef tea. Whether awake or asleep—if her ecstatic state at night could be called sleep—she engaged in spiritual labors for sinners alive and dead, helping free the latter from Purgatory. Her vocation was to suffer for Christ and the Church,[1] and she embraced that vocation wholeheartedly, expressing dissatisfaction only that her marks were visible and that she had become, against her will, the object of public attention.

Her physical and mental sufferings were greatly intensified by the intrusive medical examinations repeatedly inflicted upon her by ecclesiastical and civil authorities, both of whom were disappointed that they could neither cure her nor prove her a fraud, and thus end the embarrassment which her stigmata caused them in that "enlightened" age. Since then, the Catholic Church has officially recognized her life of sanctity—wholly apart from the stigmata and visions—and has recently announced that all the requirements for her beatification (the last step before canonization), including approval of a miraculous healing attributed to her intercession, have been fulfilled.[2]

Sister Emmerich kept silent about her visions until her later years when she felt spiritually compelled to make them public: "I implored God to withdraw my visions, that I may be relieved of the responsibility of communicating them. In this also, I was not heard. I received, as usual, the injunction to relate what I could, even if I should be ridiculed for it, even if I saw no utility in it. I was told again that no one had ever had visions of the same kind or in the same measure as I; but it is not for myself, it is for the Church."[3]

She was fortunate enough to find as a scribe not a mere note taker but a noted German poet of the time, Clement Brentano, who put aside his own career to spend six years at her side, taking her dictations. He then faced several daunting problems in transcribing them, particularly the fact that her visions did not occur in chronological order, but rather, for the most part, were triggered by the date of a Church season or feast day observance, especially Christmas, Lent and Easter.

In addition, in her weakened state, what she had to say was fragmentary and unorganized, and, very infrequently, inconsistent on minor points. Brentano wound up with thousands of pages of notes, and the task of organizing and reconciling them proved to be too much for him: he died after having completed only one volume, The Dolorous Passion of Our Lord Jesus Christ. Four volumes titled The Life of Jesus Christ, and a single volume, The Life of the Blessed Virgin Mary, were completed years later by others. Many other visions appear in a two-volume biography, The Life of Anne Catherine Emmerich.

As is the case with almost all private revelations, the Catholic Church has not taken an official position on whether Sister Emmerich's visions are worthy of belief.[4] The Church always keeps in mind that the holiness of the recipient of a vision or locution is no guarantee that he or she did not err in what was perceived, or in how those perceptions were interpreted and then retransmitted by the recipient. For her part, Sister Emmerich did not claim that her visions had the accuracy of Scripture. According to Brentano's preface to his first edition of the Dolorous Passion, she herself considered her visions as having only "a human and defective value."[5]

Moreover, Clement Brentano at times inserted his own commentary, and, speaking of the compiled revelations as a whole, the dividing line between her revelations dictated in Low German and his rendering of them in elegant language is not always clear.

Nevertheless, the reader who immerses himself in the staggering wealth of detail of her visions will surely decide for himself that, in the main, their source could only have been divine revelation. And, a study of her visions reveals that they were truly original with her: they were not shaped, consciously or subconsciously by the fantastic, apocryphal legends which had become a vital part of European culture and popular piety during the Middle Ages and the Renaissance.[6] As a

point of validation, it should be mentioned that by following Sister
Emmerich's description, in 1891 two friars were able to locate the home
of the Blessed Virgin Mary in Ephesus, Turkey. The site subsequently
was officially approved as a place of pilgrimage by five Popes including
John Paul II, who has celebrated Mass there.[7]

Apart from satisfying one's hunger to learn more about Jesus, there
are three spiritual reasons to expose oneself to Sister Emmerich's
visions. The first is to employ in meditation their wealth of information
about the Holy Land in general, and about Jesus, His family, His
disciples, His travels, His words and in particular His miracles. Her
visions provide us with exciting insights into topics ranging from how
and when Jesus called His disciples to the vital role played by the Holy
Women in His ministry, and from His teachings on marriage and
prayer to a description of how He celebrated the Last Supper.

The second reason is to comprehend with new eyes the totality
of Jesus' mission and the price He paid to accomplish it. We cannot
appreciate the full extent of what Jesus did for the Jewish people,
ministering to them in every corner of their land, and also how he
brought the good news to the gentiles, except by reading her day-to-
day description of His public ministry. The handful of miracles
recounted in the Gospels are not even a "drop in the bucket." Nor can
we appreciate just how vicious and widespread was the enmity against
Him organized by certain religious leaders in Jerusalem during the
whole of His ministry, or how horrible were the tortures that He
willingly endured, save by reading her depiction of them.

Thirdly—Sister Emmerich's visions fill, rather than empty, the
figure of Jesus Christ. They fully confirm the Gospels' depiction of
Jesus. By supplementing, and at times harmonizing the Gospels, her
visions reinforce the reader's belief that the Evangelists did indeed speak
the truth. No one who meditates on her revelations will fall prey to the
current portrayals of Jesus as a wandering country rabbi, who made
believers with conjurer's tricks (not miracles), and who was Himself
unaware of having a supernatural birth, divine nature, and salvific
mission, and a predestined Passion, Death and Resurrection.[8]

[1] For a good summary of the Catholic Church's teachings about the role of redemptive suffering, *see* Pope John Paul II, *On the Christian Meaning of Human Suffering (Salvifici Doloris)*, Apostolic Letter (Feb. 11, 1984). http://www.vatican.va/holy_father/john_paul_ii/apost_letters/documents/hf_jp-ii_apl_11021984_salvific-doloris_en.html.

[2] *See* "German Mystic Anna Katharina Emmerick to Be Raised to the Altar," *Zenit News Agency* (July 7, 2003). http://www.zenit.org/english/visualizza. phtml?sid=39572. (accessed October 2003). For background information on her cause, *see* three articles by Samuel Sinner in the weekly newspaper *The Wanderer:* "Some Further Perspectives on Anne Catherine Emmerich" (March 1, 2001), http://www.petersnet.net; "Decree Proclaiming Anne Catherine Emmerich's 'Heroic Virtue' Promulgated in the Vatican" (March 17, 2001); "Anne Catherine Emmerich's Beatification Case Moves Forward" (April 12, 2001).

[3] C. E. Schmöger, *The Life of Anne Catherine Emmerich*, v. 2, 610 (Rockford, IL: TAN Books and Publishers 1976).

[4] The Catholic Church teaches that private revelations "do not belong to the deposit of faith. It is not their role to improve or complete Christ's definitive Revelation, but to help live more fully by it in a certain period of history." *See Catechism of the Catholic Church*, (New Hope, KY: Urbi et Orbi Communications 1994, as modified 1998) § 67. http://www.christusrex.org. For an extensive discussion of the theological status and anthropological structure of private revelations, *see* Vatican Congregation for the Doctrine of the Faith, "The Message of Fatima," *Origins*, 30 (July 6, 2000) 113, 120–22. http://www.cin.org/docs/message-fatima.html. *See also*, the entry for "Private Revelations" in *The Catholic Encyclopedia*. http://www.newadvent.org/cathen. An excellent spiritual guide for persons interested in private revelations is, *A Still, Small Voice—A Practical Guide on Reported Revelations* (San Francisco: Ignatius Press 1993), by Benedict J. Groeschel.

[5] *See* Anne C. Emmerich, *The Life of the Blessed Virgin Mary*, (Rockford, IL: TAN Books 1970) viii (quoting from Brentano's preface to *The Dolorous Passion*).

[6] Numerous spurious writings were attributed to Jesus' disciples or friends, for example the so-called "Gospels" of Peter, Thomas and the Nazoraeans. Most of these were used by *heretical* sects. As one scholar recently commented: "Far from being the alternative voices of Jesus' first followers, most of the lost gospels should rather be seen as the writings of much later dissidents who broke away from an already established orthodox church." *See* Philip Jenkins, *The Hidden Gospels—How the Search for Jesus Lost Its Way* (New York: Oxford U. Press 2001) 12. They do not appear in our Bibles because the Church (at a time when it was still united) carefully sifted these works, found them not to be authentic, and barred them from the "canon" that Christians today still recognize as the "New Testament." These "apocrypha" contain at most a borrowed glimmer of divine truth amidst a profusion of ridiculous human inventions.

7 *See* Farley Clinton, "Pope Encourages Pilgrimages to Mary's House in Turkey," *The Wanderer* (January 25, 2001), http://www.petersnet.net; Pauly Fongemie, "The Discovery of Mary's House in Ephesus." http://www.catholictradition.org/ephesus.

8 TAN Books and Publishers, Inc., Rockford, IL has published the following books of visions of Sister Emmerich, which the reader of this volume is encouraged to explore: *The Life of Jesus Christ and Biblical Revelations*, vols. 1–4 (1979 & 1986); *The Dolorous Passion of Our Lord Jesus Christ* (1968); *The Life of the Blessed Virgin Mary* (1970). The *Dolorous Passion* is a shortened form of the Passion, Death and Resurrection story found in volume 4 of *The Life of Jesus Christ*. The *Dolorous Passion* is available online at http://www.emmerich1.com, as is a short biography, *Life of Venerable Anne Catherine Emmerich*. Many additional visions are contained in the two volume biography, *The Life of Anne Catherine Emmerich*, by Carl E. Schmöger, published by TAN Books, in 1976. *See also* the entry for "Ven. Anne Catherine Emmerich," in *The Catholic Encyclopedia*. http://www.newadvent.org/cathen.

*The scenes of the life of Christ set forth in this book, and the directly quoted passages, come from the four volume Life of Jesus Christ and Biblical Revelations, unless otherwise indicated, for example by a reference to Scripture.*

# CHAPTER ONE

Jesus, a prophet of God, appeared in Judea crying "Woe to Jerusalem!" — " Woe to the Temple!" — "Woe to the people!" The country was restive under Roman rule, but it was a time of prosperity, and the leaders of the Jewish people were infuriated by the dire and unsettling prophecies of this man of low estate, who lacked religious credentials. They had him beaten, then turned him over to the Roman authorities for more severe punishment. The procurator demanded to know, "Who are you?" and, "From whence have you come?" Jesus made no answer. The Romans scourged him to the bone; still, he would not ask for mercy, nor would he change his proclamation. And so, the procurator was forced to decide whether to nail Jesus to a cross in order to put an end to the civil commotion he was causing.

*Concluding that Jesus was only a madman, the procurator released him. . . .*

That is not the story we are used to hearing—but the ending is not a fiction to shock the reader. The story is about another Jesus, the son of Ananus, and a procurator named Albinus, at a time thirty-odd years after Jesus of Nazareth was crucified by Pontius Pilate.[1]

Why was one Jesus killed and the other spared? Was one more of a danger to Rome than the other? Although one scholar has gone so far as to speculate that Jesus of Nazareth mounted an open revolt against the Jewish and Roman authorities,[2] there is no evidence whatsoever that this Jesus or His followers attempted to take over the Temple by force or in any way took part in an insurrection. That would have been completely contrary to all of His ethical prescriptions, and it certainly is something which would have been noted in secular sources at the time such as the writings of Josephus, as well as in Rabbinic sources.

In fact, it must have been clear to Pilate that Jesus of Nazareth was no threat to him personally, or to Caesar, or to Rome—else Pilate would not have repeatedly resisted the calls for Jesus' death, proposing instead to release Him, as is set forth in St. John's Gospel. After all, Jesus did not preach resistance to the Roman government; He did not advocate the nonpayment of taxes; and, as St. John also recorded, He told Pilate that "my kingdom does not belong to this world." He might reasonably have been viewed as a madman who disturbed the peace, but that was not a sufficient a reason for the Romans to crucify a man, as they showed in their handling of Jesus, son of Ananus.

### Who Was to Blame for the Death of Jesus?

Trying to ascertain *why* Jesus of Nazareth met the violent and disgraceful end He did is a difficult and sensitive task because a determination of causal responsibility can readily be confused with—or lead to—a judgment about moral guilt. We understand the distinction between responsibility and guilt, and we apply it every day in our courts: the fact that one man kills another does not by itself make him a criminal, or even answerable in a civil suit for wrongful death. We look to whether the person who caused the death had a privilege to act as he did—for example, a policeman defending himself against an armed felon—and what his state of mind was—for example, did he specifically intend to cause the other's death?, and were there mitigating circumstances? News reporters go out of their way to avoid imputing guilt before trial, resulting at times in absurd TV bulletins about "alleged incidents," in which participants are called "alleged suspects" or "alleged victims, allegedly shot."

And yet, when it comes to the case of Jesus of Nazareth, *without being able to examine and cross-examine a single one of the witnesses*, we are tempted to decide the moral guilt of those involved and even of people in some way related to them who are living today, 2000 years later.

In assessing the blame for the Crucifixion of Jesus, the Catholic Church has taught explicitly *for more than 400* years that: "We must regard as guilty all those who continue to relapse into their sins. Since our sins made the Lord Christ suffer the torment of the cross, those who plunge themselves into disorders and crimes crucify the Son of God anew in their hearts (for he is in them) and hold him up to contempt. *And it can be seen that our crime in this case is greater in us than in the Jews.* As for them, according to the witness of the Apostle, 'None of the rulers of this age understood this; for if they had, they would not have crucified the Lord of glory.' We, however, profess to know him. And when we deny him by our deeds, we in some way seem to lay violent hands on him."[3]

Obviously, this teaching of the Church was not always observed by Christians interacting with Jews. In a further attempt to eliminate the charge of deicide from popular discourse, and the sort of injustices to the Jewish people which occurred at the hands of Christians ostensibly on account of the mistreatment of Jesus of Nazareth, the Catholic Church now teaches that:

> The historical complexity of Jesus' trial is apparent in the Gospel accounts. *The personal sin of the participants (Judas, the Sanhedrin, Pilate) is known to God alone. Hence we cannot lay responsibility for the trial on the Jews in Jerusalem as a whole*, despite the outcry of a manipulated crowd and the global reproaches contained in the apostles' calls to conversion after Pentecost. Jesus himself, in forgiving them on the cross, and Peter in following suit, both accept "the ignorance" of the Jews in Jerusalem and even of their leaders. *Still less can we extend responsibility to other Jews of different times and places*, based merely on the crowd's cry: "His blood be on us and on our children!" a formula for ratifying a judicial sentence.[4]

The visions of Sister Emmerich are squarely in accord with these teachings of the Church. *She saw Jesus on His knees in the Garden of Olives, contemplating His imminent Crucifixion as being necessary to satisfy the demands of His Father for justice with regard to the sins of all mankind throughout all time, including the sins of those who were or would later be His followers.*

It is with this framework in mind that we now consider Sister Emmerich's visions which illuminate the Gospel accounts of the life and death of Jesus of Nazareth, the Christ.[5]

## Simeon's Prophecy of Rejection

Not long after Jesus was born in Bethlehem, His Mother and foster father, Joseph, took Him up to the Temple in Jerusalem. According to the Gospel of Luke, it had been divinely revealed to an aged priest, Simeon by name, that Jesus was to be the Messiah—the Anointed One who was to save Israel. And so, Simeon took the infant in his arms and thanked God that he had seen "a light of revelation to the gentiles, and a glory for thy people, Israel." But then, instead of waxing eloquent about those glories to come with the Messiah, as prophets of old had done, Simeon uttered this bittersweet prophecy:

> Behold, this child is destined for the fall and for the rise of many in Israel, and for a sign that shall be contradicted. And

thy own soul a sword shall pierce, that the thoughts of many
hearts may be revealed.

The prophecy was in fact fulfilled, as to Jesus, His Mother, and
His countrymen. The story of how that came to pass begins with His
only other notable appearance in public before He entered upon His
ministry at the age of thirty.

### What and Why Did Young Jesus Teach in the Temple?

St. Luke mentioned that, as a twelve-year-old, Jesus taught in the
Temple in Jerusalem, the center of Jewish worship. Jesus had gone up
to the Temple yearly with His Mother and Joseph since the age of
eight, and had attracted attention due to His piety and intelligence.
This time, hardly had the return journey begun when Jesus slipped
away to the inn where the Holy Family had stayed at the time of His
presentation. He was not missed at first because a group of pilgrims
from Nazareth was traveling together, and He usually was with boys
His own age. It was not until the caravan stopped at Gophna (Ophni)
that Mary and Joseph realized He was not in the party. On each of
the three days that they searched for Him, Jesus attended a different
religious school in Jerusalem with boys of His acquaintance. The third
day, He appeared in the Temple itself.

The focus of St. Luke's account was the interaction between Jesus
and His Mother *following* His teaching, when she reproached Him
for worrying herself and Joseph, and He surprised her with His
explanation that He had to be in His (true) Father's house. For St.
Luke, the significance of the episode was that Jesus already, at that age,
understood His calling. As to what had occurred, the Evangelist said
only that Mary and Joseph found Him "in the midst of the teachers,
listening to them and asking them questions. All who heard him were
amazed at his intelligence and his answers."

According to the Arabic Infancy Gospel, which is an apocryphal
gospel not part of the Bible,[6] Jesus displayed great wisdom by teaching
on a variety of topics, and the occasion was an unqualified triumph.
Supposedly, when His mother Mary finally appeared, the scribes and
Pharisees lauded the excellence of Jesus' commentaries, and called her
blessed for having brought forth such a son.

But, that is not how Sister Emmerich saw the event. According
to her, by His questions and answers in the schools, Jesus had
embarrassed the teachers, and they had resolved to humble Him by
putting Him on display in a public forum, where He would be
confronted by experts in all branches of learning. So, in a lecture hall,

in the middle of the Temple porch, they seated Jesus in the large teacher's chair, and surrounded Him with learned men in priestly robes: "They now began, one by one, to dispute with Him. He remarked that although, properly speaking, such subjects did not appear appropriate to the Temple, yet He would discuss them since such was His Father's will. But they understood not that He referred to His Heavenly Father; they imagined that Joseph had commanded Him to show off His learning.

"Jesus now answered and taught on medicine. He described the whole human body in a way far beyond the reach of even the most learned. He discoursed with the same facility upon astronomy, architecture, agriculture, geometry, arithmetic, jurisprudence and, in fine, upon every subject proposed to Him. He applied all so skillfully to the Law and the Promise, to the Prophecies, to the Temple, to the mysteries of worship and sacrifice that *His hearers, surprised and confounded, passed successively from astonishment and admiration to fury and shame. They were enraged at hearing some things that they never before knew, and others that they had never before understood.*"

It is hard for us in our day and age to appreciate exactly how devastating the event was to those in attendance, given the religion and culture of that time. There was twelve-year-old Jesus, in the midst of the elders of His people—men renowned for their wisdom, their knowledge of the Law, and their devotion to God and the Jewish religion—yet He did not sit humbly at their feet as their disciple. *He* was the one who was seated in the "teacher's chair," from whence He contradicted their doctrines, and explained facts about the universe and even about the Law which were unknown to them. What was worse, He did so as one having superior authority!

They might have reflected upon the epiphany they had just witnessed—the breaking forth of divine wisdom through the mouth of young Jesus—just as it had through the mouth of young Daniel centuries before, confounding the elders of the people, when they had erroneously condemned a woman to death.[7] But, Jesus was an egregious affront to their pride, and it is very understandable that they could not bring themselves to thank God for what they had heard, and contemplate the possibility that they had seen the future hope of Israel.

The question is—why did Jesus do it, if the predictable outcome was to antagonize His elders? And why, as Sister Emmerich related, did Jesus recall to them this maddening experience when He finally came forth, years later, to teach in earnest?

*The answer, which she heard from His mouth, was that His early display of supernatural wisdom was, like the visit of the Magi, intended as a "sign"—a sign that the Messiah was at hand, even in their very midst. A sign which eventually they would have to come to grips with, and either accept that they "had a greater than Solomon here" or deny Him.*

## What Did Jesus Know and How Did He Know It?

Some would dismiss Sister Emmerich's account of Jesus' teaching in the Temple out of hand, as showing divine wisdom which no child of twelve could possibly have had—even Jesus. The issue of what Jesus knew, and how He came to know it, is one which we have to resolve, because it is vitally important to accepting many of His sayings in the Gospels. It came to the fore for His own contemporaries as soon as Jesus began to teach in the synagogue of Nazareth. His fellow townspeople could not understand how He had become so wise, for they knew that He had neither gone to Jerusalem to study in a religious school, nor traveled or engaged in any notable undertaking to gain worldly experience. As St. Mark wrote, they asked each other—sometimes innocently and sometimes sarcastically—"Where did he get all this? What is this wisdom that is given to him?"

These are questions which commentators still ask, often in the context of analyzing the verse from St. Luke's Gospel which recounted that, after teaching in the Temple, Jesus went back with His Mother and foster-father to Nazareth, where He "advanced in wisdom and age and grace before God and men." Some commentators have suggested that this passage, as well as the questions which Jesus asked of people during His ministry, show that Jesus had only human knowledge, and that His intellectual abilities grew as He matured, albeit remaining within the bounds of His humanity.

However, an orthodox theologian who has carefully considered the issue of the "consciousness" of Jesus rejects the suggestion that Jesus was limited by His human brain and what He learned from His five senses, explaining instead that Jesus had "two *channels* of knowledge, divine and human." Thus, St. Luke's comment that Jesus grew in wisdom should be taken to mean that He grew "in knowledge acquired via the human channel," or "in the manifestation of wisdom to men."[8]

Scriptural verses which show Jesus asking questions do not prove any ignorance of facts on His part. When Jesus posed a question such as, "Who touched my clothing?," or He asked Martha whether she believed that He was "the resurrection and the life," the fact that He asked the question no more showed a lack of knowledge about external facts or the person's interior thoughts than did God's questions (to Adam) "Adam, where are you?," (to Cain) "Where is your brother Abel?," and (to Eve) "Why did you do such a thing?"[9] Both God and Jesus must have known the answers to their questions, but asked them anyway for the purpose of drawing forth a vocal response, to facilitate teaching a lesson. *As will be set forth herein, Sister Emmerich's visions show that Jesus was always possessed of Divine wisdom.*

### Who Did Jesus Claim to Be?

From time to time, writers have attempted to depict Jesus as merely a wandering rabbi—not only somewhat ignorant of earthly learning, but also having no knowledge that He was the Messiah, much less that He was divine.[10] They have, to begin with, run up against the fact that Jesus, from very early on in His dealings with His disciples, used the phrase "the Son of Man" to refer to himself. Despite the eschatological connotations of the term which many readers of the Bible assume it then had based on how it was apparently used in the Book of Daniel, scholars have opined that in the ordinary speech of that time, "Son of Man" could have been used by Jesus merely like the word "myself" or the phrase "*a* son of *men*," with no special overtones identifying Himself as the Anointed One.[11]

Even if we lay aside His use of the phrase "Son of Man" as being ambiguous, and even though in most situations He refused to answer the question of whether He was the Messiah, it is clear that on other occasions He did indeed claim to be God's Son in a very unique way (*e.g.*, "No one knows the Father except the Son"), and also that He asserted His divinity in these words (from the Gospel of St. John and the Book of Revelation):

~ The Father and I are one.

~ You will surely die in your sins unless you come to believe that I AM.

~ I have come down from heaven.

~ I solemnly declare it: before Abraham came to be, I AM.

~ I am the Alpha and the Omega, the First and the Last.

Most Protestants have no trouble in deciding for themselves that these words mean exactly what they seem to, and Catholics are assured by Pope John Paul II that: "The church has no doubt that the evangelists in their accounts, and inspired from on high, have correctly understood in the words which Jesus spoke the truth about his person and his awareness of it. . . . There is no doubt that already in his historical existence Jesus was aware of his identity as the Son of God. John emphasizes this to the point of affirming that it was ultimately because of this awareness that Jesus was rejected and condemned."[12] *The visions of Sister Emmerich are completely in accordance with the teaching that Jesus always knew that He was the Messiah and "true God from true God," as the Nicene Creed states.*

## The Holy Family's Life in Nazareth

For 18 years, the Light of the World, which had flashed so briefly but brilliantly in the Temple, remained hidden under a bushel basket. Jesus lived in the obscurity of Nazareth, in a small house with his Mother and foster-father. As seen by Sister Emmerich, Mary sewed or knitted when alone, sitting on the ground with her feet crossed under her in her room. There she was joined by Joseph and Jesus, a devout and contemplative child, for the Holy Family's prayers. Jesus was cheerful and helpful to all, working with Joseph at his light carpentry work, such as constructing room dividers and furniture, in their house and in a shop outside the city walls.

Jesus' playmates in Nazareth were four sons of an Essene family related to Joachim, Jesus' late grandfather. These boys eventually became disciples of John the Baptist and, when John was killed, of Jesus Himself; one of them was Cleophas, who accompanied St. Luke on the road to Emmaus after the Resurrection. The Holy Family and other pious people such as this family made annual visits together to the Temple, to the cave of the prophet Elijah on Mount Carmel, and to a massive old pine-tree near the Cave of the Nativity outside Bethlehem (commemorating Abraham's meeting there with Melchizedek).

In His earlier years, Jesus was thought well of and held up by the townspeople as an example for their own children. However, they later came to be annoyed at His holiness, and He was persecuted beginning when He was twenty. According to Sister Emmerich: "They could not bear the sight of Him. Their jealousy often made them exclaim that the carpenter's son thought He knew every thing better than others, that He was frequently at variance with the teachings of the Pharisees, and that He always had around Him a crowd of young followers." Thus, He continued to be a sign of contradiction.

## Who Were the "Brothers and Sisters" of Jesus?

All four Evangelists (Matthew, Mark, Luke and John) mentioned that Jesus had "brothers," sometimes identified as James, Joseph (or Joses, the Greek form of Joseph), Simon, and Judas. St. Mark recorded a challenge to Him issued by the townspeople of Nazareth implying that He had "sisters" as well. These passages have given rise to a point of contention between Catholics, Eastern Orthodox and Protestants.

The latter believe that the mother of Jesus had several children,[13] a belief taught by a heretical sect during the first few centuries but condemned by the Council of Capua when the Church was still united, in 392 A.D.[14] The Eastern Orthodox faith teaches that there were *half*-brothers and sisters of Jesus—children of Joseph from a first marriage not mentioned in the Gospels. And the Catholic Church teaches that the Blessed Virgin Mary was perpetually a virgin, both before and after the birth of Jesus; intimations in the Gospels—in questions by *un*believers—that Jesus had "brothers" and "sisters," were, in accordance with the usage of the language at that time, references to people whom we would identify as "cousins."[15]

Some scholars recently claimed that the hypothesis that Jesus had true brothers was supported by the discovery of a stone ossuary (a container used to store skeletal remains after the body had decomposed) with the following inscription, ostensibly dating from the period 20 B.C.–70 A.D.: "Jacob [James], son of Joseph, brother of Jesus."[16] However, their assertion was improbable on its face,[17] and the inscription on the ossuary has since been determined to be a forgery.[18]

Thanks to the very detailed genealogical information provided by Sister Emmerich, the controversy over Jesus' relations can be resolved, if her visions are credited. Sister Emmerich's visions confirm that Jesus had no natural or step-brothers or sisters. His nominal "brothers and sisters" were indeed what we would call cousins, related to Jesus through the Blessed Virgin Mary's older sister, Mary Heli, or more distantly through her mother, Anne, or her father, Joachim. Specifically, they were:

- ~ sons of Mary Heli, viz., Sadoch, Jacob (or James), and Heliachim (all Jesus' first cousins, who followed John the Baptist before they followed Jesus);
- ~ the daughter of Mary Heli, viz., Mary Cleophas (Jesus' first cousin);
- ~ Mary Cleophas' sons and daughter by her first husband, Alphaeus, viz., James the Lesser, Simon Zelotes,[19] Jude Thaddeus, and Suzanne (all first cousins of Jesus, once-removed); and
- ~ Mary Cleophas' son by her second husband, Sabas, viz., Joses Barsabas (a first cousin, once-removed).

Sister Emmerich also noted the relationships of many other important people mentioned in the Gospels, such as the son of the Widow of Nain, and the Apostles (she recounted that all except Thomas and Judas Iscariot were related in some degree to Jesus).[20]

## The Holy Death of St. Joseph

According to Sister Emmerich, when Jesus was thirty, Joseph, then about 75 years old, experienced a holy death in Mary's arms, with Jesus by his side and angels in attendance. As would happen to the body of His foster-son three years later, Joseph's remains were laid in a beautiful tomb provided as an act of charity by a good man. In her visions, Sister Emmerich also saw Joseph's body, incorrupt, finally interred by Christians in his native town of Bethlehem.

---

[1] *See* Flavius Josephus, *War of the Jews*, at 6.5.3. http://www.ccel.org/j/josephus/works/war. Josephus was a Jewish leader in the revolt against Rome; before the bitter end, he was captured and went over to the Roman side. He lived to write histories of the war and of his people. *See* the entry for "Josephus" in *The Anchor Bible Dictionary*, (New York: Doubleday 1992) 3:981.
[2] *See* S.G.F. Brandon, *The Trial of Jesus of Nazareth*, (New York: Stein & Day 1968) 147. Another scholar suggested that Jesus had "performed some sort of subversive act that could have engendered a riot in the Temple at Passover." *See* John D. Crossan, *Who Killed Jesus?* (New York: HarperSanFrancisco 1996) 108. However, Crossan could not point to anything in the canonical Gospels as indicating that Jesus desired to, much less expressed an intent to, destroy the Temple. The only Gospel that has Jesus saying, *"I will destroy this Temple"* does not report those as Jesus' actual words, but as a *false* and inconsistent accusation about what He had said, made at His trial before the Sanhedrin. (Mk 14:57-59) Raymond E. Brown took the more modest position that "something done and/or said by Jesus prognostic of Temple/sanctuary destruction was at least a partial cause of the Sanhedrin's decision that lead to his death." *See* Raymond E. Brown, *The Death of the Messiah* (New York: Doubleday 1994) 1:458-60.
[3] *Catechism of the Catholic Church* § 598 (emphasis added)(quoting from the Catechism of the Council of Trent, which was issued by order of Pope Pius V in 1566).
[4] *See Catechism of the Catholic Church* § 597 (emphasis added). *See also,* Pope John Paul II, "The Death of Christ as a Historical Event," *The Pope Speaks* 33:4 (1988), Catechetical Address (Sept. 28, 1988).
[5] In the transcriptions of Sister Emmerich's visions, the term "the Jews" appears frequently, with its true meaning requiring a reference to the context. Usually when she used the term, it was simply to differentiate persons of the Jewish religion as a group from other peoples, especially the pagans, Samaritans and

Romans, who were living among them and interacting with them. At other times, the term appears to have had reference to some of the religious leaders of the Jewish people, especially the High Priests, or to those Jews who opposed Jesus. (In a similar vein, the Vatican Commission for Religious Relations With The Jews has stated that the use of the term "the Jews" in the Gospel of John is imprecise, and sometimes the context suggests that the Evangelist meant "the leaders of the Jews" or "the adversaries of Jesus." *See* "Guidelines and Suggestions for Implementing the Conciliar Declaration *Nostra Aetate*, No. 4" (Dec. 1, 1974).) http://www.bc.edu/research/cji/meta-elements/texts/documents/catholic/Vatican_Guidelines.htm. From the fact that Jesus and His Mother and ancestors, and His Apostles and initial supporters, were Jewish, it should be inferred that Sister Emmerich did not use the term pejoratively, but rather as a neutral descriptor. *Use of the term "the Jews" in this book is intended by the author to be a strictly neutral descriptor.*

[6] The apocryphal "gospels" are available in various collections, and also online in the library of the Gnostic Society. http://www.gnosis.org/library.

[7] *See* the Story of Susanna, which appears either as chapter 13 of the Book of Daniel, or as a separate deuterocanonical work. Carey A. Moore, *The Anchor Bible—Daniel, Esther and Jeremiah—the Additions* (Garden City, NY: Doubleday 1977) 77.

[8] William G. Most, *The Consciousness of Christ* (Front Royal, VA: Christendom College Press 1980) 41–42.

[9] *See ibid.* at 40–41.

[10] *See* Marcus Borg, "What Did Jesus Know?," *Bible Review* (December 1995) 19; Raymond E. Brown, *The Death of the Messiah* 1:480–82; Albert Nolan, *Jesus Before Christianity* (Maryknoll, NY: Orbis Books 1988) 138; James H. Charlesworth, *Jesus and the Dead Sea Scrolls* (New York: Doubleday 1993) 150–52 and n.73.

[11] *See, e.g.*, Albert Nolan, *Jesus Before Christianity* 118–20; Bruce Chilton, "The Son of Man—Who Was He?," *Bible Review* (August 1996) 34; Raymond E. Brown, *Jesus God and Man* (Milwaukee, WI: Bruce Publishing Co. 1967) 87; Louis F. Hartman, *The Anchor Bible—Daniel* (New York: Doubleday & Co. 1978) Introduction at ch. XIII. *But see* W.F. Albright & C.S. Mann, *The Anchor Bible—Matthew* (New York: Doubleday 1971), Introduction at clviii ("A study of the implications of the sayings of Jesus, especially of those in which he speaks of his Father, leaves the reader of the New Testament with precisely the same impression that Jesus' opponents had; it is hard to avoid the conclusion that Jesus meant to convey the fact of a unique relationship which he had with God, a relationship moreover which implied deity.")

[12] Pope John Paul II, "Novo Millennio Ineunte," 30 *Origins* 489, 497–98, Apostolic Letter (Jan. 18, 2001). http://www.vatican.va/holy_father/john_paul_ii/apost_letters/documents.

[13] *See, e.g.*, John P. Meier, *A Marginal Jew—Rethinking the Historical Jesus* (hereafter *A Marginal Jew*) (New York: Doubleday 1991) 1:324–32; Richard J. Bauckham, "All In the Family—Identifying Jesus' Relatives," *Bible Review* (April 2000) 20.

[14] The sect was the Ebionites, also known as the Antidicomarianites, who originally taught that Jesus was the natural son of Joseph and Mary. *See* the entry for "Antidicomarianites" in the *Catholic Encyclopedia*. http://www.newadvent.org.

[15] *See Catechism of the Catholic Church* § 500; Pope John Paul II, "Mary as 'Ever Virgin'," *The Pope Speaks* (Jan/Feb 1997) 17, Catechesis (Aug. 28, 1996). According to two orthodox biblical scholars: "While it was certainly not unknown for sons to be named after their fathers, it was at the same time uncommon." *See* W.F. Albright & C.S. Mann, *The Anchor Bible—Matthew* 9. That would suggest that Joseph, the "brother" of Jesus, probably was not a son of Joseph the foster father of Jesus.

[16] *See* André LeMaire, "Burial Box of James, the Brother of Jesus," *Biblical Archaeology Review* (Nov/Dec 2002) 24, 25, trumpeting the find as the "earliest archaeological evidence of Jesus found in Jerusalem."

[17] Assuming *arguendo* that the word "brother" meant "brother" as we use the term, there would be no good reason to infer that the Jesus referred to was Jesus of Nazareth. This can be seen by focusing on the identity of "James": (1) Neither of the two men named James who were called as Apostles had Joseph for a father: James the Great was specifically identified as the son of Zebedee (*e.g.*, Mt 4:21; Mk 1:19; Lk 5:10), and James the Lesser was specifically identified as the son of Alphaeus (*e.g.*, Mt 10:3; Mk 3:18; Lk 6:15). (2) All three Synoptic Gospels mention a James who was the son of a woman named Mary, but without any indication that Joseph was his father, and in settings which make it evident that the Mary referred to was *not* the Blessed Virgin Mary (Mt 27:56; Mk 15:40 & 16:1; Lk 24:10)—this James was the Apostle James the Lesser, the son of Alphaeus and Mary Cleophas. (3) The James who was referred to (along with Joses/Joseph, Simon and Judas) by townspeople as a "brother" of Jesus (*e.g.*, Mt 13:55), was James the Lesser. Similarly, the Jude who identified himself as "brother of James" (Jude 1), presumably was referring to James the son of Alphaeus, who had Jude Thaddeus as one of his brothers. (4) The Gospel of Luke also mentions a James, the father of the Apostle Judas (Lk 6:16), without identifying James' father, and without linking him to Jesus. (5) The visions of Sister Emmerich, though not the New Testament, identify one more James, viz., Jacob [James] the son of Jesus' aunt Mary Heli and Cleophas—a man who with his brothers Sadoch and Heliachim followed John the Baptist and only switched his allegiance to Jesus upon John's death. It was wholly implausible to postulate that the man whose bones may have been contained in the ossuary was still *another* James—a true brother of Jesus Christ, who was born of Joseph and Mary (or even a half brother born of Joseph), and yet was so unimportant to the ministry of Jesus and the life of the early Christian community that there is no record of his participation therein.

[18] *See* "'Jesus Box' Exposed as Fake," *CNN.com./science & space* (June 18, 2003). http://www.cnn.com/2003/TECH/science/06/18/jesus.box (accessed October 2003).

[19] Sister Emmerich related that Peter's father-in-law was surnamed "Zelotes" because he had won a dispute with the Romans concerning the right of

navigation on the Sea of Galilee. There may have been a family connection which resulted in the name "Simon Zelotes" being given to one of the three sons of Alphaeus and Mary Cleophas, in which case it did not connote, as commonly thought, that the Apostle Simon was a Zealot party member.

[20] (a) Bartholomew was a cousin of James the Lesser, Simon Zelotes and Jude Thaddeus, and Philip was related to Bartholomew. (b) Matthew was the stepson of Mary Cleophas, through her husband Alphaeus' first wife. (c) James the Great and John the Evangelist were grandsons of Sobe, who was a sister of St. Anne and an aunt of the Blessed Virgin Mary; their mother, Mary Salome (married to Zebedee), was a first cousin of the Blessed Virgin Mary. Thus, James the Great and John were Jesus' second cousins. (d) Peter's stepfather was an uncle of Philip and Andrew. Also, Peter may have been related to James the Lesser, Simon Zelotes and Jude Thaddeus. (e) John the Baptist was a grandson of Emerentia, who was an aunt of Sobe; His Mother, Elizabeth, was a first cousin of St. Anne. Thus, John the Baptist was Jesus' second cousin, once removed. (f) Nathanael (the bridegroom at Cana) was a great-grandson of Emerentia; His Mother, Mara, was a niece of Elizabeth. Thus, Nathanael the Bridegroom was a third cousin to Jesus. (g) Joses Barsabas (the disciple who drew lots with Matthias to replace Judas Iscariot) was the son of Mary Cleophas by her second husband, Sabas; he was a half-brother of James the Lesser, Simon Zelotes and Jude Thaddeus. (h) Martial, the resurrected son of the widow of Nain, was a grandson of Sobe; his father, Eliud, was the uncle of James the Great and John the Evangelist.

# CHAPTER TWO

## *When Did Jesus Begin to Proclaim the Good News?*

The drama of the baptism of Jesus in the Jordan was breathtaking: there, manifest in different ways to the gathered crowd, were all Three Persons of the Holy Trinity, Father, Son and Holy Spirit. It is understandable why all the Evangelists chose to begin their account of Jesus' public ministry with that milestone in the history of Salvation. *But, the events of the five month period leading up to it, following St. Joseph's death, were important too in their own way, as is revealed in Sister Emmerich's visions. During that time, Jesus set out on a series of trips, preaching the Good News from one end of Israel to the other.* Although He avoided the city of Jerusalem, He even went to the Jews living in pagan territory on the north, lodging in the house in Zarephath where Elijah had once lived with the widow whose jug of oil never ran dry despite the famine which lay over the land.

Unlike a prospective candidate for public office who first travels through his district sounding out the inhabitants on different issues, to find out if he has a popular message and sufficient support for a race, *Jesus was not trying to craft a resonating message or develop a prophetic "voice" with which to announce it, for He knew from the beginning:*

- ~ that He was the Messiah;
- ~ what the Good News was that He would preach;
- ~ what His public ministry would entail for Himself and His followers; and
- ~ how His mission on earth would end.

Thus, many themes and parables of His post-baptismal ministry as described in the Gospels were announced in these initial visits. *The teachings which Sister Emmerich heard Him give early on did not significantly change or develop—although they became more pointed and poignant as His Passion drew near.*

His hearers then at public and private discourses included the future Apostles Peter, Andrew, James the Greater and James the Lesser, John, Philip, and Levi (later renamed Matthew), as well as Lazarus and Nicodemus. Some of these were then disciples of John the Baptist, and their coming and going between John and Jesus spread word everywhere of what Israel's two prophetic voices were saying.

Just as the Baptist did, Jesus called people to repentance. In public, Jesus proclaimed the necessity of John's baptism, and in private He exposed secret sins to lead penitents to amend their lives. But this was only a prelude to Jesus' main message, which focused on the advent of the Messiah. *He said that the signs of the times bore witness that the prophecies were then fulfilled—the Messiah was at hand, in their very midst, although they did not recognize him because they were looking for the wrong kind of man. He told His listeners: "Ye wish to see a conqueror, an illustrious personage, a man surrounded by magnificence and eminently learned companions. Ye will not recognize as the Messiah one that comes among you destitute of wealth and authority . . . whose companions are unlettered peasants and laborers, whose followers are made up of beggars, cripples, lepers and sinners."*

Jesus did not confine Himself to platitudes about the Messiah and his kingdom: from the outset He taught people how they should live. He rejected divorce, and He censured Herod for his adultery. At the same time, He told His listeners that they should not judge others, lest they be judged themselves. He even criticized some for their hard hearts. At Jezreel, the home of the Nazirite sect, he warned them that an excess of piety was dangerous, because there were different ways to salvation. Instead of looking down on their neighbors who were weaker in the faith, they should be succoring them.

He gave a similar warning to His fellow Jews in Nazareth who despised the Canaanites in nearby Endor and treated them like slaves. Jesus went to instruct these pagans about the Messiah, and urged them to be baptized, but they felt themselves too unworthy for that. And so, when He returned to Nazareth, Jesus told the Jews that they should take their pagan neighbors to John's baptism.

The Parables which Jesus used in this period were among those most often ultimately set forth in the Gospels, from the time of His later preaching: the man about to erect a tower; the power of faith as great as a mustard seed; the unjust steward; the son sent by his father to take possession of a vineyard; the laborers in the vineyard; and the grain of wheat, which must die before producing fruit.

Already, Jesus gave evidence of His prodigious healing powers. For example, in Sepphoris, He visited with his great aunt Maraha and her sons, and taught at a school run by Sadducees where a hall in the rear was reserved for a group of demoniacs and lunatics. These unfortunates, who had been in convulsions prior to His appearance, were instantly cured when He drove out their demons. However, He did not announce that He was conducting a healing ministry or cure at every opportunity to do so.

Jesus customarily blessed the little children when He was entering or leaving a synagogue, using the "Patriarchs' blessing"— made with three strokes of the hand, one from the head and one from each shoulder, down to the heart. He blessed the girls in the same way as the boys, except that He did not lay His hands upon the girls, and He made a sign on their lips. While the parents were happy to have Him do this, Pharisees in Nazareth grumbled about this show of apparent religious authority on His part.

At this very early stage, persecution of Jesus by the Pharisees was limited and unorganized. The Sanhedrin in Jerusalem had heard reports of John's preaching, and had sent letters to synagogues and schools throughout the country warning against a "man to come," whom John had been speaking about, but John had not yet named this man and the authorities did not know he was Jesus. Still, they took special interest in Jesus' doings when they learned that He was the boy who had silenced the Doctors of the Law in the Temple years before. They tried to get Him to say who was greater, He or John the Baptist. He turned away that question, replying with words He so often used: "The greatest is he who serves as the least and last of all."

## What Great Sacrifice Did Jesus Require of His Mother?

The day came when He told His Mother that He was going to go to John's baptism, and then retire alone to the desert for forty days. As one might expect of a mother, she beseeched Him not to go where He might die of hunger or thirst. Now, He loved her as dearly as God could love a human being, and He understood better than anyone the commandment about honoring one's father and mother, but He was God as well as man, and, according to Sister Emmerich's visions, He told her that a new relationship must exist between them, despite the pain it would entail for her:

*"Jesus replied that henceforth she should not seek to deter Him by human considerations, for He must accomplish what was marked out for Him; a very different life was now about to commence for*

*Him, and they who would adhere to Him must suffer with Him; that He must now fulfill His mission, and she must sacrifice all purely personal claims upon Him. He added that although He would love her as ever, yet He was now for all mankind. She should do as He said and His Heavenly Father would reward her, for what Simeon had foretold was about to be fulfilled, a sword should pierce her soul."*

In her visions, Sister Emmerich heard Jesus deliver two equally discomfiting messages to those who were thinking of becoming His followers. The first was that if they separated themselves from Him, they would be lost, like those who ridiculed Noah and did not enter the Ark, or like Lot, who parted company with Abraham, to settle in Sodom and Gomorrah. He told them: "Look not around after the glory of the world, which fire from heaven shall destroy, that ye may not be turned into pillars of salt! Remain with me under every trial. I will always help you!" The second was that this "help" might not be the comfort they were looking for—*those who would follow Him must give up all their earthly possessions, and leave parents and friends, to suffer with Him and be buffeted and persecuted.*

### John the Baptist in the Wilderness

Those words fit perfectly the situation of one who was already hard at work preparing the way for Jesus, namely John the Baptist, Jesus' second cousin, once removed. *As to worldly possessions,* John had had none since he was taken into the wilderness by his mother Elizabeth at age two, to escape the murderous designs of Herod. *As to parents,* John's own miraculous birth had attracted the attention of Herod's spies, and eventually, having not found the child, Herod had a group of soldiers waylay John's father, Zachary, when the latter was traveling to the Temple, and kill him when he would not reveal John's hiding place. Of necessity, John saw his mother only on a few occasions thereafter. *As to friends,* John had no human ones, though Sister Emmerich saw John playing with birds and animals, and constantly being taught by angels. *As to suffering and being persecuted,* he had already led a harsh life of penitence, and execution awaited him shortly.

When John finally appeared in civilization, he immediately attracted attention. He was a daunting, powerfully built, ascetic figure, striking both in appearance and in behavior, as Sister Emmerich described: "John allowed nothing to prove an obstacle in his way. He walked boldly up to all he met, and spoke of one thing only, penance and the near coming of the Lord. His presence everywhere excited wonder and made the lightest grave. His voice pierced like a sword.

It was loud and strong though tempered with a tone of kindness. He treated all kinds of people as children. The most remarkable thing about him was the way in which he hurried on straight ahead, deterred by nothing, looking around at nothing, wanting nothing. It was thus I saw him hastening on his way through desert and forest, digging here, rolling away stones there, removing fallen trees, preparing resting-places, calling together the people who stood staring at him in amazement, yes, even bringing them out of their huts to help him."

## Where and How Did John Baptize?

When he had sufficiently "prepared the way" by his physical labors, John intensified his spiritual ones, by initiating a baptism of repentance at three different locations on the Jordan River. These were only about 20 miles apart in a direct line, but many more miles apart by foot. One spot was near Ainon on the east bank, opposite Salem, where he built a hut on the foundation of Melchizedek's tent-castle. Another site was at Ono, on the west bank, south of Jericho and north of Beth-hoglah, opposite Beth-barah; the third, in between those two sites, was on the east bank opposite Gilgal.

Why did he choose those places? As will be explained below, one had a particular spiritual importance, and all three were strategically located near well traveled roads. Ainon was on the west-east trade route which led from Caesarea on the coast, across the Jordan Valley to Philadelphia, a city of the Decapolis. The other two places were on the south-north route which led from Heliopolis in Egypt, to Hebron and Jerusalem, up the Jordan to the Sea of Galilee, and finally to Damascus in Syria. Thus, although John did not himself move around the country, large numbers of people were exposed to his preaching and his fame spread everywhere.

At Ainon, the baptismal candidate would stand waist deep in the water between two tongues of land, with the hand of an already baptized person, standing at either side, on his shoulder. The upper half of his body was clothed only in a white scarf, leaving his shoulders bare. John, wearing a long white garment and standing on one of the strips of land, would scoop water with a shell and pour it on the head of the neophyte. Only men were baptized. (Sister Emmerich did not see even the Holy Women being baptized until the Pentecost after Jesus' Resurrection.) Among those who went to John's baptism were most of the future Apostles, excepting Judas, but including the publican Levi, who was converted by John's preaching and amended his life.

We have a narrow picture of John from the Gospels—he is portrayed in rough garb, and acting in an unorthodox, even crude, manner. But, Sister Emmerich also saw him on one occasion attired in an elaborate, long white robe, serving as the priest for an incense ceremony held in a large lattice-work tent which he had built at the place was where Jesus was later baptized. He had a small shield hanging over his chest from gold chains; a precious stone was set in it for each of the Twelve Tribes, with the names inscribed. Exactly such a shield was described by Josephus, the Jewish historian, who attributed special significance to it: "God foreshadowed a victory in battle by means of the shining of the 12 stones which the high priest wore upon his breast stitched into the *essen* [breastplate]."[1]

In light of John's conduct, arrogating to himself religious authority and attracting an immense following, it is no wonder that the Jewish leaders in Jerusalem continuously dispatched spies and emissaries to the sites of John's baptism, and attempted to bring John under their control. One scene related by Sister Emmerich showed some twenty representatives of the Sanhedrin appearing for the purpose of summoning him to Jerusalem, there to attempt to validate his mission. John told them that if they waited, they would see the One from whom he had his mission. While adding that he had not seen this person, John went on to give them a description of his background—in terms which obviously fit Jesus. The deputies left in anger, without John.

Herod fared no better with John the Baptist than did the representatives of the Sanhedrin. According to Sister Emmerich, Herod visited John twice in the hope that John would accommodate Herod's desire to marry Herodias, his brother's wife, with whom he was already living. The Sanhedrin had refused to approve their union, and Herod hoped to quell public controversy with a favorable opinion from this prophet esteemed by the masses. John would not allow Herod to meet him at the place of baptism, to avoid having it defiled, and when they did come together the first time, John rejected Herod's petition out of hand.

A second time, Herod journeyed out to meet John. Sister Emmerich related the conversation of the two men as follows: "Herod inquired of John whether he knew a man by the name of Jesus of Nazareth of whom the whole country was talking, whether or not he kept up communication with Him, and whether that man was the One whose coming he was constantly announcing. He urged that John need not hesitate to inform him on these points, for that he intended to lay his case before Him. John answered that that man would give him

(Herod) just as little quarter as he himself did, that he (Herod) was and would always be an adulterer."

### What Happened at the Baptism of Jesus?

John answered rightly about Jesus, for John knew that sin was a complete anathema to Jesus. (Indeed, by this time, Jesus had already preached against Herod's adultery.) The apparent incongruity—if not *lese majesty*—of Jesus submitting to a baptism of repentance like a publican was captured by St. Matthew, who wrote that when Jesus presented Himself at the Jordan, John, recognizing the Messiah, protested that Jesus should be baptizing *him* and not the other way around. Jesus assured John that, nevertheless, it was fitting for John to proceed.

The reason Jesus gave was that so that "righteousness" would be fulfilled. In some biblical translations, in place of "righteousness," words such as "justice" or "holiness" or "God's will" are used—but the underlying meaning is the same, namely that Jesus' baptism was part of the grand design of salvation on the part of God the Father, which would be accomplished through the actions of Jesus and the people who interacted with Him.[2] Sister Emmerich provided information as to the specific purposes of His baptism, in the form of teachings by the Baptist and Jesus on that very occasion, but before turning to that, let us set the scene.

Where did the baptism occur? The Jordan River stretches from the base of Mount Hermon south to the Sea of Galilee, and still further down to the Dead Sea, a distance of over 200 miles if its twists and turns are measured. The four Gospels are silent about the location of Jesus' baptism,[3] but Sister Emmerich pinpointed the exact location as being the west bank site used by John at Ono, about five miles north of the Dead Sea.

Did Jesus' appearance at the Jordan take the Baptist by surprise? No, not according to Sister Emmerich's visions—confirming St. Mathew's account. Jesus had instructed his own followers to tell John the Baptist's disciples that He was on His way. Moreover, John learned from his angel companions that Jesus would appear imminently, and they gave him many directions to carry out in preparation for the occasion.

This particular spot which John used for baptisms had great spiritual resonance: it was the place where, centuries before, Elijah had divided the waters with his mantle. Even before that, the Ark of the Covenant (a sacred cultic object, like a chest, closely associated by the ancient Hebrews with the presence of God)[4] had crossed the Jordan there, borne by Joshua's men on their way to take possession of the land which God had given the Israelites. As they stepped into the river with the Ark, the water had ceased to flow, piling up beside them as had the Red Sea when Moses led the Hebrew people out of Egypt. The twelve stones which Joshua had the twelve tribes choose to commemorate the crossing, and place in the bed of the river at that time, were recognized and used by John in constructing a baptistry for Jesus.

Where the Ark had once rested in the riverbed, an island miraculously rose up as a sign to John's disciples verifying his testimony to the coming of the Messiah. By placing large stones in the water and overlaying them with tree trunks and branches, and white gravel, a short connecting bridge was made from the western bank of the Jordan. On the island, they planted bushes and twelve small trees, connecting their upper branches into an arbor. The central feature of their work was an octangular well[5] about five feet in diameter, whose bottom was lined with the stones upon which the Ark had rested. Water entered through underground channels.

As Sister Emmerich described the high point of John's ministry, Jesus arrived early one morning with other pilgrims, listened to John's instruction, and waited patiently as many others were baptized at the usual site. When He finally stepped forward, although John had never seen Him as an adult, John recognized Him spiritually. Sister Emmerich's visions accord with the Gospel passages showing that John knew well who Jesus was—indeed that he recognized Jesus as being more than just the Messiah: "John saw the Lord always in spirit, for he was generally in the prophetic state. He saw Jesus as the accomplishment of his own mission, as the realization of his own prophetic vocation. Jesus was not to John a contemporary, not a man like unto himself. He was to him the Redeemer of the world, the Son of God made man, the Eternal appearing in time, therefore he could in no way dream of associating with Him."

*To John's suggestion that he should be receiving rather than performing the baptism, Jesus replied not merely by calling upon John to play his assigned role, but also by answering John's own plea for baptism. In that brief interchange, Jesus said that John would be receiving the baptism of the Holy Ghost and of blood.*

In a tent erected in advance for Him, Jesus shed most of His clothes. He was led to the edge of the special baptismal well; there, He took off his brown, woven undergarment, leaving on only a linen band around his loins. At last He stepped into chest high water, holding onto a tree with his left arm. John scooped a sea shell into the water, raised it, and let streams from three perforations in the shell flow over Jesus' head.

Obviously, John had never heard of baptism "in the name of the Father, the Son, and the Holy Ghost"—the formula all Christians are familiar with today. So, what words did John use in baptizing Jesus? According to Sister Emmerich, John said: "May Yahweh through the ministry of His cherubim and seraphim pour out His blessing over Thee with wisdom, understanding and strength."[6] The latter three signified gifts of the mind, soul and body.

When Jesus came up out of the well, John's disciples Andrew and Saturnin threw about Him a large cloth so that He could dry Himself, and then put on Him a long white baptismal robe. The theophany (manifestation of God to man) described in the Gospels occurred next, as Jesus was standing alone, praying. This is Sister Emmerich's account:

*"There came from Heaven a great rushing wind like thunder. All trembled and looked up. A cloud of white light descended, and I saw over Jesus a winged figure of light as if flowing over Him like a stream. The heavens opened. I beheld an apparition of the Heavenly Father in the figure in which He is usually depicted and, in a voice of thunder, I heard the words: "This is My beloved Son in whom I am well pleased." Jesus was perfectly transparent, entirely penetrated by light; one could scarcely look at Him. I saw angels around Him."*[7] (Note that what she saw hover over Jesus was not a dove or any other bird but rather "a winged figure of light," which was how she customarily saw the Holy Spirit. Her vision was not a contradiction of the Gospel accounts, for they declared that the Holy Spirit had descended *"like* a dove," and not that it had descended *"in the form of* a dove.")

### What was the Significance of Jesus' Baptism—Then and Now?

*Since Jesus was born sinless and maintained Himself in that state, was John's baptism of Him a superfluous act, of no real consequence?* That is a question which every Christian should ponder, because it has several profound answers.

After Jesus reclothed Himself in a tent, He stood in the open while John spoke to the crowd. *John cited the prophecies that had been fulfilled, reminded them that they had heard the voice of God, and gave witness to Jesus as the Son of God and promised Messiah.*[8]

*Thus, we can see that an essential purpose of the baptism was to allow the Father and the Holy Spirit to witness to the divine favor resting on Jesus, in front of John and John's disciples, and the assembled pilgrims, including most of the men who later became Apostles, as well as Lazarus and Joseph of Arimathea.*

Why was it necessary to do this? Precisely because in His own discourses, for strategic reasons, Jesus was refraining from claiming the title of Messiah, and He was not even hinting at His divine origin and nature. In God's wisdom, in order to effect our salvation, it had been necessary for Jesus to be born and live as a man among men, and it was necessary that men lacked understanding of His divinity until He was resurrected. If Jesus had intimated His divinity at the outset of His ministry, the Jewish religious leaders would certainly have moved immediately to crush such apparent blasphemy.

*Even assuming that they could not have done so, because His "hour" had not yet come, how would it have been possible for His disciples, or anyone else, to relate to Jesus as a mere man?* Some in the audience, hearing a claim of divinity, would have thought Him possessed and a blasphemer, and would not have stayed to listen to the Good News. Others, thinking only of the glory of being disciples of the Messiah, if His claim proved true, would have swarmed to His side. And finally, there were those who would have tried to worship Him, then and there. Recall what happened to the Apostles Paul and Barnabas in Lycaonia, as recorded in the Acts of the Apostles: when they worked a miraculous cure, the pagan populace jumped to the conclusion that they were the gods Hermes and Zeus, and the priest of the temple of Zeus hastened to bring oxen to sacrifice to them! The two were able to prevent the people from worshiping them only by rending their garments and declaring forcefully that they were mere men, and not gods—a *declaration which Jesus could not have made.*

And, if it had been recognized, during His ministry, that He had a divine nature, that understanding might well have pushed aside recognition that He also had a human nature. Exactly such a heresy, called docetism, did arise in the early Church: its adherents believed that Jesus' body was only an illusion (like the human form which the angel Raphael assumed in dealing with Tobit and Tobias[9]).

Thus, in order to set Christianity on the right track from the beginning, it was essential that His followers not know at first of His divine origin and nature, so that they would become familiar with and convinced of His human nature. At the same time, it was also essential that His prospective Apostles understand that He was no ordinary man—that He was the "Son of Man" upon whom God's favor rested. And that is precisely what was accomplished through the theophany at the Jordan.[10]

Jesus Himself spoke to the crowd after His baptism, confirming what John had just told them about it, and stating that He would withdraw from view for a while before coming back to lay the foundation for the kingdom given Him by His Father; further, upon His return, they should bring their sick to Him to be healed.

A truly striking and significant detail added by Sister Emmerich's visions concerning Jesus' baptism is her account of Jesus' preaching about it in the days immediately following, before He entered the desert. These are the words she heard Jesus say, in instructing the people on penance, baptism and the Holy Ghost:

*"'When I was baptized, my Father sent down the Holy Ghost and uttered the words, 'This is My beloved Son in whom I am well pleased.' These words are addressed to every one that loves his Heavenly Father and is sorry for his sins. Upon all that will be baptized in the name of the Father and of the Son and of the Holy Ghost, He sends His Holy Spirit. They then become His sons in whom He is well pleased, for He is the Father of all that receive His baptism and to Him by the same are born again.'"*

Consider that Jesus would have been entitled to use His Father's benediction at the Jordan to glorify Himself, and to assert His right to the honors due His unique status. Instead, in His remarks to the multitude, He went to the other extreme—opening up the way to glory for all men, gentile as well as Jew, by becoming God's adopted children. *Therefore, the theophany at the Jordan River has meaning for us today going far beyond being an imprimatur on Jesus and his teachings—it is a promise from God the Father addressed to each of us who is born again in the baptism established by His Son.*[11]

---

[1] See *The Anchor Bible Dictionary* 2:620.
[2] According to W.F. Albright & C.S. Mann: "'Righteousness' must be seen as the whole purpose of God for his people, and not . . . as a moral quality only. Psalm cxix frequently describes the commandments and ordinances of God as 'righteous,' and the same sense underlies Jesus' reply. 'To fulfill all righteousness' must therefore be seen as meaning the fulfillment not only of the demands of God upon his people, but also the fulfillment of those Scriptures in which those demands are set out—law, prophets, writings." *The Anchor Bible—Matthew* 31-32.
Hippolytus gave us this exegesis: "Do you see, beloved, how many and how great blessings we would have lost if the Lord had yielded to the exhortation of John and declined baptism? For the heavens had been shut before this. The region above was inaccessible. We might descend to the lower parts but not

ascend to the upper. So it happened not only that the Lord was being baptized—
he was also making new the old creation. He was bringing the alienated under
the scepter of adoption. For straightway 'the heavens were opened to him.' A
reconciliation took place between the visible and the invisible." *See Ancient
Christian Commentary on Scripture* (Downers Grove, IL: InterVarsity Press
1998) NT II: 11–12.

[3] While not fixing the place of Jesus' baptism, St. John referred to John's
preaching "in Bethany, across the Jordan." (Jn 1:28) However, Bethany is not
on the river: it is on the outskirts of Jerusalem, about 15 miles west of the
Jordan, and it may be that the word 'Bethany' is a mistranslation, with the
actual word having been 'Bethabara' as Origen thought. *See* the entry for
"Bethany Beyond the Jordan" in *The Anchor Bible Dictionary* 1:703–05. In any
event, while John did frequently baptize on the east bank of the Jordan, that
was not where, according to Sister Emmerich, he baptized Jesus. (However,
the Greek Orthodox Church, believing the contrary, has selected the east bank
site at Wadi Al-Kharrar for its church honoring the Baptism. *See The Wanderer*
(February 6, 2003) 8.)

[4] *See* the entry for "Ark of the Covenant" in *The Anchor Bible Dictionary*
1:386.

[5] It has become traditional for baptistries to be octagonal, "to show that Baptism
is birth into the eighth day, into the Resurrection of Christ and into the new
time that opened up with the Resurrection." *See* Joseph Ratzinger, *The Spirit
of the Liturgy* (San Francisco: Ignatius Press 2000) 97.

[6] As to the ministry of angels, recall the greeting from John to the seven
communities in Asia: "grace to you and peace from He Who is and was and is
to come and from the seven spirits which are before His throne." Rv 1:4. The
reference may have been to the seven throne angels of Jewish tradition. Also
recall Tobit 12:15.

[7] Note that in her vision, Sister Emmerich saw all three members of the Holy
Trinity, and heard God the Father speak (St. John's account lacks this detail).
Also, she heard the Father address His words to the assembled crowd (as St.
Matthew wrote), rather than to Jesus alone (as St. Mark and St. Luke wrote).

[8] Some scholars have suggested that John the Baptist thought he was preparing
the way *for Elijah to return* (rather than for Jesus), and that there was no
theophany at the baptism of Jesus. *See, e.g.*, Raymond E. Brown, *The Birth of
the Messiah* (New York: Doubleday 1979) 283, 30 & n.16; Raymond E. Brown,
*The Anchor Bible—John* (New York: Doubleday 1966) 1:64–66; John P. Meier,
*A Marginal Jew* 2:106–10. Such suggestions are contrary both to the letter of
Scripture and to the teachings of the Catholic Church. *See Catechism of the
Catholic Church* §§ 523, 535–36. Note also the Apostolic Letter of Pope John
Paul II, who proposed five new "Mysteries of Light" for the Rosary, beginning
with Jesus' baptism in the Jordan. *See* 32 *Origins* (October 31, 2002) 345, 350.

[9] St. Ignatius of Antioch composed a Creed to counter this heresy. *See* Harold
O.J. Brown, *Heresies* (Garden City, NY: Doubleday 1984) 52.

[10] A second purpose was revealed in the Baptist's subsequent preaching: the baptism of Jesus worked an exorcism of water—the evil that was in that element was cast out, and it was thereby sanctified, making it suitable for conferring grace.

[11] Hilary understood this. In his commentary on Matthew, he wrote that: "We knew from those who were immersed in Christ that after baptism with water the Holy Spirit would descend to us from the heavenly gates. Then would we be filled with the anointing of heavenly glory and become God's children through the adoption the Father's voice announced. Truth prefigured the image of the sacrament through these very happenings." *See Ancient Christian Commentary on Scripture*, NT Ia:53-54.

# CHAPTER THREE

## *Jesus Resumes His Public Ministry*

In her visions, Sister Emmerich saw Jesus after His baptism continuing His itinerant public ministry, with friends and disciples joining Him and then going back to their normal pursuits, for several weeks before He went into the desert. (Because the Evangelists related only a very small fragment of their experiences with Jesus, and not even one of them was present at all times with Him, it is not surprising that the three Synoptic Gospels (Matthew, Mark and Luke) all segued from His baptism immediately into his temptation in the desert.)

One of Jesus' first stops was Bethel, where Sister Emmerich, in her visions, heard Him give a long discourse in the synagogue in which He contrasted the Law with grace, speaking of "the Ark of the Covenant and of the severity of the Old Law, for whoever approached so near the Ark as to touch it instantly fell dead;[1] but now was the Law fulfilled and grace poured forth in the Son of Man." He also told His disciples that they should give up everything and not worry about their daily needs, "for it was a far greater thing to be regenerated than to find nourishment for the body. But if they would be born again of water and the Holy Ghost, He who had regenerated them would also nourish them."

It was understandable that His disciples did not take His instruction to heart when they were hungry: en route to the next town, they asked Him whether they might eat some dates which had fallen by the wayside. As He was to do with so many people on similar occasions, He tried to turn their thoughts to spiritual matters, instructing them not to be concerned about what they ate—rather, He said, they should cultivate purity of soul and holiness of speech.

At the beginning, while the disciples went along primarily to learn from Him, they were useful in giving witness to the people they would gather to hear Jesus, of what they had seen and heard at Jesus' baptism. This was necessary because everyone was so accustomed to thinking of John the Baptist as the Prophet of their time, that Jesus was at first regarded by the people as being merely John's helper.

Jesus traveled on to the valley of the shepherds near Bethlehem and taught them with parables of sheep and shepherds. They had been given special graces, and when He appeared, they knelt or prostrated themselves before Him, and greeted Him with the words of psalms that foretold the coming of the Messiah. The shepherds, including some who had actually been present at His birth in the Cave of the Nativity, delighted in recounting all that had happened then. They led him to the Cave, which even before His ministry had already been developed by them as a place for devotion. They had physically altered it, to let in more light, and decorated it with tapestries and carpets left by the Three Kings.

At this point, Jesus released His disciples for a period, and went on a journey alone, to lead to salvation all those people who had acted hospitably to the Holy Family on their flight into Egypt when He was an infant. Sister Emmerich described a visit to such a man, an innkeeper at the southern border of Herod's territory. Immediately upon Jesus entering his inn, he felt a ray of grace touch him, bringing with it salvation. Jesus explained that He had come to repay the man's good deed many years before, for every action, good or bad, bears its own "fruit." When the man volunteered his own sinfulness, Jesus reassured him that He had come to "cleanse sinners from their iniquity and lead them back to God." And when the man mentioned that his grandchildren were ill, Jesus promised to heal them—provided that the man would believe in Him and be baptized.

Those who read Sister Emmerich's accounts of this and other healings will see that in no case did Jesus bring salvation or heal a person in recompense for good deeds. Rather, what He specifically asked for was faith in Himself and His teachings.[2] Moreover, Jesus made it clear to the innkeeper that He was not thrusting salvation on him: it was a gift, which could be rejected or lost once received.

Jesus proceeded to cure the man's relatives, and then had them bathe, adding to their bath some water which He had brought with Him from the Jordan in a flask. He did not baptize them, but instead urged them to go to John's baptism. According to Sister Emmerich, when they asked whether the Jordan was special: "He answered that the channel of the Jordan had been hollowed out and its course directed; that all holy places of this land had been allotted to special purposes by His Heavenly Father long before man had existed there, yea, even before the land or the Jordan had sprung forth from nothing."

Next, Jesus traveled north to Ephron in the Bethel Hills, where He was met by His disciples. He led them to a cave where both the prophet Samuel and David, when a shepherd, had stayed in times past. Mary and Joseph also had rested there, exhausted, on their flight. Jesus used their hardships as an example of what lay in store for His disciples.

### Why Was Jesus Born in Bethlehem?

When asked why His Mother had gone to Bethlehem for His birth instead of remaining in comfort in her house, He answered that He was to be born in poverty at Bethlehem among the shepherds, since He was to gather the flocks together. That surprising response was in keeping with His character. Jesus might well have referred to the Messianic prophecy of where the Savior was to be born, or to His Davidic ancestry—but instead of emphasizing the glory of His inheritance, he emphasized the humility of his calling, for shepherds were of the lowest class in society.

### Jesus Intended to Raise a New "Temple" to His Father

His next stop was Mizpah, located a few hours away from Bethlehem. *He gave an instruction in the synagogue, at which, according to Sister Emmerich, He said that "the Promise would be withdrawn from the unbelieving Jews and handed over to the heathens." She also recounted that when "His hearers boasted the magnificence of the Temple and the superiority of the Jews over the heathens, Jesus explained to them that the end for which the Chosen People had been called and their Temple erected was now attained, since the One promised by God through the Prophets was now come to establish the Kingdom of His heavenly Father, and to raise to Him a new Temple." Devoted readers of the Gospels will be familiar with these severe messages of Jesus, but they may be surprised at learning that He first delivered them so early in His ministry, only weeks following His baptism. Is it any wonder why, when such teachings were reported to them, pious—albeit uncomprehending—leaders of the religious establishment might have been appalled and hostile to Jesus from the outset?*

At a nearby place where He stopped, Jesus spoke about John the Baptist, "likening him to one knocking at the house of a sleeping man, to rouse him for the coming of the Lord; to one breaking a path through the wilderness, that the king might safely travel over it; and lastly to an impetuous torrent that rushing along purifies the channel through which it flows." He again was asked who was the greater, He or John? This time, His answer was not evasive: "He of whom John gives testimony." When the people remarked upon Jesus' handsome figure, He predicted that a few years in the future, "they would see no beauty in Him, they would not even recognize Him, so disfigured would He be." Of course, they could not understand these words at the time.

Jesus had His disciples baptize very few people in the locations He visited during this period; for the most part He urged penitents to go to John for baptism. Sister Emmerich said that those who had already been baptized by John were not baptized again by Jesus' disciples until Pentecost after the Resurrection, and she noted that there were differences between John's baptism and that of Jesus. For example, there was only a general confession of sins at the former, while sins were individually confessed at the latter, at times under Jesus' prompting.

### Foes—and Friends—in the Sanhedrin

The Sanhedrin of Jesus' day has been the subject of much obloquy for the persecution of Jesus. It was a body of self-chosen priests, nobles, elders, scribes and teachers of the Law, from the Pharisee and Sadducee sects.[3] At the time of Jesus' ministry, it was the most notable center of religious power in Israel, a power with a physical dimension which was exercised not only by the guard at the Temple itself, but throughout the country in the local synagogues. The Sanhedrin was able to cause the arrest and questioning of people, their expulsion from the religious life of the community, and even their death. As related in the Acts of the Apostles, the day of the stoning of Stephen, with Saul of Tarsus acting as the official witness, "saw the beginning of a great persecution of the church in Jerusalem," and Saul, "breathing murderous threats against the Lord's disciples, went to the high priest and asked him for letters to the synagogues in Damascus which would empower him to arrest and bring to Jerusalem anyone . . . living according to the new way."[4]

Sister Emmerich was privileged to see in her mystical visions not only what Jesus and His disciples were doing, but also the actions of His enemies in the Sanhedrin, who were conspiring against Him even at that very early stage. *At the same time, it should be noted that Sister Emmerich also saw that Jesus had admirers in the Sanhedrin, members who assisted Him secretly, and that some of the things said and done against Him, at least initially, could be attributed only to a minority of the whole Sanhedrin.*

According to her, at that early time, "the Sanhedrin in Jerusalem again held a long consultation on the subject of Jesus. Everywhere they had spies bribed to give them information of His words and actions. The Sanhedrin consisted of seventy-one priests and doctors, of whom twenty were again divided into fives, thus forming so many sub-committees for deliberating and disputing together.

"They examined the genealogical register, and could in no way deny that Joseph and Mary were of the House of David, and Mary's mother of the race of Aaron. But as they said, these families had fallen into obscurity, and Jesus strolled around with vagrants. He also defiled Himself with publicans and heathens, and sought the favor of slaves. They . . . thought that He must have designs to raise an insurrection with the aid of such hangers-on. Some gave it as their opinion that He was very likely an illegitimate child, because He had once proclaimed Himself the son of a king. Others declared that He must in some way receive secret training from the devil, for He often retired apart and spent the night alone in the wilderness or on the mountains.

"Among these twenty deliberators were some who knew Jesus and His family very well, who were most favorably inclined toward Him, who were indeed His friends in secret. Nevertheless, they did not contradict what was said against Him. They kept silence in order to be the better able to serve Him and His disciples and to give them information of whatever might come to their knowledge. The majority of the committee concluded at last that Jesus was in communication with the devil from whom He received instruction, and this was the opinion they publicly proclaimed and which was spread throughout Jerusalem."

## The Devil Has Many Disguises

While some members of the Sanhedrin were spreading word that Jesus was *in league with* the Devil, Jesus was actually preparing to *combat* him alone in the desert. Jesus walked south from Bethany toward the Jordan River, avoiding towns. About an hour from Jericho, He came to Mt. Quarantania,[5] a wild place, with many chasms and grottoes. Elijah had dwelt there in the distant past; also, the Israelites had pitched their camp there when they marched around Jericho before destroying it. After spending days in prayer, Jesus left the mountain and crossed the Jordan near Beth-barah, heading southeast to a place in the desert near Bozrah/Bezer in Moab.

Here he remained in a cave, praying constantly, and taking neither food nor drink.

The authors of the Synoptic Gospels wrote about the three main temptations of Jesus, based, according to Sister Emmerich's visions, on what Jesus Himself told the disciples immediately thereafter and again in an instruction given before His Passion. Sister Emmerich saw these three, and more besides. (The Gospel of St. Luke can be read as implying that there were many temptations.)

According to her, the Devil first appeared at Jesus' cave in different disguises: as various disciples of His; an old Essene friend; an angel; one of Herod's officers; a traveler; a magician, and so forth. The theme of the minor temptations was that He should break his fast. The Devil suggested that His health would suffer, or that His followers were feeling abandoned without Him, or that there was an opportunity to gather His supporters and free the Jewish nation. Each time, Jesus' responded in one of three ways—by ignoring the Devil completely, by praying that His Father would remove the temptation, or by directly telling Satan to withdraw.

As for the three main encounters with the Devil, Sister Emmerich saw them in the order recorded by St. Matthew. Following the temptation to turn stones into bread, when the Devil took the form of a large man, the Devil appeared as an angel in military dress, like St. Michael the archangel. Sister Emmerich saw the Devil seize Jesus by the shoulders and carry Him through the air to the tower on the corner of the Temple which was on the west side, opposite the Antonia fortress. The Devil encouraged Jesus to throw Himself off the Temple, presumably causing angels to come to His aid and thereby prove that He was the Son of God.

Finally, came the third temptation, after the Devil had carried Jesus back to Mt. Quarantania. Sister Emmerich described it as follows: "Satan flew with the Lord to the highest peak of the mountain, and set Him upon an overhanging, inaccessible crag much higher than the grotto. It was night, but while Satan pointed around, it grew bright, revealing the most wonderful regions in all parts of the world. The devil addressed Jesus in words something like these: 'I know that Thou art a great Teacher, that Thou art now about to gather disciples around Thee and promulgate Thy doctrines. Behold, all these magnificent countries, these mighty nations! Compare with them poor, little Judea lying yonder! Go rather to these. I will deliver them over to Thee, if kneeling down Thou wilt adore me!' . . . Satan pointed out in each the features of special attraction. He dwelt particularly upon those of a country whose inhabitants were unusually tall and magnificent looking. . . . Satan advised Jesus to go there above all to teach. He showed Him Palestine, but as a poor, little, insignificant place. . . . The only words uttered by Jesus were: 'The Lord thy God shalt thou adore and Him only shalt thou serve! Depart from Me, Satan!' Then I saw Satan in an inexpressibly horrible form rise from the rock, cast himself into the abyss, and vanish as if the earth had swallowed him."

Clearly, the Devil was trying to steer Jesus off course in different directions,[6] as though He was merely a holy man, like the Prophets, who might be tempted to desist from His holy practices. Sister Emmerich said that she herself wondered how Satan could have been so blind, but the Lord told her: *"Man knew not that the serpent tempting him was Satan; in like manner, Satan was not to know that He who redeemed man was God."* And so, Satan was not aware of Jesus' divine nature until He descended into hell after His death, there to rescue the souls who were not eternally condemned.

*Given not only that Jesus was God, but also that the Devil didn't know who or what he was really facing, we may wonder whether Jesus' desert experience was truly a meaningful trial, apart from the physical discomforts felt by Jesus' human body. The answer to that doubt is to be found in an extraordinary vision of Jesus being tempted by angels, even before the diabolic temptations began.*

### How God the Father Tempted His Son

Sister Emmerich had a vision of temptations sent by God the Father:

"And now I beheld the angelic band bending low before Jesus, offering Him their homage, and begging leave to unfold to Him their mission. They questioned Him as to whether it was still His will to suffer as man for the human race. . . . When Jesus answered in the affirmative, accepting His sufferings anew, the angels put together before Him a high cross, the parts of which they had brought with them. . . . Three carried a ladder. Another had a basket full of ropes, cords, and tools, while others bore the spear, the reed, the rods, the scourges, the crown of thorns, the nails, the robes of derision—in a word, all that figured in His Passion.

"The cross appeared to be hollow. It could be opened like a cupboard, and then it displayed the innumerable instruments of torture with which it was filled. In the central part, where Jesus' Heart was broken, were entwined all possible emblems of pain in all kinds of frightful instruments, and the color of the cross itself was heartrending, the color of blood. The various parts presented different tints symbolical of the pain there to be endured, but all like so many streams converged to the heart. The different instruments were likewise symbolical of future pains. In the cross were also vessels of vinegar and gall, as well as ointment, myrrh, and something like herbs, prefiguring perhaps to Jesus His death and burial.

*"On another occasion, I saw the angels placing before Jesus the ingratitude of men, the skepticism, the scorn, the mockery, the treachery, the denial of friends and of enemies up to the moment of His death and after it."*

*These were real temptations—for Jesus truly had a human nature which, like our own, could fear pain and death, and could be tempted not to suffer horribly for such an ungrateful race.* And these were temptations which He could not reject out of hand by telling Satan "Begone!," for these came from His Father, not from the Devil.

Why might God the Father have directed angels to tempt Jesus in the desert? Perhaps for the same reason that a commander, before he sends troops into battle, trains them with realistic combat exercises, so that when they come face to face with the enemy they can master their fears and perform their mission. In the garden on the Mount of Olives, the human nature of Jesus was tempted to the point where He prayed that the cup of suffering would pass by Him, but, perhaps strengthened by His experience on Mount Quarantania, He was able to collect Himself and accept the will of His Father.[7]

---

[1] I Ch 13:9–10.

[2] The Catholic Church teaches that good works alone are neither sufficient nor necessary for salvation (although, as St. James wrote, "faith without works is as dead as a body without breath"). Rather, "all persons depend completely on the saving grace of God for their salvation," and "whatever in the justified precedes or follows the free gift of faith is neither the basis for justification [the forgiveness of sins] nor merits it." See the Lutheran-Catholic "Joint Declaration on the Doctrine of Justification" 28 Origins (July 16, 1998) 120 at §§ 19, 25–27, 31. http://www.vatican.va/roman_curia/pontifical_councils/chrstuni/documents/rc_pc_chrstuni_doc_31101999_cath-luth-joint-declaration_en.html. In that declaration, Catholics and Lutherans proclaimed that "We confess together that sinners are justified by faith in the saving action of God in Christ." 28 Origins 123 at § 25.
Is there, then, salvation for those who do not believe in Christ? That very meaningful question has been answered for Catholics by "Dominus Iesus," a

Declaration of the Unicity and Salvific Universality of Jesus Christ and the Church, issued by the Congregation for the Doctrine of the Faith (August 6, 2000): "For those who are not formally and visibly members of the Church, 'salvation in Christ is accessible by virtue of a grace which, while having a mysterious relationship to the Church, does not make them formally part of the Church, but enlightens them in a way which is accommodated to their spiritual and material situation. This grace comes from Christ; it is the result of his sacrifice and is communicated by the Holy Spirit. . . .'" *Ibid.* § 20. http://www.ourladyswarriors.org/teach/domiiesu.htm.

[3] For a description of the Sanhedrin, *see generally*, Raymond E. Brown, *The Death of the Messiah* 1:339–57.

[4] Acts 8:1 and 9:1.

[5] It is two miles northwest of Jericho, and is referred to variously on maps as Jebel Qarantal, Mt. Dok or Mt. Docus.

[6] A modern analysis of the symbolism of the three temptations was given by W.F. Albright & C.S. Mann, in *The Anchor Bible—Matthew*: "The first test would be to see if he would identify his mission with what nowadays would be called 'social reform,' working as a popular leader for the eradication of hunger and poverty. . . . The second temptation . . . would, in this view, be a temptation to trade upon the Messiah's relationship with God, to achieve a reputation as a wonder worker and so succeed in securing the attention of man. The third test would be to compromise with evil, and recognize the devil's dominion to the point of regarding some men, some situations, as beyond hope of redemption." *Ibid. 36.*

[7] If the idea that the Father would cause His Son to be tempted seems outlandish, consider that, according to the Synoptic Gospels, Jesus was led into the desert by the Holy Spirit. Further, in the Lord's prayer, we petition the Father, "lead us not into temptation. . . ."

# CHAPTER FOUR

### How Did Jesus Call His Apostles?

One day, a man appeared along the shore of the Sea of Galilee and, without explaining who he was or what he was about, he ordered some fisherman to "Come after me," telling them that He would make them "fishers of men." Contrary to all expectations about human behavior, they abandoned their livelihood with alacrity to follow him. *Or did they?*

Preachers understandably revel in the story of the calling of the Apostles found in the Synoptic Gospels, which seems to describe a spontaneous act of faith and commitment as a model for future followers of Jesus to emulate. *While the response of each future Apostle to Jesus' call was indeed an act of faith, and a generous one, for most of them it was not an immediate reaction on his part, according to the visions of Sister Emmerich. Rather, they were very hesitant about laying aside their work and becoming dependent upon divine providence, especially those with family responsibilities. Only after they had many times alternated between traveling with Him and resuming their occupations, and only after He had apprised them of the imminence of their "final call," did they bring their ships to shore and lay down their nets, as depicted in the Synoptic Gospels.*

If the seaside event was only the end of a process, how and when did Jesus begin to call His Apostles? He began, as was recorded in St. John's Gospel, at the Jordan River. Jesus had just climbed down from His cave on Mt. Quarantania and emerged from forty days in the desert. Crossing to the east bank of the Jordan, He had gone along it to the point where John was baptizing on the other side. Seeing Him, John proclaimed to his own disciples—"Behold the lamb of God who taketh away the sins of the world."

Now, John's disciples had attended Jesus' baptism, and two of them, Andrew and Saturnin, had subsequently followed Him from time to time in the weeks thereafter. These two were moved to cross the river and hurry after Jesus, catching up to Him outside of Beth-barah. Jesus spoke to them about His mission, His own preparation in the desert for it, and the necessity of preparation before commencing an important work. They volunteered to be His disciples, and Andrew commended his brother Peter, and Philip and Nathanael, to Jesus.

Andrew and Saturnin were exceptions—one of the problems which plagued Jesus during His ministry was that some of the disciples of John the Baptist felt such a strong attachment to their master that they refused to go over to Jesus, and at times they even expressed hostility to Him. And those who did leave John sometimes felt a divided loyalty. When Jesus commissioned several of His followers—formerly John's disciples—to begin baptizing at the pool which John had been using on the east bank, about an hour north of Beth-barah, they objected that this was John's territory. Jesus informed them that John's work was almost completed, and so they did as He had instructed.

*There, they baptized neophytes with a triple pouring of water over their heads, in the name of the Father, Son and Holy Ghost— the first time that the true Trinitarian formula was used in baptizing.* Those of John's disciples who had remained at his side saw what was going on and vehemently protested to him that Jesus was poaching converts; John did his best to set them straight, and encouraged them to follow Jesus instead of himself, but such was their loyalty to John and pride in being his disciples, that they would not leave him for a new master.

In Abel-meholah, Jesus met with Andrew, Peter and John. Confirming St. John's Gospel, Sister Emmerich related that Jesus gave Peter his new name at this very first meeting, even though Peter, unlike his brother, had not made any commitment to Jesus. Sister Emmerich mentioned that Andrew and Peter were of very different temperaments: whereas Andrew had eagerly volunteered at the earliest opportunity, Peter thought that serving as a disciple of Jesus was beyond his abilities, and so hung back.

The time was then drawing near for the Wedding at Cana, but before setting out for it, Jesus' relatives and disciples assembled at Mary's house, which was in between Capernaum and Bethsaida.[1] After giving a detailed and inspiring explanation of His teachings in the synagogue, Jesus took some followers to a nearby vale where they could converse privately. Philip hung behind, out of humility, but Jesus said to him, "Follow me!," which Philip was happy to do. Sister Emmerich recounted the following scene, when Jesus told them to make ready to answer His future summons to them:

"When He should call them, they should follow Him immediately. The disciples questioned Him unrestrainedly as to how they should manage with regard to their families. Peter, for instance, said that just at present he could not leave his old stepfather, who was also Philip's uncle. But Jesus relieved his anxiety by His answer, that He would not begin before the Paschal feast; that only in so far as the heart was concerned, should they detach themselves from their occupations; that exteriorly they should continue them until He called them. In the meantime however they should take the necessary steps toward freeing themselves from their different avocations."

## What Was Behind the Story of Nathanael and the Fig Tree?

Jesus and His disciples then proceeded toward Cana on a path which ran through Gabara, where Nathanael Chased had his business. Nathanael was not an Apostle, but he was an important disciple, and the story of his calling was told by St. John: when Nathanael first met Jesus, Jesus said that He had previously seen him under a fig tree. St. John did not explain Jesus' remark, and many homilists try to flesh out St. John's story with the assumption that Jesus had clairvoyantly seen Nathanael sitting under a fig tree shortly before he was summoned to meet Jesus. Sister Emmerich's explanation was very different.

The episode when Jesus saw Nathanael under the fig tree had occurred months before—in this fashion. Nathanael had been standing under a fig tree in a park, struggling internally with sexual temptation as he watched some beautiful women playing a game, when he happened to notice a stranger looking at him. That man said nothing to him, but Nathanael understood the meaning of his gaze—it was a warning to observe propriety. When Nathanael met Jesus, he realized that Jesus had been the stranger, for a look from Him now reminded Nathanael of the earlier occasion and convinced him that Jesus had read his mind then and had acted like a guardian angel. And so, the impetuous and joyful Nathanael acknowledged Jesus on the spot as His savior!

*The story of the calling of Nathanael, thus, did not relate to Jesus' ability to see events far in the distance, but rather His knowledge of a person's innermost thoughts.* According to Sister Emmerich, Jesus usually carried on conversations as ordinary people do, and listened to them tell Him about things He already knew. He also asked them questions, not because He did not know the answer, but because He wanted to hear something from their own mouth—think, for example, of His questions, "Who do men say I am?" and, "Who do you say I am?" Occasionally, though, He showed His disciples that He could read their minds (for example, St. Mark recorded that He did so after they were arguing privately about who among them was the most important).

And, He repeatedly demonstrated he read the minds of His opponents. (Recall St. Matthew describing how Jesus read the minds of the Pharisees who were secretly criticizing His forgiving of sins, and how St. Luke described Him acting to answer the unvoiced thought of Simon the Pharisee, when a fallen woman tended to Him at Simon's house.) *It is precisely because God can indeed read our minds that we should expect to see fulfilled Jesus' declaration, reported in the Gospels of Matthew and Luke, that "Nothing is concealed that will not be revealed, nor secret that will not be known."*[2]

### Why Was the Wedding at Cana So Important—Then and Now?

Having secured Nathanael Chased as a disciple, Jesus proceeded to Cana, for the wedding which St. John recognized as one of the highpoints of His entire public ministry. *The miracle Jesus performed there, transforming large jugs full of water into wine when the wine ran out, has from the very beginning of the Church been a crucial factor in its belief in the Holy Eucharist and in the bounteousness of God's Kingdom. Sister Emmerich's visions make clear that the miracle was highly significant for a second reason. For the first time, Jesus was in the midst of His own community—more than a hundred relatives and two dozen disciples. All at the wedding had seen for themselves His baptism or some of His miraculous cures, or else they had heard of them, and they were in awe of Him. But, the time had drawn nigh for the chosen ones to make the decision whether to answer His call to abandon everything they had to follow Him—and they needed the reassurance of a great sign.*

Thanks to St. John, we do know about the miracle, but his description of the event was so sparse that it leaves us with significant unanswered questions, especially these: Why did Jesus' Mother approach Him, a guest, about the need for more wine—and why did He accede to her request?; Why did Jesus publicly address His Mother as "Woman!"?; and *Did the guests truly understand the epiphany— the breaking forth of the supernatural world into their natural world— which occurred in their presence?* To answer such questions, we turn to Sister Emmerich's visions.

The first point to note from Sister Emmerich's account is that Jesus was not there by accident. He had, many years before, predicted that He would be in attendance at the wedding of this Nathanael (not Nathanael Chased), who was related to Jesus through Sobe, His grandmother Anne's sister. And, He had certain roles to play in the celebration.

The wedding ceremony itself was performed by a priest in front of the synagogue, with wedding rings blessed by Jesus, on the morning of the third day after Jesus had arrived. Back at the public hall where the banquet was to be given, Jesus acted as "master of the feast," awarding prizes of fruit for certain decorous games which the wedding party played. According to Sister Emmerich's account, these were no ordinary fruits, and the bridegroom and bride won a remarkable specimen: "There were two pieces on a single stem: one was like a fig, the other, which was hollow, more like a ribbed apple. They were of a reddish color, the inside white and streaked with red. I have seen similar in Paradise." "I heard Jesus saying that those fruits could produce effects far greater than was the remarkable signification attached to them." After eating the fruit, the couple appeared to her to be "much brighter and purer, yes, even transparent" compared to how they had been before.

To appreciate the foregoing description, it is helpful to be aware of Sister Emmerich's mystical account that: "The vegetable kingdom before the Fall was endowed with certain supernatural virtues, but since the taint of sin the power of plants remains for man a secret. The form, the taste, the effects of the various herbs and fruits, are now but simple vestiges of the virtues they possessed before sin touched them. In my visions, I have seen upon the celestial tables fruits such as they were before the Fall."

It was during the wedding banquet itself that the incident recorded by St. John occurred. It had a background not known to him. Visions related by Sister Emmerich explain the basis of Mary's request of her Son, and also the nature of His answer. Prior to the feast, Jesus had agreed to supply the second course—birds, fish, confections and fruits—together with the wine for the whole affair. He relied on His good friend Lazarus, who was attending with the latter's sister Martha, to pay for the provisions; the foods were prepared under the supervision of His Mother and Martha. The wine which had been purchased ran out, as Jesus knew it would, and thus it was wholly understandable why Mary approached Him with her concern.

*Sister Emmerich explained why He responded to her as He did: "Jesus addressed her as 'Woman,' and not as 'Mother,' because, at this moment, as the Messiah, as the Son of God, He was present in divine power and was about to perform in presence of all His disciples and relatives an action full of mystery. On all occasions when He acted as the Incarnate Word, He ennobled those that participated in the same by giving them the title that best responded to the part assigned them. Thus did the holiness of the divine action shed as it were some rays upon them and communicate to them a special dignity. Mary was the 'Woman' who had brought forth Him whom now, as her Creator, she invokes on the occasion of the wine's failing. As the Creator, He will now give a proof of His high dignity. He will here show that He is the Son of God and not the Son of Mary. . . ."*

In meditating upon Jesus' interchange with the Blessed Virgin Mary on this occasion, it is helpful to keep in mind the instruction He gave Her immediately prior to His baptism, that she must now sacrifice all purely personal claims on Him, and that He was thereafter to be for all mankind.

Events then proceeded as described by St. John, with Jesus issuing a command and the servants taking three wine jugs and three water jugs to the cellar, where they were filled from a cistern. The earthen jugs, now so heavy that it took two men to carry each, were brought up, and the newly created wine drawn off and presented first to the wine steward and then to the bridegroom and the bride's father.

According to Sister Emmerich, "the miracle gave rise to no alarm or excitement; on the contrary, a spirit of silent awe and reverence fell upon them." *"His listeners were filled with fear and wonder, and the wine produced a change in all. I saw that, not by the miracle alone, but also by the drinking of that wine, each one had received strength, true and interior, each had become changed. . . . His disciples, His relatives, in a word, all present were now convinced of Jesus' power and dignity, as well as of His mission. All believed in Him. Faith at once took possession of every heart. All became better, more united, more interior."*

As described by Sister Emmerich, the bride and bridegroom were particularly affected, as they had been previously by eating the fruit Jesus gave them: after the banquet they approached Jesus separately, expressing the feeling that they were dead to carnal desires, and were willing to live a life of continence if their spouse would agree. Jesus then brought them together and counseled them: "He referred to many of the prophets and other holy persons who had lived in chastity, offering their body as a holocaust to the Heavenly Father. They had thus reclaimed many wandering souls, had won them to themselves as so many spiritual children, and had acquired a numerous and holy posterity." The two, manifesting Essene spirituality, took a vow to live in continence for three years.

Consider this contrast: whereas Adam and Eve had sinned through eating fruit forbidden them by God the Father, this couple conquered their sins by eating fruit expressly given them by God the Son—fruit which was described by Sister Emmerich as being exactly like that of the forbidden tree in Paradise. And this too was a contrast: far from directing the bridal pair to be fruitful and multiply, as the Father had done with Adam and Eve, on this occasion the Son heartily approved of marital continence, albeit within limits, prescribing only a three-year period, rather than the lifelong one which they were willing to undertake.

As we might expect, Jesus used the miracle as an occasion for an extended teaching—even giving those assembled a hint of the true Eucharistic miracle which would come at the end of His ministry: "He told them that they should witness greater miracles than this; that He would celebrate several Paschs, and at the last would change wine into Blood and bread into Flesh, and that He would remain with them till the end to strengthen and console." *The eschatological implication of His transformation of the water was thus taught by Jesus at the marriage feast itself, just as the Catholic Church teaches it still: "The sign of water turned into wine at Cana already announces the Hour of Jesus' glorification. It makes manifest the fulfillment of the wedding feast in the Father's kingdom, where the faithful will drink the new wine that has become the Blood of Christ."*[3]

---

[1] It should be noted that Sister Emmerich did not see Capernaum as being directly on the Sea of Galilee in those years. According to her visions, at that time, Capernaum lay on a plateau and southern slope of a mountain, northwest of the Sea, accessible by a valley through which a stream ran into the Sea. This will seem strange to those who have made a pilgrimage to the Holy Land and have visited the partial reconstructions of what are believed to have been the Synagogue of the Centurion, and the House of St. Peter, right next to the Sea. *See* James F. Strange and Hershel Shanks, "Synagogue Where Jesus Preached Found at Capernaum," *Biblical Archaeology Review* (Nov/Dec 1983), and "Has the House Where Jesus Stayed in Capernaum Been Found?," *Biblical Archaeology Review* (Nov/Dec 1982).

In general—the identification of locations in the Holy Land has proven to be problematic, as most sites have long been in ruins, and archaeologists do not find artifacts bearing the name of the town they are excavating, so many of the current attributions should still be regarded as provisional. *See, e.g.,* J. Maxwell

Miller, "Biblical Maps—How Reliable Are They?," *Bible Review* (Winter 1987) 33.

In particular—Jesus cried "Woe!" over three towns in Galilee: Chorazin, Bethsaida and Capernaum. (Mt 11:20–24; Lk 10:13–15); all three were utterly destroyed and were lost track of for many centuries. Identifying the ruins of them now is complicated by the fact that there are earthquake fault systems running up the Jordan and north from the Sea of Galilee. *See* Amos Nur and Hagai Ron, "Earthquake!—Inspiration for Armageddon," *Biblical Archaeology Review* (July/Aug 1997) 48. It seems likely that the shoreline and course of the Jordan River have changed significantly since the time of Jesus: for example, the harbors of Galilee in Jesus' time are now underwater—proving that the water level was lower then than now. *See* Mendel Nun, "Ports of Galilee," *Biblical Archaeology Review* (July/Aug 1999).

Sister Emmerich had a vision of an earthquake occurring at the time of Jesus' death, one which not only opened tombs and did other damage in Jerusalem, but also caused the Sea to flood the valley which had been east of Capernaum. That suggests that Capernaum has been correctly identified as now being on the Sea. However, if her visions are correct, the ruins of Bethsaida now lie east of it under the Sea of Galilee, and not, as some archaeologists believe, at a tell on the eastern side of the Jordan, more than a mile north of the Sea. *See* Rami Arav, et al., "Bethsaida Rediscovered," *Biblical Archaeology Review* (Jan/Feb 2000). Sister Emmerich referred to the latter site as Bethsaida-*Julias*. Further, the possible identification of ruins northwest of Capernaum as those of Great Chorazin, *see* Ze'ev Yeivin, "Ancient Chorazin Comes Back to Life," *Biblical Archaeology Review* (Sept/Oct 1987), is inconsistent with Sister Emmerich's visions, which locate that city east of the Sea.

[2] Not only have commentators challenged *New* Testament accounts of Jesus' ability to read minds, they have even argued that the *Old* Testament does not depict God as always being able to read the minds of men. *See* Michael Carasik, "Can God Read Minds?," *Bible Review* (June 2002), 32. *Accord*, David N. Freedman, "Is it Possible to Understand the Book of Job?," *Bible Review* (April 1988) 26, 32–33. A compelling written record exists that at least two priests of modern times, great saints, demonstrated the power to read the minds of sinners: St. John Vianney and St. Francesco Forgione (Padre Pio). Their feats were attested to by penitents themselves, with regard to sins forgotten or concealed. *See, e.g.*, Francis Trochu, *The Curé D'Ars* (Rockford, IL: TAN Books 1977) 295; Clarice Bruno, *Roads to Padre Pio* (Norristown, PA: National Centre for Padre Pio 1981) 78–80, 187–88; C. Bernard Ruffin, *Padre Pio: The True Story* (Huntington, IN: Our Sunday Visitor 1991) 265.

[3] *See Catechism of the Catholic Church* § 1335. Pope John Paul II has proposed the "self-manifestation" of Jesus at the Wedding at Cana as the second "Mystery of Light" for the Rosary—an event "when Christ changes water into wine and opens the hearts of the disciples to faith, thanks to the intervention of Mary, the first among believers." *See* Pope John Paul II, "On the Most Holy Rosary," Apostolic Letter (Oct. 16, 2002 ), 32 *Origins* (October 31, 2002) 345, 350. http://www.petersnet/research/retrieve_full.cfm?RecNum=4466.

# CHAPTER FIVE

*Are Modern Doubts About Jesus' Miraculous Healings Valid?*

The late author Flannery O'Connor was deeply distressed by the general lack of appreciation of the *power* of God: "Miracles seem in fact to be the great embarrassment for the modern man, a kind of scandal. If the miracles could be argued away and Christ reduced to the status of a teacher, domesticated and fallible, then there'd be no problem."[1]

The "embarrassment" seems especially pronounced in biblical scholarship. As two leaders in that field noted with dismay: "A premise underlying much modern writing on miracles holds that because there is nothing which cannot ultimately be proved or disproved by rational understanding, then *miracles in the sense of God's overruling of the natural order cannot happen.*"[2]

There are academics who are determined to find scientific explanations for all the events in Scripture, even if their efforts are less believable than the miracle stories themselves. Charlotte Allen, who studied two hundred years worth of such creative apologetics, described some of the attempts to avoid the appearance of the supernatural as "the most bizarre forms of fiction imaginable."[3] Even among the group of scholars most favorably inclined to the veracity of the miracle texts, there are very few who embrace them all as historically valid. It is usual to find a commentator adopting a "nuanced" approach: in some cases he admits that an event "most likely" had a historical foundation and that the onlookers believed it to be miraculous (without the author crediting their belief); other verses are taken as creative expansions of events which actually happened, but were not regarded as miracles at the time; still other accounts are rejected outright as having been "created whole and entire" to illustrate some doctrine or pedagogical point.[4]

One prominent Catholic professor and cleric wrote, with regard to the category of so-called "nature miracles"[5]: "With the sole exception of the feeding of the multitude, all these stories appear to have been created by the early church to serve various theological purposes."[6] Exorcisms are dismissed out of hand as reflecting superstitious nonsense about demons,[7] and instances of Jesus raising the dead are denigrated with the suggestion that at the bottom, they may only have been stories of the healing of a very sick person.[8] Accounts of cures of the living suffer only somewhat less at the hands of the skeptics.

As an antidote to such scoffing, it is appropriate to consider the historical context in which Jesus lived, and to answer the question: How did He become the most important person who ever lived? He was not the son of an earthly king. He was not even born into a wealthy or powerful family. He was not a noted warrior, scholar, merchant, or a man of any great attainment when He first burst on the public scene. He did not attract attention by mobilizing His countrymen against the Romans or even against their puppet-king Herod. He was not commissioned by the religious establishment to expound upon the Law and the Prophets. He walked around barefoot, depending on charity for His food. *And to those who, nevertheless, were considering following Him, He made no promises about rewards in this world—rather, He told them that they would have to leave their work and their families, and suffer hatred and persecution. He had nothing whatsoever with which to draw an audience to listen to His parables, instructions and prophecies, and nothing whatsoever to draw to Himself disciples, except the miracles He performed—and these were sufficient because they clearly demonstrated that the divine favor rested upon Him.*

At the same time that He deliberately performed "signs," Jesus refused to work miracles merely for the sake of making an impression, as is shown by the case of the adopted son of the Centurion of Capernaum. This is one of the miracles always brought up by academics who try to disparage the historicity of the Gospels by pointing out apparent inconsistencies between different accounts of the same event. Sts. Matthew, Luke and John all told of the healing of a boy by Jesus, at the behest of a someone who was variously described as a centurion or a royal official (or servant of a royal official), and who was either the boy's father or his master. In the case of the Gospels of Matthew and Luke, the person requesting the favor expressed his unworthiness to have Jesus come under his roof, and so asked that the boy be cured from a distance. *While the academics assume that there was only one underlying healing incident, which the three Evangelists described differently based on unreliable reports from others, Sister Emmerich had visions of two distinct healings.*

One was conformable to the Gospels of Sts. Matthew and Luke, and involved the Centurion Cornelius, a young Roman military officer; the other was conformable to St. John's Gospel, and involved Centurion Zorobabel, a retired royal official, and his chief steward.

As to the latter, Sister Emmerich identified Zorobabel (the Centurion of Capernaum) as being a retired officer who had once been Governor of a part of Galilee under Herod Antipas. Recently, the Centurion had protected the disciples against the Pharisees and had supported them monetarily. He had no natural children, but had adopted the son of his chief steward as his own son. Because the boy was ill, he sent his servants to find Jesus and request that He return with them to Nazareth. Although they were accompanied by Andrew and Nathanael, they were rebuffed by Jesus because of the spirit in which they had requested the miracle: both the Centurion and Jesus' own disciples were motivated not only by concern for the boy, but also by a desire to show up the Pharisees.

The boy's condition grew worse, and the Centurion's chief steward[9] himself approached Jesus, who by then had arrived in Cana and was teaching a crowd. The man was not able to make his way through the throng to Jesus, and so instead cried out, imploring Jesus to come with him in haste, for his son was dying. Here is what Sister Emmerich saw:

"When he cried so impatiently, Jesus turned His head toward him and said loud enough for the people to hear: 'I know your case well. You want to boast of a miracle and glory over the Pharisees, though you have the same need of being humbled as they. My mission is not to work miracles in order to further your designs. I stand in no need of your approbation. I shall reserve My miracles until it is My Father's will that I should perform them, and I shall perform them when My mission calls for it!' And thus Jesus went on for a long time, humbling the man before all the people." Ultimately, as we know, when the man pleaded that his son was in the agony of death, Jesus relented and cured him at a distance. But when Jesus arrived in Capernaum and was met by the overjoyed Centurion, Jesus took the occasion to chastise him too for the improper motive he had in asking for boy's cure.

Reader of the Gospels know that Jesus' most often performed miracle was the healing of physical infirmities, and yet, if we were to count up every time an Evangelist recorded a specific cure, we would find only about a dozen such incidents. Still, it is clear that many, many more cures were effected by Jesus, for the Evangelists repeatedly commented about people thronging to Him, bearing their ill on litters, and laying them where He would pass by. *Indeed, Sister Emmerich's visions indicate that a true count of His healings would be in the thousands—perhaps over ten thousand!*

She saw that in most cases, at least with healings of the Jews, a period of time passed before there was a full recovery, in some cases minutes, in others, hours or days. This was to give them time to reflect on the mercy of God and their own situation. She noted that healings of pagans often appeared more sudden and miraculous, for such people needed to see a stronger sign. While Jesus frequently touched the affected part of the body, He could and did heal with a glance or simply prayer at a distance.

### How Did Jesus Link Illness with Sin?

*The single most significant point to be drawn from Sister Emmerich's visions of the cures worked by Jesus, is that Jesus always dealt with illness as being linked together with sin—albeit that the ill person himself might not be the sinner.* Her understanding was that: "As every malady of the body symbolized some malady of the spiritual order, some sin or the chastisement due to it, so did every cure symbolize some grace, some conversion, or the cure of some particular spiritual evil." Jesus always demanded not only belief in Himself, but also, from those who had sinned, contrition and a prospective reformation of life. The merit, or lack thereof, of the individual, had an effect on whether he was cured and if so, to what extent and for how long.

A story illustrating this was told by St. John of a man, crippled for 38 years, being healed by Jesus at the Pool of Bethesda. At that particular point in time, Jesus was able to move freely in Jerusalem because the important Sadducees and Pharisees were not in town, and there were no crowds of people by whom He might have been recognized. After teaching in the Temple precincts without disturbance, together with His disciples He slipped through a back door into the hall surrounding the pool, where the invalids were sitting or lying. His disciples distributed clothes, covers and food to them, while Jesus moved from one to the next. Ultimately, He attended to the man whose cure was memorialized for all time in St. John's Gospel.

As the Evangelist told the story, after the man complained that there was no one to plunge him into the waters when they happened to be stirred up (it was believed that an angel did this, from time to time, and thus imparted healing powers to the water), Jesus ordered him to stand, and he was instantly cured; Jesus then slipped away, but later found the man and told him: "Remember, now, you have been cured. Give up your sins so that something worse may not overtake you." It is not clear from the Gospel exactly when the later encounter occurred—whether hours or days afterwards.

Because St. John condensed the story, readers are left to wonder what the man's sins were, why Jesus brought them up, and why Jesus only referred to them *after* curing him. The visions of Sister Emmerich supply details which explain these points. According to her, when Jesus went over to the man, He spoke for a while to him, "*placed his sins before his eyes, excited his heart to sorrow, and told him that he should no longer live in impurity and no longer blaspheme against the Temple, for it was in punishment of such sins that his sickness had come upon him. Then He consoled him by telling him that God receives all and assists all that turn again to Him with contrition.* The poor man, who never before had received a word of consolation . . . was now deeply touched at Jesus' words." Only after that did Jesus command: "Arise! Take up thy bed, and walk!"

Sister Emmerich saw the cure itself as taking place at a lesser feast, while it was months later, at the second Pasch of Jesus' ministry, that Jesus came up to the formerly lame man and warned him. The lapse of time between the two incidents would explain Jesus' reminder to him to give up his sins.

No Gospel story so well illustrates the connection between illness and sin as the incident reported by St. Mark and St. Luke of a paralyzed man being lowered through a roof to be pardoned and cured by Jesus. As Sister Emmerich described it, the event at the synagogue in Capernaum was even more impressive than is set down in the Gospels, for there was not just one paralytic but four, each carried by two friends who themselves were ambulatory but partially lame. They lifted the litters over a wall and forced their way through the crowd, which drew back. The Pharisees expressed their anger that public sinners were daring to come near, causing the malades to fear that they would be ejected without being treated by Jesus, but Jesus came to their rescue, crying out to them that their sins were forgiven! *In response to the furious exclamations of the Pharisees, Jesus said to them sharply: "If ye do not want salvation yourselves, yet should you not grudge it to the repentant!"*

And, Jesus remonstrated with them over their anger that He would cure on a Sabbath. In a number of passages in the Gospels, when that subject came up, Jesus is pictured as defending Himself by pointing out that His accusers would have no hesitation about rescuing their own ox or ass which had fallen into a pit on the Sabbath. This time, He justified Himself not by comparing it with how His accusers themselves acted, but by reference to the actions of His heavenly Father on the Sabbath: "Does the hand of the Almighty rest on the Sabbath-day from doing good and punishing evil? Does He not feed the hungry, cure the sick, and shed around His blessings on the Sabbath? Can He not send sickness on the Sabbath? May He not let you die on the Sabbath? Be not vexed that the Son does the will and the works of His Father on the Sabbath!"

When Jesus reached the sick men, He ordered the Pharisees to stand in a row at some distance, saying: "Stay here, for to ye these men are unclean, though to Me not, since their sins have been forgiven them! And now, tell Me, is it harder to say to a contrite sinner, 'Thy sins are forgiven thee,' than to say to a sick man, 'Arise, and carry thy bed hence?'" The Pharisees had not a word to answer. Then Jesus approached the sick men, laid His hands on them one after the other, uttered a few words of prayer over them, raised them up by the hand, and commanded them to render thanks to God, to sin no more, and to carry away their beds.

"All four arose. The eight who had carried them and who were themselves half-sick, became quite vigorous, and they helped the others to throw off the covers in which they were wrapped. These latter appeared to be only a little fatigued and embarrassed. Putting together the poles of their portable beds, they shouldered them, and all twelve went off through the wondering and exulting crowd joyfully intoning the song of thanksgiving: 'Praised be the Lord God of Israel! He has done great things to us. He has had mercy on His people, and has cured us by His Prophet!'"

If we were asked the same question—whether it is easier to forgive sins or to cure an illness—we might well say the latter, since there are many who can heal, but only God can forgive sins. So it is helpful to our understanding of the point that Jesus was making that, on yet another occasion in Capernaum when the Pharisees criticized Jesus for pardoning sinners, *Sister Emmerich heard Jesus explain why it was easier to forgive sins: he that sincerely repents sin will not lightly sin again; but the sick who are cured in body often remain sick in soul, and make use of their body to relapse into sin.*

Sister Emmerich explained a difference in His treatment of those whose maladies were especially grave, from those with lesser ills. "The great and most violent maladies I saw Jesus, in His wisdom, cure at once. They that were afflicted with them, like the possessed, had no will whatever to remain in the state in which they were, or again, self-will was entirely overcome by the violence of the malady. But as to those that were less grievously affected, whose sufferings only opposed an obstacle to their sinning with more facility, and whose conversion was insincere, I saw that Jesus often sent them away with an admonition to reform their life; or that He only alleviated without curing their bodily ills that through their pressure the soul might be cured.

"Jesus could have cured all that came to Him and that instantaneously, but, He did so only for those that believed and did penance, and He frequently warned them against a relapse. Even those that were only slightly sick He sometimes cured at once, if such would prove beneficial to their soul. He was not come to cure the body that it might the more readily sin, but He cured the body in order to deliver and save the soul."

The foregoing rationale explains Jesus' actions in this poignant scene which she saw in her visions: "I saw Him several times pass by some that were able to stand. They were those that had frequently received slight relief from Him, but their conversion not being earnest, they had relapsed in body and soul. As Jesus was passing by them, they cried out: 'Lord, Lord! Thou dost cure all that are grievously sick, and Thou dost not cure us! *Lord, have pity on us! We are sick again!' Jesus responded: 'Why do ye not stretch forth your hands to Me?' At these words, all stretched out their hands to Him, and said: 'Lord, here are our Hands!' Jesus replied: 'Ye do indeed stretch forth these hands, but the hands of your heart I can not seize. Ye withdraw them and lock them up, for ye are filled with darkness.'* Then He continued to admonish them, cured several who were converted, slightly relieved others, and passed by some unnoticed."

Similarly, along the route from Capernaum to Nazareth, when Jesus was approached by two men who were possessed and wanted Him to cure them. He put to them this question: "If a man was sick from overloading his stomach, and wanted to get well in order to indulge in new excesses, what would they think of him?" He refused their request, telling them to amend their ways.

In the city of Regaba, northeast of the Sea of Galilee, in the land of Bashan, Jesus opened the ears and loosened the tongue of a deaf and dumb man, as reported by St. Mark. On this occasion, as He had done many times before, Jesus enjoined the recipient of the grace to keep silent. It may be wondered why Jesus did so, since He was then engaged in proclaiming the advent of the Kingdom. Would it not have been appropriate to have such proclamations made also by those who had been healed?

As Sister Emmerich explained, Jesus commanded silence first and foremost to forestall boasting on the part of the cured person which would prevent his reflection upon the mercy of God. Also: "Jesus desired that the cured should enter into themselves instead of running about enjoying the new life that had been given them, and thereby falling an easy prey to sin. Another reason for enjoining silence was that Jesus wanted to impress upon the disciples the necessity of avoiding vainglory and of performing the good they did through love and for God alone. Sometimes again, He made use of this prohibition in order not to increase the number of the inquisitive, the importunate, and the sick who came to Him not by the impulse of faith. Many indeed came merely to test His power, and then they fell back into their sins and infirmities."

While the people believed—and Sister Emmerich was given to understand—that there was a link between bodily infirmity and sin, this did not necessarily mean that the ill person was himself the sinner. It was in accordance with the times to believe that punishment for sins could be visited upon later generations—as, indeed, God told the Children of Israel He would do, right in the First Commandment: "I, the Lord, your God, am a jealous God, inflicting punishment for their fathers' wickedness on the children of those who hate me, down to the third and fourth generation."[10]

In that context, Sister recounted the cure of a deaf and dumb boy in Shunem, and the guidance Jesus gave the boy's father: *"During the evening Jesus had a private interview with the father upon whom a great crime committed by his own father was still resting. The man asked Jesus whether the chastisement was to fall even to the fourth generation. Jesus answered that if he did penance and atoned for the crime, he might blot out its consequences."*

We know that certain particularly holy people, such as St. Francis and St. Pio (Padre Pio)—and Sister Emmerich herself—deliberately chose to suffer for the sins of others. Sister Emmerich related that such suffering may also come upon us involuntarily, as was the case with a group of possessed persons whom Jesus cured: "There are such good possessed people of whom the demon has taken possession by no fault of their own. I cannot clearly explain it, but I saw on this occasion as well as upon others, how it happens that a guilty person may by the mercy and long-sufferance of God be spared, while Satan takes possession of one of his weak, innocent relatives. It is as if the innocent took upon himself a part of the other's punishment. I can not make it clear, but it is certain that we are all members of one body.

It is as if a healthy member, in consequence of a secret, intimate bond between them, suffers for another that is not sound."

Sister Emmerich detailed some of the benefits of sacrificial suffering—even for an *inherited* sinfulness—in describing the story of a paralyzed girl named Michol, who lived in Antipatris: "She had been chained down by sickness during the most perilous years of her childhood, years full of danger to innocence; and in consequence of the same, her parents had an opportunity for the exercise of charity and patience. Had she been well from infancy, what would perhaps have become of both her and her parents? Had the latter not sighed after Jesus, Michol never would have been so blessed. Had they not believed in Him, their daughter would never have been cured and anointed, which anointing had imparted wonderful strength and energy both to body and soul. *Her sickness was a trial, a consequence of inherited sinfulness, but at the same time, a loving discipline, a means of spiritual progress for Michol's soul, as well as for her parents.* The patience and resignation of the parents resulted from their cooperation with grace. It brought to them the crown, the recompense of the struggle decreed for them by God, namely, the cure through Jesus of soul and body. *What a grace! To be bound down by sufferings, and yet to have the spirit free for good until the Lord comes to deliver both body and soul!*"

Those who are familiar with Sister Emmerich's own life will realize that the last two sentences perfectly expressed her view of her own painful, yet grace-filled existence.

---

[1] *See* Sally Fitzgerald (ed.), *The Habit of Being— Letters of Flannery O'Connor* (New York: Vintage Books 1980) 231.

[2] *See* W.F. Albright & C.S. Mann, *The Anchor Bible—Matthew*, Introduction at cxxvii. As Cardinal Ratzinger has noted: "the preconception that what is most improbable in the world is also impossible for God conceals the tacit presupposition that it is impossible both for God to reach into earthly history and for earthly history to reach him. His field of influence will be limited to the realm of the spirit. And with this we have landed back in pagan philosophy. . . ." *See* Joseph Ratzinger, *Daughter Zion* (San Francisco: Ignatius Press 1983) 60.

[3] *See* Charlotte Allen, *The Human Christ—The Search for the Historical Jesus* (New York: The Free Press 1998) 134.

[4] *See*, e.g., John P. Meier, *A Marginal Jew* 2:968. A representative example of the scholars' attack on miracles is Jarl Fossum, "Understanding Jesus' Miracles," *Bible Review* (April 1994) 16.

[5] Msgr. Meier identified the "nature miracles" as the stories of the Temple tax, the cursing of the fig tree, the miraculous catch of fish, the walking on water, the stilling of the storm at sea, the changing of water into wine, and the feeding of the multitude(s). *See* John P. Meier, *A Marginal Jew* 2:874–970.

[6] *See ibid.* 970.

[7] According to Raymond E. Brown, "in the area of demonology . . . Jesus seems to draw on the imperfect religious concepts of his time." *See Jesus God and Man* 59.

[8] *See, e.g.,* John P. Meier, *A Marginal Jew* 2:831; Peter Joseph, "Did Lazarus Rise?," *The Latin Mass—A Journal of Catholic Culture* (Spring 2002) 22 (disputing a learned commentary that Lazarus was merely sick).

[9] St. John referred to the boy's father as a *basilikos*, which appears in translations as a "royal official," but the word also could be understood to mean a servant of a royal official, which the chief steward was.

[10] Ex 20:1–6.

# Chapter Six

*Mary Magdalene*

Mary Magdalene still provokes much interest and commentary today, as she has for centuries, despite—or perhaps because of—the fact that so little is really known about this woman who had a special devotion to Jesus.

All four Evangelists told of her going to the tomb of the Risen Christ and encountering Him there, and all except St. Luke also reported that she had been present at the foot of the Cross with His Mother and John. As to how she had fit into Jesus' life, and He into hers, before that terrible moment, the only certain clues we have are from a passing reference by St. Mark that Jesus had cast seven devils out of her, and the mention by St. Luke, that on His journeys, Jesus was accompanied by the Apostles "and also some women who had been cured of evil spirits and maladies; Mary called the Magdalene, from whom seven devils had gone out. . . ."

That is all we know for sure, and so we are left to wonder: Was she truly "possessed?" Is the popular imagination of her as a great sinner correct, and, if so, what converted her? Was this the Mary who anointed Jesus' feet with perfume and dried them with her hair? Was she the sister of Martha and Lazarus—the Mary who chose "the better part," listening to Jesus while her sister scurried around with the tasks of hospitality?

Many stories have been created to fill in the gaps of her history and assess her significance for believers. One of these inventions was the so-called "Gospel of Mary." The few surviving fragments of this second century apocrypha[1] show a holy and enlightened Magdalene, the embodiment of wisdom, providing gnostic revelations to the Apostles about the journey of the soul through the planetary spheres.[2] (Understandably, the Church refused to include this heresy in its Canon of Scripture!) People in the Middle Ages were familiar with stories of a more human, albeit not much more believable,

Magdalene—this one a reformed sinner, who herself performed many miracles after the Resurrection.[3] Times change, and our own era exalts unrepressed sexuality, rather than penitence or holiness; and so it is not surprising that the carnal side of Magdalene is the one which writers now choose to emphasize. Shockingly, they have taken artistic license to the point of blasphemy about the Lord, by portraying Him with Magdalene in an unchaste liaison.[4] In this, they also libel *her* memory, for she is a canonized saint of the Church, still held up to believers as the model penitent.

As a corrective to such fictions, it is well to refer to the extensive visions which Sister Emmerich had of Magdalene's life. These clear up the mysteries surrounding her, and describe the long process of suffering she went through while being freed from demonic possession. According to Sister Emmerich, Mary Magdalene was the sister of Martha and Lazarus. Their parents, who were very wealthy and owned great properties in Jerusalem and Galilee, had had 15 children, of whom only four remained alive at the time of Jesus' ministry: Lazarus, Martha, Mary Magdalene, and a third sister, called "Silent Mary," who lived in seclusion and was thought by everyone to be a simpleton. The following is part of what Sister Emmerich saw in her visions of Magdalene's childhood:

"Magdalene, the youngest child, was very beautiful and, even in her early years, tall and well developed like a girl of more advanced age. She was full of frivolity and seductive art. Her parents died when she was only seven years old. She had no great love for them even from her earliest age, on account of their severe fasts. Even as a child, she was vain beyond expression, given to petty thefts, proud, self-willed, and a lover of pleasure. She was never faithful, but clung to whatever flattered her the most. She was, therefore, extravagant in her pity when her sensitive compassion was aroused, and kind and condescending to all that appealed to her senses by some external show. . . . I never saw that she either really loved or was loved. It was all, on her part at least, vanity, frivolity, self-adoration, and confidence in her own beauty. I saw her a scandal to her brother and sisters whom she despised and of whom she was ashamed on account of their simple life." Magdalene continued to give scandal as she grew up in the castle at Magdalum, which she had inherited, to the point that people talked of her being possessed of a devil.

*However, Jesus, who knew her heart and her future, predicted at the beginning of His ministry that Mary would eventually rise to higher sanctity than her sister Martha.*

*How Did Jesus Drive the Devils Out of Mary Magdalene?*

The first, small step on the road to her sanctification occurred when she was invited to go with the Holy Women to hear Jesus for herself. She accompanied them, but did not stay for the instruction. A mere glance from Jesus so agitated and internally humiliated her that she ran away.

Her initial conversion—a genuine one, but one which did not last—came at another teaching by Jesus, which she stayed to attend in Gabara, where Jesus taught on a mountainside. As recounted by Sister Emmerich, Jesus gave a severe instruction, demanding conversion, and referring to the fate of Sodom and Gomorrah. Having brought the possibility of damnation home to His listeners, Jesus did not dwell on it, but offered relief through another message delivered with great emotion—this one a message of compassion for sinners, even for His enemies:

*"He implored His Father to touch their heart that some, a few, yes, even one, though burdened with all kinds of guilt, might return to Him. Could He gain but one soul, He would share all with it, He would give all that He possessed, yes, He would even sacrifice His life to purchase it. He stretched out His arms toward them, exclaiming: 'Come! come to Me, ye who are weary and laden with guilt! Come to Me, ye sinners! Do penance, believe, and share the Kingdom with Me!' Then turning to the Pharisees, to His enemies, He opened His arms to them also, beseeching all, at least one of them to come to Him."*

This exhortation greatly affected Magdalene, who wept under her veil. She wanted to fly to Jesus, but was restrained by her companions, who feared a disturbance. Jesus noted her movement, however, and spoke some words which brought consolation to her: *"'If even one germ of penance, of contrition, of love, of faith, of hope has, in consequence of My words, fallen upon some poor, erring heart, it will bear fruit, it will be set down in favor of that poor sinner, it will live and increase. I Myself shall nourish it, shall cultivate it, shall present it to My Father.'"*

Following His instruction, and His healings of sick people brought there from all over, Jesus repaired for a feast at the home of Simon, the head of the local synagogue. Magdalene followed and, seeing that the Pharisees had failed to accord Jesus any of the honors due a guest, in the middle of a debate at table she darted in to anoint him from a little flask. This was the occasion described by St. Luke, when Jesus proposed to Simon the parable of the two bankrupt debtors, one owing a great deal and one a relatively small amount, whose creditor forgave them both; just as the debtor who owed more would be more grateful, so would this woman be very grateful that her many sins were forgiven. After telling Magdalene to go in peace, Jesus spoke out against "the criticizing of others, public accusations, and remarks upon the exterior fault of others while the speakers often hid in their own hearts much greater, though secret evils."

Magdalene withdrew to the inn, where she met with the Blessed Virgin Mary and the other Holy Women. She said that she must follow Jesus, and she wanted to join them, which they were more than willing to accommodate; they pleaded with her to accompany them back to Bethania, but she determined to go back to her castle at Magdalum, to make arrangements for her household. Unfortunately, once there, Magdalene was subject to the baneful influences of the dissolute men in her life, and she relapsed into sin, now becoming possessed and falling into convulsions.

Finally, Magdalene's sister Martha visited her for the purpose of trying to persuade her to attend a great instruction to be given by Jesus in Azanoth, a little town just south of Dothan. Magdalene was haughty and defiant, treating her sister very rudely, but consented to go; she sent Martha on ahead because Martha was dressed so simply that Magdalene was ashamed to be seen with her. In her extravagant finery, Magdalene made a grand appearance with her dissolute friends who set down their seats, cushions and rugs right up front, scandalizing the Pharisees.

It was another of Jesus' dire sermons, crying woe to the towns of Capernaum, Bethsaida, and Chorazin, but, then, surprisingly, Jesus began an exorcism of the assembled group, and especially of Magdalene. Sister Emmerich recounted the proceeding as follows: "Making allusion to Magdalene, Jesus said that, when the devil has been driven out and the house has been swept, he returns with six other demons, and rages worse than before. These words terrified Magdalene. After Jesus had in this way touched the hearts of many, He turned successively to all sides and commanded the demon to go out of all that sighed for deliverance from his thralldom, but that those who wished to remain bound to the devil should depart and take him along with them.

"At this command, the possessed cried out from all parts of the circle: 'Jesus, Thou Son of God!'—and here and there people sank to the ground unconscious." Magdalene went into convulsions, which Jesus observed with equanimity, saying: "The death she is now dying, is a good death, and one that will vivify her!"

After several such convulsive spells, Magdalene was led down the mountain, where the Holy Women took charge of her. Beginning to come to her senses, she shed some of her rich attire, donned a veil, and appeared at an instruction given by Jesus at the synagogue. Once more she was convulsed as an evil spirit was driven out. Now, the tears flowed in a torrent, and she tore her garments and ran about like a madwoman, proclaiming to all that she was a wretched sinner. Finding Jesus again, she threw herself down before Him and asked if she might still be saved. The Pharisees wanted Him to banish her, but instead, He comforted her with the counsel that she would soon find peace.

Her deliverance came the next morning, as described by Sister Emmerich: Jesus taught against the sin of impurity, blaming it as the vice that had called down fire upon Sodom and Gomorrah, while Magdalene listened in misery, sitting with the Holy Women. But, Jesus assured His listeners that it was a time of grace and that pardon was still available if they asked for it. Jesus exorcised Magdalene one last time, as she sat there, leaving her faint and desiring to confess her sins. Then, the Holy Women led her away to a private place, to await Jesus.

"She cried for pardon, confessed her numerous transgressions, and asked over and over: 'Lord, is there still salvation for me?' Jesus forgave her sins, and she implored Him to save her from another relapse. He promised so to do, gave her His blessing, and spoke to her of the virtue of purity, also of His Mother who was pure without stain. He praised Mary highly ... and commanded Magdalene to unite herself closely to her and to seek from her advice and consolation. *When Jesus and Magdalene rejoined the Holy Women, Jesus said to them: 'She has been a great sinner, but for all future time, she will be the model of penitents.'*"

Magdalene's conversion was complete and lasting. Sister Emmerich observed that thereafter: "She followed Jesus everywhere, sat at His feet, stood and waited for Him everywhere. She thought of Him alone, saw Him alone, knew only her Redeemer and her own sins. . . ." That corresponds exactly to the incident St. Luke reported, when Jesus visited the home of Martha and Mary: Martha busied herself as a hostess, while Mary left the work to her sister and simply sat in His presence and listened to Him talk. Sister Emmerich further noted that Magdalene was physically changed and gave outward evidence of her newfound humility: "Her countenance and bearing were still noble and distinguished, though her beauty was destroyed by her penance and tears. She sat almost always alone in her narrow penance-chamber, and at times performed the lowest services for the poor and sick."

A reader of Sister Emmerich's visions might be struck by the thought that Magdalene didn't do anything much out of the ordinary in her "possessed" state: sexual promiscuity is a common vice, and we aren't used to thinking of it as being caused by demonic possession. Indeed, going beyond Magdalene's case, after surveying all of the instances in the Gospels where Jesus was reported to have driven demons out of a person, a noted theologian wrote that: "Moderate or liberal Christians would probably . . . [see] most or all of the instances of 'possession' as various types of mental or psychosomatic illnesses."[5]

For those who believe that miracles *cannot* exist, it is natural to deny the existence of demons and the possibility of demonic possession. *But for those who accept the veracity of the Gospels, there is no way to get around the accounts that Magdalene, and certain other people, were truly possessed: the Gospels did not portray them either as simply lacking in moral character, or as being ill in a way which Jesus could cure like He cured leprosy or broken bones. Rather, they had to be healed with an exorcism—and in difficult cases with prayer and fasting—and the Evangelists frequently verified the fact of possession through the anguished words of the embedded demons, acknowledging Jesus as the "Son of God"—acknowledgments which He repeatedly had to stifle with a command.*

### The "Legion" of Devils, and the Swine of Gergesa

Verification of demonic possession was given in three different and very dramatic ways in the story of Jesus driving a troop of demons called Legion out of two possessed men into a herd of swine. The incident began when Jesus and His disciples went ashore at Magdala, a little boat landing on the southeast side of the Sea (not to be confused with Magdalum on the opposite shore). The purpose of Jesus' visit was to deliver the possessed of Gergesa,[6] a town a little way up the mountain to the east of Magdala. Jesus explained to the disciples that the possessed were particularly numerous there because the inhabitants were so focused on material goods, and practiced sorcery.

The local people urged Him not to go near a dark ravine which ran down to the Sea near Magdala, for there were two wild men there, suffering from possession. He replied that, to the contrary, He would indeed go that way, for He had been sent on earth for the sake of the miserable. And when the people suggested that He should at least stay the night with them because it was already dark, He replied that He feared not that sort of darkness—but they should fear remaining in eternal darkness, when the Word of God was shining upon them.

Going to the ravine the next day, Jesus confronted the two possessed men, who had long been practicing devilish magic. They were running around sepulchres, beating themselves with bones of the dead, and the demons in them set up a cry. In a vineyard nearby was a great wooden vat, big enough to hold twenty men, in which was mixed juices from grapes and also from an intoxicating herb; the resulting potion was used by the inhabitants to bring about diabolical ecstasies. Jesus commanded the possessed men to overturn the huge, full vat, which they did, to the consternation of the vineyard workers. (This herculean feat was a second proof of their demonic possession: an experienced exorcist of our own time, Father Gabriele Amorth, confirms that superhuman strength of the victim is one of the customary signs of demonic possession he encounters in his work.[7])

It was at this point that the legion of devils in the possessed men begged to be allowed to enter the swine. Jesus agreed to their proposal; the men were thrown into convulsions, while the thousands of swine went berserk, as reported in the Synoptic Gospels. The noises of the animals mingled with the cries of the herdsmen, as the swine rushed heedlessly around, plunging down the mountainside toward the Sea. And so, there was yet another verification given that the men had been possessed by demons.

Sister Emmerich's visions answer a question that a perceptive reader of the Gospels may have wondered about: "Would not thousands of pig carcasses have made the Sea of Galilee and its fish 'unclean' to the Jews?" Indeed, Jesus' disciples were worried about that possibility, but the animals did not actually go into the Sea, but rather into a whirlpool at the end of the ravine, which was blocked from the Sea by a sandbank, with water entering the whirlpool but not exiting into the Sea.

The herdsmen were furious, and they complained to Jesus, but He showed no sympathy for them. Now, some preachers profess to be concerned that Jesus would cause great economic loss to the supposedly innocent owners of the swine, and they have suggested that, because pigs were unclean animals under the Mosaic Law, perhaps they should not have been raised in the first place. But, Gergesa was in pagan territory, and Sister Emmerich's visions do not indicate that Jesus was in any way influenced in what He did by the fact that the swine were unclean. Rather, He was furious with the godless people of the area, who were deeply involved in idolatry and devilish practices, and He viewed the loss of the swine as the price they had to pay to save two of their guilty neighbors.

Jesus then approached the town and attempted to lecture the people who had gathered on a hillside, but the authorities and pagan priests, who regarded Jesus as a great sorcerer,[8] beseeched Him to leave their area and not do the people further injury. Sister Emmerich recounted Jesus' response: "Jesus bade them dismiss their fears, because He would not trouble them long. He had come for the sake of the poor sick and possessed alone, since He knew well that the unclean swine and the infamous beverage were of more value to them than the salvation of their souls. But the Father in heaven, who had given to Him the power to rescue the poor people before Him and to destroy the swine, judged otherwise. Then He held up to them all their infamy, their sinful dealings in sorcery, their dishonest gains, and their demonolatry. He called them to penance, to baptism, and offered them salvation." Fixated on their losses, they turned a deaf ear to His exhortation and sent Him on His way.

### Jesus Exposes Pagan Deviltry

Fortunately, Jesus was better received in other places where there were pagans, and He was able to cast out demons, heal the sick and begin to lead them to the true God. In Gadara, a heathen city which had a small Jewish quarter, a pagan women approached Him with a plea to cure her ill three-year-old son, who was in imminent danger of dying. Jesus went to her house and, together with Judas Barsabas and Nathanael the bridegroom, ministered to the boy. When he was cured, the mother threw herself at Jesus' feet, crying out "Great is the God of Israel! . . . Henceforth I will serve no other gods!" The commotion drew a crowd, and soon other mothers appeared with their ill children, complaining that their priestess was of little use to them in such matters.

Jesus ordered the priestess to be brought to Him; she was possessed, and tried to keep her face hidden. After Jesus drove demons out of her in forms which the crowd could see, He commanded her to tell them what she had done to their little boys and girls. She was forced to confess that she had deliberately made them sick by witchcraft, so that she could then cure them to honor the gods. Taking her in tow, Jesus led the people to a group of tombs, where the idol of Moloch was kept in a vault. Jesus ordered the pagan priests to bring Moloch to the surface.

Sister Emmerich described the idol and its workings: "Moloch was seated like an ox on his hind legs, his forepaws stretched out like the arms of one who is going to receive something upon them. . . . His gaping mouth disclosed an enormous throat, and on his forehead was one crooked horn. He was seated in a large basin. Around the body were several projections like outside pockets. On festival days long straps were hung around his neck. In the basin under him fire was made when sacrifices were to be offered. . . . Children used to be laid on his arms and consumed by the fire under him and in him, for he was hollow. He drew his arms in when the victim was deposited upon them, and pressed it tightly that its screams might not be heard. There was machinery in the hind legs by which he could be made to rise."[9]

Jesus called upon the priestess to praise her god—but, like Balaam the Prophet,[10] the woman could only speak in praise of Israel's God, and against the horrors of Moloch. And when Jesus' disciples turned over the idol and shook it; all sorts of demons seemed to emerge, crawl about, and disappear into the earth. These demonstrations had their desired effect, for the pagans asked Jesus to instruct them, which He did.

"Jesus spoke to them of baptism, exhorting them in the meantime to remain tranquil and persevere in their good resolutions. He spoke to them of God as of a father to whom we must sacrifice our evil inclinations, and who asks no other offering from us than that of our own heart. When addressing the pagans, Jesus always said to them more plainly than He did to the Jews, that God has no need of our offerings. He exhorted them to contrition and penance, to thanksgiving for benefits received, and to compassion toward the suffering."

Jesus knew that His war against the Devil and his minions would continue right up to the end of time, and He made it one of the missions of the Church He was establishing. *First*, when He commissioned the Apostles, "He gave them authority over unclean spirits"; *second*, the disciples did indeed drive out demons by invoking His name; and *third*, after the Resurrection, Jesus said that those who profess their faith "will use my name to expel demons." It is in keeping with such teachings that, even in this age when "demonic possession" is considered by most to be a relic of the superstitious past, the Catholic Church still includes exorcism among its sacramentals.[11]

### Jesus Frees Prisoners in Tirzah

In a metaphorical sense, we can speak of someone suffering from demonic possession, or a crippling illness or blindness, as being a captive to his condition, and in that sense Jesus did set prisoners free. (And, of course, Jesus did come to free those imprisoned by sin.) But the prophecy of Isaiah, that the Messiah would proclaim liberty to captives,[12] can also be interpreted as having the Messiah going to places of imprisonment and freeing the inmates unjustly held there. Although the Gospels do not report that type of action on the part of Jesus, Sister Emmerich saw it in her visions.

She recounted that He went to Tirzah, in Samaria, specifically because it was the site of a combined hospital and prison, where the inmates were particularly neglected on account of the cruelty of the Sadducees and Pharisees. Sister Emmerich described the place: "Women were imprisoned, some for their excesses, some on account of their bold speech, while many others of their number were innocent. In the same building many poor men underwent the rigors of grievous imprisonment, some for debt, others for having joined in a revolt, many also the victims of revenge and enmity, while others were confined merely to get them out of the way. Many of these poor creatures were quite abandoned, left to starve in their prison-cells."

Jesus healed the sick, and provided abundant alms, but the Roman commandant of the establishment told Jesus that he could not release any prisoners without the concurrence of the Jewish authorities of the town. Jesus promised to return with them, and then went off to teach in the synagogue, delivering as could be expected a very pointed instruction on the Beatitude "Blessed are the merciful," and explaining the parable of the Prodigal Son. He chastised the trustees of the jail and others who had misappropriated the funds intended for the support of the prisoners. "Here too Jesus related the parable of the compassionate king and the unmerciful servant. He applied it to those that allow the poor prisoner to languish on account of an insignificant debt, while God suffers their own great indebtedness to run on."

The leading Pharisees and Sadducees were too hardened to repent of their sins, and they would not assist the unfortunate inmates. Jesus was able to secure their grudging acceptance of the release of inmates only by arranging to pay a large ransom with funds to come from the sale of Mary Magdalene's castle. No longer possessed, she had ordered it sold to benefit the work of Jesus. The wretched men and women were dragged out of their cells, sick and in tatters, to be bathed, clothed, fed and sent home, through the ministrations of Jesus and the disciples. And thus did the Messiah set prisoners free, as had been prophesied by Isaiah.

[1] In current usage, the word connotes a spurious writing or writings, but originally it connoted writings whose wisdom was "hidden" from all but the initiated.

[2] In the process of lecturing the disciples, Magdalene faced down the Apostle Peter, who was depicted as frightened, ignorant and a misogynist. The Gospel of Mary can be found in various collections of apocrypha, including Edgar Hennecke, *New Testament Apocrypha* (Philadelphia, PA: Westminster Press 1963) 1:340, and James M. Robinson (ed.), *The Nag Hammadi Library in English* (New York: HarperSanFrancisco 1990) 523.

[3] *See* Jacobus de Voragine, *The Golden Legend* (Princeton, NJ: Princeton U. Press 1993) 1: 374.

[4] *See* Nikos Kazantzakis, *The Last Temptation of Christ* (New York: Simon and Schuster 1960) 446–50 (Jesus depicted as having, while He was nailed to the Cross, a reverie of copulating with Mary Magdalene); Dan Brown, *The Da Vinci Code* (Doubleday 2003)(Jesus presented as the *husband* of Mary Magdalene, who bore His children).

[5] *See* John P. Meier, *A Marginal Jew* 2:661.

[6] It is not easy to identify the locale from the Gospels, but St. Jerome and Eusebius thought that Gergesa (the modern El Kursi) was the site of the miracle of the swine. A lavish 5th century church has been excavated there. The fact that various early Biblical manuscripts are not in agreement on where the incident occurred may simply be due to the fact that Gerasa, Gadara and Gergesa, the three names mentioned of places east of the Sea of Galilee, are all spelled somewhat similarly in Greek. *See The Anchor Bible Dictionary* 2:991.

[7] *See* Gabriele Amorth, *An Exorcist Tells His Story* (San Francisco, CA: Ignatius Press 1999) 70, 72.

[8] There is no doubt that the people of that time believed that diabolical powers could be invoked through magic—as witness the reference to Simon Magus in the Acts of the Apostles. (Acts 8:9.)

[9] For a confirming description of child sacrifice to Molech, *see* Lawrence E. Stager & Samuel R. Wolff, "Child Sacrifice at Carthage—Religious Rite or Population Control?," *Biblical Archaeology Review* (Jan/Feb 1984).

[10] Nb ch. 23–24.

[11] "When the Church asks publicly and authoritatively in the name of Jesus Christ that a person or object be protected against the power of the Evil One and withdrawn from his dominion, it is called *exorcism*. Jesus performed exorcisms and from him the Church has received the power and office of exorcising. In a simple form, exorcism is performed at the celebration of Baptism. The solemn exorcism, called 'a major exorcism,' can be performed only by a priest and with the permission of the bishop. The priest must proceed with prudence, strictly observing the rules established by the Church." *See Catechism of the Catholic Church* § 1673. A recent working paper prepared by the Vatican on the role of bishops noted that: "In the fight against evil and the Evil One, the bishop must enlist, according to canon law, priests endowed with piety, knowledge, prudence and integrity of life to perform exorcisms and practice prayer so as to obtain healing from God." *See* Vatican Synod Secretariat

Working Paper, "The Bishop: Servant of the Gospel of Jesus Christ for the Hope of the World" 31 *Origins* (June 14, 2001) 65, 99. A first-hand account of the need for, and practice of, exorcisms in our own day has been written by a priest specializing in exorcisms. *See* Gabriele Amorth, *An Exorcist Tells His Story*; *see also* the interview with Fr. Amorth published in *30 Days* (June 2000). http://www.thecatholiclibrary.org/Articles. Pope John Paul II himself has conducted exorcisms. *See* "On File," 30 *Origins* (Sept. 21, 2000) 226.

[12] Is 61:1.

# CHAPTER SEVEN

## *Who Can Forgive Sins But God?*

"Who is this that speaks blasphemies?" "Who can forgive sins but God only?"

These two challenges to Jesus were repeatedly made by the scribes and Pharisees, as reported in the Synoptic Gospels. In the light of the Law and Tradition, their complaints were not unreasonable: sin was an offense against God—and who but God could forgive it? *We know Jesus could forgive sin because Jesus was God—but the religious leaders should not be blamed for not knowing that, as even His own disciples were ignorant of His divinity at the time.* Moreover, what Jesus did conflicted with the established rituals which enabled penitents to implore the Most High for forgiveness.

## *"Arise, Child of God!"*

Sister Emmerich had a vision of just such a reconciliation service which Jesus attended in the synagogue at Succoth during the festival of Tabernacles. Men laid their sin-offerings on tables by the altar, and then confessed their sins. They could do this either publicly in front of the assembled priests, or privately behind a curtain with a single priest. The penitent expressed his contrition, often with tears, and promised fidelity to the Law and to the Holy of Holies in the Temple at Jerusalem. A penance was imposed, and incense was burned on the altar. While confessions were being heard, those in the assembly chanted and prayed. After the men had been confessed, it was the turn of the women.

There are very significant similarities between this rite from 2,000 years ago and the Rite of Reconciliation celebrated by the Catholic Church today. Catholics who are conscious of only venial sin may content themselves with a general penitential service in church, while those conscious of mortal sin must make an individual confession to a priest, normally done privately, behind a curtain. In the Catholic rite, the sinner expresses his remorse, promises to amend his conduct, and receives a penance.[1]

However, there are also very great differences. In the old Jewish rite, an essential element was making a sin-offering to God. As Christians, we believe, as St. Paul wrote in his Letter to the Hebrews, that: "when Christ appeared as a high priest of the good things that have come . . . He entered once for all into the Holy Place, taking not the blood of goats and calves but His own blood, thus securing an eternal redemption. For if the sprinkling of defiled persons with the blood of goats and bulls and with the ashes of a heifer sanctifies for the purification of the flesh, how much more shall the blood of Christ, who through the eternal Spirit offered Himself without blemish to God, purify [our] conscience from dead works to serve the living God." Moreover, whereas the Jews believed that only God could forgive sins—the Catholic Church teaches that Jesus authorized Simon Peter and the Apostles to do so; further, that His power to forgive sins has been validly delegated by the Church to ordained priests acting in His name.

*It is very understandable that when Jesus taught that God no longer desired the sacrifice of animals, but rather a broken and contrite heart, and when He claimed that the Son of Man had authority to forgive sins, many pious Jews of His time thought it was a grave scandal.* Nor was Jesus content with merely making such a claim of authority in the abstract—He actually purported to forgive sins, and He did this everywhere He went, even in the reconciliation service described above.

According to Sister Emmerich, while Jesus was present there, a distinguished lady became too agitated by her desire for reconciliation to wait for the turn of the women, and she entered a place where women were forbidden to go. She kneeled in front of the priests, begging to be reconciled, but they told her to leave as they could not hear her there. "One of them, however, younger than his brethren, took her by the hand, saying: 'I will reconcile thee! If thy corporal presence belongs not here, not so thy soul, since thou art penitent!' Then turning with her toward Jesus, he said: 'Rabbi, what sayest Thou?' The lady fell on her face before Jesus, and *He answered: 'Yes, her soul has a right to be here! Permit this daughter of Adam to do penance!'* and the priest retired with her into the curtained enclosure. When she reappeared, she prostrated in tears upon the ground, exclaiming: 'Wipe your feet on me, for I am an adulteress!' and the priests touched her lightly with the foot. Her husband, who knew nothing of what was transpiring, was sent for.

"At his entrance, Jesus occupied the teacher's chair, and His words sank deep into the man's heart. He wept, and his wife, veiled and prostrate on the ground before him, confessed her guilt. Her tears flowed abundantly, and she appeared to be more dead than alive. *Jesus addressed her: 'Thy sins are forgiven thee! Arise, child of God!'* and the husband deeply moved reached out his hand to his penitent wife. Their hands were then bound together with the wife's veil and the long, narrow scarf of the husband, and loosened again after they had received a benediction. It was like a second nuptial ceremony. The lady was now after her reconciliation quite inebriated with joy."

There are two points of great importance to take away from Sister Emmerich's vision. The first is that Jesus did not content himself with giving a rabbinic opinion as to whether it was proper for the woman to make her confession then and there. Rather, He publicly interjected Himself into the process of reconciliation between her and the Most High, by proclaiming that her sins were forgiven!

*The second point is that He intimated that her atonement had effected a change in her spiritual status, by the difference in how He referred to the adulteress before and after she confessed her sins and was reconciled. Before, He called her "Daughter of Adam"— signifying that she was born only of sinful man; afterwards, He called her "Child of God"—signifying that she was reborn of the Spirit.*

### Who is Free of Spiritual Adultery?

Sister Emmerich saw that Jesus' forgiveness of the sins of another adulteress became the subject of controversy with the Pharisees of Ainon. Mary of Supha was a Jewish descendent of Orpah, the daughter-in-law of Naomi who had remained in Moab when the other daughter-in-law, Ruth, accompanied the widowed Naomi to Israel.[2] Estranged from her husband, she lived with her three illegitimate children. John's preaching had touched her, and she had repented and done penance. Still, she was still harassed by five devils—one for her husband and one for each of her lovers. She sought to confess her sins to Jesus, but was kept away by the Pharisees, who would not let her come near Jesus while He taught in the synagogue.

Going to her home, Jesus exorcised her demons by breathing upon her, and He laid His hand on her head and said, "Thy sins are forgiven thee!" He blessed her children and assured her that they would turn out well. He also consoled her with the thought that one day she might join the Holy Women in furthering His work. Jesus then went on to an entertainment prepared by the Pharisees. While He was sitting there, first her children and then she herself, veiled, entered the room with costly gifts of perfume to anoint Him. The Pharisees complained of the waste of money, but, as He later did for Magdalene, Jesus defended the woman with eloquence as well as charity.

"He said to the Pharisees: 'All gifts come from God. For precious gifts, gratitude gives in return what it has the most precious, and that is no waste. The people that gather and prepare these spices must live.' Then He directed one of the disciples to give the value of them to the poor, spoke some words upon the woman's conversion and repentance. . . . *Which among them, He asked, felt himself free from spiritual adultery? He remarked that John had not been able to convert Herod, but that this poor woman had of her own accord turned away from her evil life, and then He related the parable of the sheep lost and found.*"

### Can All Sins Be Pardoned?

Jesus' pardoning of adulteresses was especially poignant as they were subject to a cruel fate under the Law—a fate which heretics in the first few centuries after Jesus wanted to see preserved, for they taught that certain sins, especially adultery, could on no account be forgiven.[3] In His own ministry, Jesus spoke against severe practices in Ephron, a Levitical city north of the Jabbok River, in the ancient kingdom of Bashan. The Jews there belonged to the Rechabite sect,[4] whose people had descended from Jethro, Moses' father-in-law. According to Sister Emmerich, they had strict rules regarding purity, and regulated which members had to marry, or were forbidden from marriage. The Rechabites secretly kept three lists with regard to everyone's charitable contributions: one called "the Book of Life," one "the Middle Way," and the third, "the Book of Death." Despite their apparent piety, Jesus chastised the Rechabites for their mercilessness to adulterers and murderers, whom they were unwilling to see pardoned.

*Sister Emmerich, in her visions, saw Jesus teach the possibility of multiple pardons for repeated sins—even adultery.* Two adulteresses of Capernaum in penitential garb threw themselves at His feet. They wanted to confess their sins openly, but Jesus replied that He knew their sins and that public confession would only scandalize their neighbors. He not only forgave them their sins, He instructed them that if they relapsed into sin, they should not despair, but should turn to God and do penance. This comports with Jesus' instruction to Peter, recorded in the Gospels of Matthew and Luke, that he must forgive his sinning brother as often as his brother repented. But note this: according to the Synoptic Gospels, while even blasphemies against

Jesus could be pardoned, "whoever blasphemes against the Holy Spirit never has forgiveness." [5]

## A Dead Sinner Is Given a Second Chance

To those who questioned His authority to forgive sins, Jesus offered the powerful witness of His raising of the dead—a miracle which Sister Emmerich, in her visions, saw Him perform on a number of occasions, not just the three related in the Gospels. One of these other miracles concerned a rich but sinful herdsman, who had misappropriated the land of some poor shepherds: "Standing in front of the corpse, Jesus spoke of the deceased. He asked of what advantage was it to him now that he had once pampered and served his body, that house which his soul had now to leave? He had, on account of that body, run his soul into debt which he neither had nor could discharge." Sister Emmerich added: "I saw the state in which the soul of the deceased was. I saw it in a circle, in a sphere above the spot upon which he had died. Before it passed pictures of all its transgressions with their temporal consequences, and the sight consumed it with sorrow. I saw too the punishments it was to undergo, and it was vouchsafed a view of the satisfactory Passion of Jesus."

The widow of the herdsman expressed a belief that the Jewish King from Nazareth could bring her husband back to life. Jesus replied that the Jewish King could indeed do that—and said that if they would believe in Him and His doctrines, He would raise the man, for his soul was not yet judged. They promised to do so, and Sister Emmerich had a mystical vision of what then transpired: "Torn with grief, [the soul] was about to enter upon its punishment, when Jesus prayed, and called it back into the body by pronouncing the name Nazor, the name of the deceased. . . . I saw the soul at Jesus' call floating toward the body, becoming smaller, and disappearing through the mouth, at which moment Nazor rose to a sitting posture in his coffin. I always see the human soul reposing above the heart from which numerous threads run to the head. . . . On the following morning He washed the feet of the resuscitated Nazor and exhorted him for the future to think more of his soul than of his body, and to restore the ill-gotten property."

## The People of Nain Stand on the Brink of The Grave

One of the three resurrections performed by Jesus which has been preserved in the Gospels was that of the son of the widow of Nain. St. Luke depicted this event in such brief fashion that the reader might infer that it occurred accidentally, when Jesus happened on the scene as the funeral procession left the town and was spontaneously moved by pity for the mother. Sister Emmerich, however, saw that Jesus' appearance was not a matter of chance; rather it was clear that He had timed His arrival for dramatic purposes.

According to Sister Emmerich, while Jesus was then in Capernaum, the widow had beseeched Him to come to cure her gravely ill twelve-year-old son Martial, and He had agreed, without specifying when He would do so. Now, we know that Jesus could have cured the boy right then at a distance—as He did Centurion Zorobabel's adopted son. But, in this case, He decided to perform a much greater miracle in person. And so, after His preaching in Capernaum was finished, He set out for Nain, a town about six miles southeast of Nazareth, with about 30 followers. It was a long journey, and His party did not arrive until the next morning, when it met the funeral party en route to the grave.

Jesus' disciples formed rows on either side of the road, and He walked between them to meet the procession. He ordered the four men who bore the coffin on a framework of poles to stop and set it down, which they did. There was a crowd with the widow, for she was well known and loved for her charitable works, and everyone gathered close to see what would happen. He told her not to weep, and He asked for a little branch of hyssop and a cup of water. Then He raised His eyes to heaven and prayed words which we know from *other* passages of the Gospels of Matthew and Luke, unrelated to the story of the widow of Nain:

"I confess to Thee, Oh Father, Lord of heaven and earth, because Thou hast hidden these things from the wise and prudent, and hast revealed them to little ones. Yea, Father, for so it hath seemed good in Thy sight. All things are delivered to Me by My Father, and not one knoweth the Son but the Father; neither doth any one know the Father but the Son, and he to whom it shall please the Son to reveal Him. Come to Me, all you that labor and are burdened, and I will refresh you. Take up My yoke upon you, and learn of Me, because I am meek and humble of heart, and you shall find rest to your souls, for My yoke is sweet and my burden light!"

Jesus then blessed the water, and used the hyssop to sprinkle the people (as priests do in the rite of Asperges); He did this because there were wicked people mingled in the group, and the ceremony drove evils spirits out of them. Jesus also sprinkled the corpse, which by then had been unwrapped. He made the sign of the Cross over it, and gave the command, "Arise!"

Martial sat up and looked around, bewildered, not knowing what had happened or why he was there. Attendants quickly clothed the

boy, and Jesus led him to his mother, saying to her: "Here, thou hast
thy son back, but I shall demand him of thee when he shall have been
regenerated in baptism." The widow was in tears, momentarily too
speechless even to give thanks.

The procession, now joyful, retraced the route to the widow's
house, where shortly a great distribution was made to the poor of
clothing, food and money. A feast was spread for all, with Peter doing
the honors since he was related to the widow by marriage. Meantime
Jesus instructed the crowds assembled in the courtyards, using the
occasion to make moving remarks about sin and death. It is worth
citing Sister Emmerich's account at length because of the sheer beauty
of Jesus' teaching on this occasion:

"His words implied that death, which had entered the world by
sin, had bound [the boy], had enchained him, and would have dealt
him the mortal blow in the tomb; furthermore, that Martial with eyes
closed would have been cast into the darkness and later would have
opened them where neither mercy nor help could be extended to him.
But, at the portals of the tomb, the mercy of God, mindful of the piety
of the boy's parents and of some of his ancestors had broken his bonds.
Now by baptism he was to free himself from the sickness of sin, in
order not to fall into a still more frightful imprisonment.

"*Then Jesus dilated upon the virtues of parents. Their virtues
profit their children in after years. It was in consideration of the
righteousness of the Patriarchs that Almighty God down to the
present day had protected and spared Israel, but now enchained in sin
and covered with the veil of mental blindness, they had become like
unto this youth. They were standing on the brink of the grave, and
for the last time was mercy extended to them. John had prepared the
way and with a powerful voice had called upon their heart to arise
from the slumber of death. The Heavenly Father had now for the last
time pity upon them. He would open to life the eyes of those that did
not obstinately keep them closed.

"Jesus compared the people in their blindness to the youth shut
up in his coffin who, though near the tomb, though outside the gate
of the city, had been met by salvation. 'If,' He said, 'the bearers had
not heeded my voice, if they had not set down the coffin, had not
opened it, had not freed the body from its winding-sheet, if they had
obstinately hurried forward with their burden, the boy would have
been buried—and how terrible that would have been!' Then Jesus
likened to this picture He had drawn the false teachers, the Pharisees.
They kept the poor people from the life of penance, they fettered them*

with the bonds of their arbitrary laws, they enclosed them in the coffin of their vain observances, and cast them thus into an eternal tomb. Jesus finished by imploring and conjuring His hearers to accept the proffered mercy of His Heavenly Father, and hasten to life, to penance, to baptism!"

### Why Did Jairus' Daughter Die a Second Time?

Such scenes of resurrection which Jesus performed are among the most moving visions recounted by Sister Emmerich, and they provide much food for thought. The Synoptic Gospels contain the story of a resurrection of the daughter of a synagogue official named Jairus, whose town was not named, but which Sister Emmerich identified as Capernaum. Sister Emmerich's visions support the Gospel accounts— but even more wonderfully, for she saw *two* resurrections of the same little girl—the later being the one memorialized by the Evangelists.

In speaking with His disciples after He had raised the girl the first time, Jesus decried the parents' lack of faith, and predicted that the girl would now have to struggle with temptations that might result in a more serious death than that of her body. Sister Emmerich saw that what led to her second death a few weeks later was the shameful conduct of the girl's mother, her sister and her mother-in-law. They not only lacked gratitude for the healing, but they actually responded with frivolity and ridiculed Jesus—and the little girl was influenced to join in this conduct. Soon, she was seized with a burning fever. The parents were afraid to acknowledge their fears that their own conduct was responsible for this development, until she lay near death and their despair overcame their shame. Jesus again responded to Jairus' summons, and again brought the girl to life, but this time He remonstrated with the family:

"Jesus earnestly exhorted the parents to receive the mercy of God thankfully, to turn away from vanity and worldly pleasure, to embrace the penance preached to them, and to beware of again compromising their daughter's life now restored for the second time. He reproached them with their whole manner of living, with the levity they had exhibited at the reception of the first favor bestowed upon them, and their conduct afterward, by which in a short time they had exposed their child to a much more grievous death than that of the body, namely, the death of the soul. The little girl herself was very much affected and shed tears. Jesus warned her against concupiscence of the eyes and sin. While she partook of the grapes and the bread that He had blessed, He told her that for the future she should no longer live according to the flesh, but that she should eat of the Bread of Life, the Word of God, should do penance, believe, pray, and perform works of mercy." Sister Emmerich reported that the parents were now converted, and accepted Jesus' command to reform. As evidence of his determination to begin a new life, Jairus gave away many of his possessions to the poor.

### What Happened When Lazarus Came Forth from the Tomb?

The most impressive resurrection described in the Gospels was the raising of Jesus' dear friend Lazarus, which only St. John wrote about—and his account ends with Jesus' command to untie Lazarus and let him go free. If we would picture more, we must turn to Sister Emmerich, who saw the events develop as St. John described, from the first news of Lazarus' sickness, which Jesus deliberately ignored, to his resurrection. Her account adds a number of details, including the fact that it happened months before Jesus' triumphal entry into Jerusalem rather than only days before His Passion as many have inferred from St. John's Gospel. Moreover, according to Sister Emmerich, Lazarus had been dead for eight days when Jesus appeared—his sisters had kept him unburied for four days in the hope that Jesus would appear and raise him. During the time of its separation from his body, Lazarus's soul was in a peaceful place, lighted by only a glimmering twilight, with the souls of the Just, who were awaiting the Lord to set them free. The scene with Mary and Martha and the mourners at the home of Lazarus was as described by St. John. When Jesus appeared, after speaking with Lazarus' sisters, He went with them to the tomb in the cemetery of Bethania. The Apostles opened the tomb and removed the cover from the woven coffin. Jesus prayed, and cried out an order to Lazarus to come forth. Sister Emmerich next saw the following:

"At this cry, the corpse arose to a sitting posture. The crowd now pressed with so much violence that Jesus ordered them to be driven outside the walls of the cemetery. The Apostles, who were standing in the tomb by the coffin, removed the handkerchief from Lazarus's face, unbound his hands and feet, and drew off the winding-sheet. Lazarus, as if awakening from lethargy, rose from the coffin and stepped out of the grave, tottering and looking like a phantom. The Apostles threw a mantle around him. Like one walking in sleep, he approached the door, passed the Lord and went out to where his sisters and the other women had stepped back in fright as before a ghost. Without daring to touch him, they fell prostrate on the ground. At the same instant, Jesus stepped after him out of the vault and seized him by both hands, His whole manner full of loving earnestness.

"And now all moved on toward Lazarus's house. The throng was great, but a certain fear prevailed among the people, consequently the procession formed by Lazarus and his friends was not impeded in its movements by the crowd that followed. Lazarus moved along more like one floating than walking, and he still had all the appearance of a corpse. Jesus walked by his side, and the rest of the party followed sobbing and weeping around them in silent, frightened amazement. . . ."

Physical resurrection was only the first step. Jesus had raised Lazarus not for show, but for a purpose. Without waiting for Lazarus to shed his grave clothes, Jesus proceeded with this ceremony in the dining hall: "The Apostles formed a circle around Jesus and Lazarus, who was kneeling before the Lord. Jesus laid His right hand on his head and breathed upon him seven times. The Lord's breath was luminous. I saw a dark vapor withdrawing as it were from Lazarus, and the devil under the form of a black winged figure, impotent and wrathful, clearing the circle backward and mounting on high. By this ceremony, Jesus consecrated Lazarus to His service, purified him from all connection with the world and sin, and strengthened him with the gifts of the Holy Ghost.[6] He made him a long address in which He told him that He had raised him to life that he might serve Him, and that he would have to endure great persecution."

News of the raising of Lazarus traveled quickly the short distance to Jerusalem, where Lazarus was a well known and respected property owner. The event was so stupendous that it should have led the enemies of Jesus finally to acknowledge Him as the Messiah and heed His call to conversion. But, Jesus had prophesied that they would not, in His parable which St. Luke related of Lazarus *the beggar* and the rich man who died and was in torment for his sins. The latter, seeing how well off Lazarus was in the afterlife, begged Father Abraham to send someone back from the dead to warn his brothers so that they would not meet his fate, but Father Abraham replied: "If they do not listen to Moses and the prophets, they will not be convinced even if one should rise from the dead." *It was as Jesus had foreseen: the resurrection of Lazarus occasioned not an acceptance of Jesus but, according to St. John, a plot to kill Him. And so, for a period, Jesus withdrew from public view, traveling to distant regions, before returning for a final confrontation with His enemies.*

---

[1] The sacrament of Penance is described generally in the *Catechism of the Catholic Church* §§ 1491–97. Its effects are to reconcile the penitent with God and with the Church. *See ibid.* at §§ 1468–69.

[2] *See* Ru 1: 1–19.

[3] One such heretical sect was the Montanists in the second century. *See* John P. Markoe, *The Triumph of the Church* (Bronx, NY: Catholic Viewpoint Pub. 1962) 9. The Novatians in the third century also held to this heresy. *See ibid.* at 11; Harold O.J. Brown, *Heresies* 197–98.

[4] *See* the entry for "Rechab/Rechabite" in *The Anchor Bible Dictionary* 5:630.

[5] An excellent commentary on that passage is as follows: "To speak against *The Man* in *this age* of the Kingdom's proclamation may be due to all manner of misunderstanding, for The Man has not yet entered upon his reign. But speaking against the *Spirit*, either in *this age* of proclamation, or in the *age to come* . . . is the ultimate sin." *See* W.F. Albright & C.S. Mann, *The Anchor Bible—Matthew* 156.

[6] The seven gifts of the Holy Spirit are: wisdom, understanding, counsel, fortitude, knowledge, piety, and fear of the Lord. *See Catechism of the Catholic Church* § 1831.

# CHAPTER EIGHT

## What Would We Have Heard at a Teaching by Jesus?

If we had been seated on a hillside overlooking the Sea of Galilee, what might we have heard in the course of an afternoon's teaching by Jesus? That is a very difficult question to answer from the Gospels, for nowhere do the Evangelists attempt to relate a single discourse at length—with the exception of St. John's rendering of the unique instruction He gave to His disciples immediately before His Passion. Not only that, in certain Scriptural passages, unrelated sayings of Jesus appear one after the other. We do not know whether these were artificially tacked onto one another by the Evangelists, or whether the sayings were truly sequential, but were recorded without Jesus' transitions between one and the next.

The examples given by Sister Emmerich of His preaching show that He was a very skillful orator, who often spoke for hours without stop, all the while moving fluidly from topic to topic. The following, from her visions, is a summary description of points in just a three-hour sermon, delivered on the mountain northeast of the Sea of Galilee where the multiplication of loaves and fishes had taken place. *It shows how Jesus segued from one topic to another, and how fully packed His discourses were, so that a listener at even one long discourse would have been exposed to many of His principal teachings* (citations are given to show how these lessons are scattered in the Gospels):

- ~ "Blessed are ye when men hate and persecute you for the Son of Man's sake." (the Eighth Beatitude) [Mt 5:11-12; Lk 6:22-23];
- ~ "Woe to the rich, to them that are filled with the goods of this world, for in them they already have their reward; [Lk 6:24] but as for you, rejoice that it is still in store for you.";
- ~ the salt of the earth [Mt 5:13; Mk 9:49-50; Lk 14:34-35];
- ~ the city on the mountain [Mt 5:14];

~ the light on the candlestick [Mt 5:14-16; Mk 4:21; Lk 8:16];

~ the fulfilling of the Law [Mt 5:17-20; Lk 16:16-17];

~ the hiding of good works [Mt 6:1-4];

~ prayer made in the privacy of one's chamber [Mt 6:5-6];

~ fasting, which should be practiced joyously with anointing of the head, and not be turned into a sanctimonious parade of piety [Mt 6:16-18];

~ the laying up of treasure in heaven [Mt 6:19-21; Lk 12:33-34];

~ freedom from worldly solicitude [Mt 6:25-34; Lk 12:22-32];

~ the impossibility of serving two masters [Mt 6:24; Lk 16:13];

~ the narrow gate and the broad road [Mt 7:13-14; Lk 13:23-24];

~ the bad tree with its bad fruit [Lk 6:43]; and

~ the wise man who built on a solid foundation, while the fool built upon sand [Lk 6:47-49].

### Why Did He Teach in Parables?

Readers of the Bible will recognize the above as figures of speech and parables, which is how He customarily couched His message. The three Synoptic Gospels give an explanation for why He taught in that manner, referring explicitly to the following vision of the Prophet Isaiah:

And he [a seraphim] replied: Go and say to this people:
Listen carefully, but you shall not understand!
Look intently, but you shall know nothing!
You are to make the heart of this people sluggish,
to dull their ears and close their eyes;
Else they will see, their ears hear, their heart understand,
and they will turn and be healed.[1]

As that passage was used in the Gospels of Mark and Luke, it would appear that Jesus spoke in parables so that certain people would *not* understand, would *not* repent and would *not* be saved. But, that would indeed be strange, considering His repeated efforts to win over even the hardened Pharisees. A different explanation of Jesus' use of the prophecy of Isaiah is set forth in the Gospel of Matthew, namely, that He spoke in parables not to conceal the truth, but because certain listeners were not genuinely looking for it—having at least partially closed their eyes and ears.

That is very close to the explanation which Sister Emmerich related that He gave on an occasion in Capernaum. From this explanation, it is clear that Jesus did want all to understand His teachings—but that He knew that for listeners who were only casually interested, He had to use similes and metaphors which could be unpacked reflectively at a later time:

"It was principally James the Greater who told Jesus that he and his companions did not understand Him, and he asked Him why He did not speak more clearly. Jesus answered that He would make all intelligible to them, but that on account of the weak and the pagans the mysteries of the Kingdom of God could not then be exposed more plainly. As even with such precautions, these mysteries alarmed His hearers who in their state of depravity, esteemed them too sublime for them, they must at first be presented as it were under the cover of a similitude. They must fall into their heart like the grain of seed. In the grain the whole ear is enclosed, but to produce it, the grain must be hidden in the earth."

In most circumstances, Jesus was similarly indirect about His own authority to teach, refraining from admitting that He was the Messiah, and deflecting questions on that topic. However, the Truth was always contained in what He said: a properly disposed listener would have been able to see Him for who He was. That was shown, for example, when Jesus taught on the Eight Beatitudes in the synagogue at Hukkok, a town five hours by foot from Capernaum:

"He said that the Messiah had already come upon earth, that they (His hearers) were living in His time, that they were listening to His teachings. He spoke of the adoration of God in spirit and in truth. . . . At these words, the Doctors of the synagogue humbly begged Him to say who He really was, whence He came, whether they whom they looked upon as His parents were not His parents, His relatives not His relatives, whether He was really the Messiah, the Son of God.

"But Jesus answered them evasively. If He said, 'I am He!' they would not believe Him, but would say that He was the Son of these people of whom they had spoken. They should not inquire into His origin, but should hear His doctrine and observe His actions. Whoever does the will of the Father is the Son of the Father, for the Son is in the Father and the Father is in the Son, and whoever fulfils the will of the Son fulfils the will of the Father. Jesus spoke so beautifully on this subject and on that of prayer that many cried out: 'Lord, Thou art the Christ! Thou art the Truth!' and falling down they wished to adore Him. But He repeated to them: 'Adore the Father in spirit and in truth!' and He left the city with His disciples."

## The Need for Prayer

Those who followed Jesus' injunction to "observe His actions," would have seen that in everything He did, Jesus prayed, briefly but visibly. And, if He had a moment at night when He was not active, He retired by Himself to pray in secret. A place which He frequently went to for that purpose was the cave of the garden on the Mount of Olives. According to Sister Emmerich's visions of the ancient past, that Mount was where Adam and Eve had lived after their ejection from Paradise, and where God had confronted Cain for murdering his brother. It was in this same cave that Jesus spent His last hour of freedom, in agony of mind and spirit, before Judas and the soldiers arrived to take Him prisoner.

Seeing Jesus so often in prayer, His disciples naturally asked Him to instruct them, as mentioned by St. Luke. He taught them what we call "The Lord's Prayer," not only once, but repeatedly, as He did also with the crowds. Sister Emmerich described an occasion when the whole area around Capernaum was a big encampment of Jews and pagans from everywhere, drawn by what they had heard of Jesus. Every space in the valleys and hills was taken by people and their animals. The Apostles were pressed into service, sent off in different directions teaching and healing, while Jesus was doing the same at Peter's house. He taught the multitude the Our Father, explaining each of the petitions, and exhorting all to pray continually, using the parable of the widow who demanded justice from the unjust judge, and of the child who would not be refused if he begged his father for bread or a fish to eat.

One of the most interesting instructions which Sister Emmerich noted on the subject of prayer was the one Jesus gave on the significance of the word "Amen!" Those who are familiar with the Gospels may have noticed that more than 50 of Jesus' pronouncements recorded there began with the words "Amen, I tell you" (or, in the Gospel of John, "Amen, amen, I say to you").

## The Power of "Amen!"

According to Jesus, "'Amen' was the whole summary of prayer. Whoever pronounces it carelessly, makes void his prayer. Prayer cries to God; binds us to God; opens to us His mercy and, with the word 'Amen,' rightly uttered, we take the asked-for gift out of His hands.' Jesus spoke most forcibly of the power of the word 'Amen.' He called it the beginning and the end of everything. He spoke almost as if God had by it created the whole world. He uttered an 'Amen' over all that He had taught them, over His own departure from them, over the *accomplishment of His own mission, and ended His discourse by a solemn 'Amen.'"*

### Teachings on Marriage and Divorce

What were the temptations which Jesus told His hearers to pray for help in avoiding? Judging by the number of instructions He gave on the subject, as reported by Sister Emmerich, it would seem that sexual impurity was one of the most serious and frequent—that was what had doomed Sodom and Gommorah.

Jesus' teachings on sexual purity often were delivered in the context of preparing couples for marriage, as He did at the Wedding at Cana. As seen in Sister Emmerich's visions, on one occasion, he related the parable of the wise and foolish virgins, and delivered a sermon which was exactly in line with what St. Paul later wrote in his letters to the Ephesians and to the Colossians, including the injunction that: "The wife should now obey through reverence and humility, and the husband command with love and moderation."

Sister Emmerich reported in detail the discourse which Jesus gave on marriage at a festival observed for the homecoming of people from the Pasch in Jerusalem: "He began by saying that in human nature much evil is mixed with good, but that by prayer and renunciation, the two must be separated and the evil subdued. He who follows his unbridled passions works mischief. Our works follow us and they will at some future day rise up against their author. Our body is an image of the Creator, but Satan aims at destroying that image in us. All that is superfluous brings with it sin and sickness, becomes deformity and abomination. Jesus exhorted His hearers to chastity, moderation, and prayer. Continence, prayer, and discipline have produced holy men and Prophets."

Discipline in marriage was needed to avoid the temptation to divorce. Jesus taught frequently about the indissolubility of a marriage, often in the context of a challenge by the Pharisees, as recorded in the Gospels of Matthew and Mark. According to the visions of Sister Emmerich, one of the repeated charges made by Jesus against the Pharisees was that they had altered the Law—an act forbidden by the Law itself[2]—and he attacked them for doing just that to facilitate the obtaining of divorces. This was the scene described by her in Lower Sepphoris, which was only a few miles from Nazareth:

Jesus pointed to a place in a scroll of the Law where an addition had been made in recopying it, and identified one of the elders of the synagogue as having committed the fraud. Surprisingly, the old man repented, acknowledged his fault and was converted by Jesus. The next

day, however, when Jesus taught at a school outside the town, a group
of Pharisees disputed with Jesus about His teachings, for divorces were
easily obtained in that town on pretexts. They were vexed at His
repudiation of the now expunged addition to the scroll, as several of
them were planning to avail themselves of the loophole it created.
Jesus demonstrated that they were in the wrong, and rebuked them
for their general readiness to approve divorces.

Jesus gave a graphic demonstration of His teachings against
divorce in Nain, when two women approached Him, asking whether
He could give them bills of divorce, He bade them bring Him a
container of milk and also one of water. Taking the two, he mixed the
liquids together, and said: "Separate the two again, so that the milk
shall be again by itself and in like manner the water. Then I shall give
you a bill of divorce."

*However, according to what Sister Emmerich heard Him say to
the two women, and in other instructions, spouses were not condemned to living in an abusive marriage: if two could not live together
in peace, and without sin, they could separate, but with these strict
conditions: the weaker party had to agree to it; the husband must
support the wife and children; and neither party could marry again.*

### Teachings on the Need for Humility

Jesus was also constantly inveighing against the temptation to
pride, which sometimes reared its ugly head even among His disciples.
He found Himself having to chastise them repeatedly with the
injunction: "Let him that will be first among you, become the last, the
servant of all." He set before them a little child, and told them to
enter Heaven as little children. And, most dramatically, He
washed their feet—a profound act of servitude. He did this not only
at the Last Supper, but, according to Sister Emmerich, also in
Bethsaida when the disciples returned from their missions in need of
care and hospitality:

"As Jesus was very busily lending a helping hand in their service,
Peter entreated Him to desist. 'Lord,' said he, 'art Thou going to serve!
Leave that to us.' But Jesus replied that He was sent to serve, and that
what was done for these disciples was done for His Father. And again
His teaching turned upon humility." *He made a further point:
"whoever does not serve from a motive of charity, whoever lowers
himself to help his neighbor, not in order to comfort a needy brother,
but in order to gain distinction at that cost, he is a double-dealer, a
server to the eye. He already has his reward, for he serves himself and
not his brother."*

Jesus delivered a particularly fine lesson on humility in the synagogue at Capernaum, in explaining the Beatitude "Blessed are the poor in spirit." *"He said that they who are learned, ought not to he conscious of it, just as the rich ought not to know that they possess riches. Then the Jews murmured again and said: 'Of what use would such knowledge or such riches be, if the owner did not know that he possessed either the one or the other?' Jesus answered: 'Blessed are the poor in spirit,' adding that they should feel themselves poor and humble before God from whom all wisdom comes, and apart from whom all wisdom is an abomination."*

Jesus even had a cautionary lesson for people of great piety. In Aser, Jesus was received by Obed, the chief magistrate, who was a pious old man. Obed had 18 children, yet gave large gifts to the poor and the Temple. Obed's wife ran a school for young girls. These were the very sort of people whom we would expect Jesus to have praised unreservedly. *Instead, Jesus "warned Obed and his people against the feeling of conscious rectitude and self complacency to which they were predisposed. They in a measure distinguished themselves from their neighbors, and on account of their well regulated life, their temperance, and the fruits of salvation amassed thereby, they esteemed themselves good and pleasing in the sight of God. Such sentiments might very easily end in pride.* To guard against such a consequence, Jesus related the parable of the day laborers."

## Teachings on Detachment from Possessions

From the very beginning of His ministry, Jesus warned His disciples that they must renounce all their earthly possessions. Ordinary people were not subjected to such a severe discipline, but Jesus encouraged them to be satisfied with what they had. Near Gennabris, Jesus stayed overnight with a farmer who complained that a neighbor had long infringed upon his rights. No doubt the farmer thought that Jesus would insist that the wrong be righted, but instead, Jesus counseled forbearance: "Jesus asked whether he still had sufficient for the support of himself and his family. The man answered, yes, that he enjoyed competency. Upon hearing this, *Jesus told him that he had lost nothing, since properly speaking nothing belongs to us, and so long as we have sufficient to support life, we have enough. The owner of the field should resign still more to his importunate neighbor, in order to satisfy the latter's greed after earthly goods. All that one cheerfully gives up here below for the sake of peace, will be restored to Him in the Kingdom of his Father.* That hostile neighbor, viewed from his own standpoint, acted rightly, for his kingdom was of this world, and he sought to increase in earthly goods. But in Jesus' Kingdom, he should have nothing."

According to Sister Emmerich, Jesus gave children the same hard-to-practice lessons about meekness and forbearance which He gave to their parents. "He counseled the boys to bear with one another. If one should strike a companion, or throw him down, the ill-treated party should bear it patiently and think not of retaliating. He should turn away in silence forgiving his enemy, and his love should become twice as great as it was before, yes, for they should show affection even to enemies. They should not covet the goods of others. If a boy wanted the pen, the writing materials, the plaything, the fruit belonging to his neighbor, the latter should relinquish not only the object coveted, but give him still more if allowed to do so. They should fully satisfy their neighbor's cupidity, if permitted to give the things away, for only the patient, the loving, and the generous should have a seat in His Kingdom. This seat Jesus described to them in childlike terms as a beautiful throne."

### Teachings on Charity

One of the major teachings of Jesus was to avoid the temptation to become a slave to earthly things, especially greed in acquiring money and goods. As a corrective to such inclination, He exhorted His listeners to give alms from the heart, especially alms which called for a sacrifice on the part of the giver. *"He said that what they deprived themselves of in food and drink and superfluous comforts, they should place with confidence in the hands of God, imploring Him to allow it to benefit the poor shepherds in the wilderness and others in need. The Father in Heaven would then like a true father of a family hear their prayer, if they like faithful servants shared the abundance He had given them with the poor whom they knew, or whom they lovingly sought out. This was real cooperation, and God works with His true servants strong in faith."*

Jesus gave many examples to show that He practiced what He taught, and His own distribution of food saved from His table was one of them. If a feast was given in His honor after He had given an instruction at a synagogue or school, Jesus saw to it that the poor also were fed, waiting on them Himself. On one such occasion in Capernaum, the Pharisees got an unwelcome double dose of instruction in humility from Jesus by word and deed. Apart from His disciples, the guests were all friends and relatives of the host, and they had taken the best places for themselves, prompting Jesus to lecture them on humility, and the need to take a low place unless one was called by the host to come up higher. As recorded in St. Luke's Gospel, He proceeded to lecture the host about the need to invite to the feast the poor and others who could not repay him, and He related the parable of the king's marriage feast for his son. Jesus then caused the poor to be assembled there, and when it was confirmed that the entertainment had been prepared for Him, He fed the poor with the leftovers of the meal.

Another instruction on how one should use the goods of this world was given when Jesus taught the farmer who was complaining about his neighbor taking his land. Jesus told him that he should *"take a lesson from his neighbor in the art of enriching himself, and should strive to acquire possessions in the Kingdom of God.* Jesus drew a similitude from a river which wore away the land on one side and deposited the debris on the other. *The whole discourse was something like that upon the unjust steward, in which worldly artifice and earthly greed after enrichment should furnish an example for one's manner of acting in spiritual affairs. Earthly riches were contrasted with heavenly treasures. . . .* Abraham had given far more land to Lot than the latter had demanded.[3] After relating the fact, Jesus asked what had become of Lot's posterity, and whether Abraham had not recovered full propriety. Ought we not to imitate Abraham? Was not the kingdom promised to him, and did he not obtain it? This earthly kingdom however was merely a symbol of the Kingdom of God, and Lot's struggle against Abraham was typical of the struggle of man with man. But, like Abraham, man should aim at acquiring the Kingdom of God."

The foregoing lesson is especially fascinating because it provides a clear guide to interpreting the perplexing parable of the unjust steward, which was recounted by St. Luke. The steward, who was about to be called to account for dissipating his master's property, had his master's debtors falsely alter the records to minimize what they had received, so that they would befriend him when he lost his position. Surprisingly, the parable concluded with the master praising the enterprise of his devious employee, and Jesus adding this moral for His disciples: "Make friends for yourselves through the use of this world's goods, so that when they fail you a lasting reception will be yours." In the light of what Jesus told the farmer, we can look again at how Jesus ended the parable of the unjust steward and see the significance of the phrase, "a lasting reception": Jesus was saying that the disciples should use this world's goods in such a way as to make friends for themselves in heaven and thus secure their heavenly reward.

*Teachings Against Exploiting the Poor*

In some discourses inveighing against greed, He focused on the exploitation of the poor by the rich. One of the most famous passages in the Synoptic Gospels records Him as expressing the severe judgment that: "It is easier for a camel to pass through a needle's eye than for a rich man to enter the kingdom of God." Sister Emmerich saw this instruction taking place in Chesulloth, a Levitical city.

The disciples, with thick ropes run through stakes had cut off a space in front of the inn in order to keep back the crowd. It was from that space that Jesus preached. As among His audience there were many of the rich merchants from the city, He taught upon riches and the danger attending the love of gain. Their position, He told them, was even more perilous than that of the publicans, who more easily than they would reform. Saying these words, Jesus pointed to the ropes that separated Him from the crowd, and uttered the words: "A rope like one of those would go more easily into the eye of a needle than a rich man into the kingdom of heaven." The ropes were of camel's hair, as thick as one's arm, and drawn four times through the stakes around the enclosure. *The rich people defended themselves by saying that they gave alms out of all their profits. But Jesus replied that alms that have been expressed from the sweat of the poor, bring down no blessing.* This instruction was not pleasing to His hearers."

Translating the Greek word in the Synoptic Gospels as "cable" rather than "camel" would be consistent with a persuasive case made by a linguistics scholar based in part upon a somewhat similar passage in the Quran, and in part on other support, including the reasoning of Cyril of Alexandria (c. 370–444), who identified the word as meaning a cable such as a sailor would use.[4] Either way the word is read, the lesson suggests very graphically the impossibility for a rich man to attain heaven without the aid of God, and makes the added point that alms given out of ill-gotten gains bring no spiritual benefit to the donor.

Sister Emmerich saw the latter lesson also being taught by Jesus at the home of a Pharisee: "A heathen slave, or servant, laid upon the table a beautiful dish of many colors filled with confectionery, made of spices kneaded together in the shape of birds and flowers. One of the guests raised the alarm. There was, he said, something unclean on the dish, and he pushed the poor slave back, called him opprobrious names, and put him last among the other servants. Jesus interposed: 'Not the dish, but what is in it is full of uncleanness.' The master of the house replied: 'Thou mistakest. Those sweetmeats are perfectly clean and very costly.' Jesus responded in words like these: 'They are truly unclean! They are nothing else than sensual pleasures made of the sweat, the blood, the marrow, and the tears of widows, orphans, and the poor,' and He read them a severe lesson upon their manner of acting, their prodigality, their covetousness, and their hypocrisy." Thus, while Jesus refused to conform to the ritual cleansings prescribed by the Pharisees, He taught them a lesson about the true nature of purity.

### Teaching on God's Mercy

The paradigm of Christian forgiveness—and God's mercy—is the story of the Prodigal Son, found in the Gospel of Luke. As Jesus told it, it was meant not just for lost sheep of the House of Israel, but for people of all nations and tribes. Sister Emmerich heard Jesus tell it in a locale where the "lost sons" present were the pagans as well as Jewish penitents: "He spoke so feelingly, so naturally of the lost son that one would have thought Him the father who had found his son. *He stretched out His arms, exclaiming: 'See! See! he returns! Let us make ready a feast for him!' It was so natural that the people looked around, as if all that Jesus was saying was a reality.*"[5]

---

[1] Is 6:9-10.
[2] Dt 4:1-2; similarly, Pr 30:6.
[3] Gen 14:8-11.
[4] *See* Saul Levin, "A Camel or a Cable Through a Needle's Eye?," *14th Forum of the Linguistic Association of Canada and the United States* (1987) 406.
[5] A particularly good exposition of this parable is Henri J.M. Nouwen's *The Return of the Prodigal Son* (New York: Doubleday Image 1992).

# CHAPTER NINE

Those who think of Jesus primarily as a "saintly" man whose mission was to dispense earthly wisdom and spread peace, have truly missed the point of His incarnation, life and death. There were many sages both before and after Him, and He does not deserve to be demoted to their rank. And as for peace, St. Matthew quoted Jesus Himself as saying: "Do not think that I have come to bring peace on earth; I have not come to bring peace, but a sword." Yes, Jesus *did* bring peace—but it was *His* peace, not peace as the world knows it, and it was not for everyone, but only for those who accepted Him as Lord.

*To really understand Jesus, it is essential to recognize that His unique and overriding missions were: to proclaim that the Kingdom of God was at hand; to show that God wanted to adopt people of all races—and not just the Jews—as His beloved children; and to give His life as a ransom for the many. Each of these missions involved Him in battles with the religious establishment.*

## Was Jesus' Spirituality Outside the Mainstream of Judaism?

While the Gospels record many of His battles with religious leaders, and His harsh words for the scribes and Pharisees, *it would be a mistake to think that His spirituality was outside the mainstream of Judaism in His day or that there was no group which looked upon Him favorably. Jesus, being God, could not be pigeonholed into the tenets of any particular sect, but according to Sister Emmerich, He had ties with the Essenes and exhibited Essene spirituality.*

The Essenes were the third largest sect in Israel, as distinct from the Pharisees and the Sadducees as those two were from each other.[1] Sister Emmerich had visions of the ancestors of the Blessed Virgin Mary as divinely chosen members of that sect who had cooperated with God's grace. Sister Emmerich saw the Essenes as being descended from priests who had carried the Ark of the Covenant at the time of Moses and Aaron. Their members had lived dispersed until they were organized by Isaiah and later by Jeremiah. Originally, they were called Eszkarenes, derived from the term 'Azkarah', which referred to the unbloody sacrifice of the Hebrews, generally made with fine flour, oil and incense. Later they were called Chasidees, derived from the term 'Hasid', which was used to designate a group of devout and observant Jews, including the Maccabees and those who joined them in their fight for freedom. Lastly, they were called Essenes.[2]

There were two centers of Essene life: Mt. Horeb (Mt. Sinai), where there were many cells in the mountain's slopes, and Mt. Carmel. In Jerusalem, they had their own entrance gate and quarter to live in,[3] and a separate place in the Temple, with their own priests. Many remained single, living in community like a religious order, under strict discipline. Essenes went to Jerusalem three times a year to worship at the Temple, after having prepared themselves by prayer, fasting and penance, even scourging.

What particularly set the Essenes apart was that they lived lives of self-denial, sexual continence, mortification and penance. Other Jews disliked them for their ascetical practices, whose purpose was to hasten the advent of the Messiah—for they believed that just as His coming in time would be retarded by the sins of His ancestors, it would be advanced by their good works. Sister Emmerich heard Jesus Himself, in a confidential discussion with an old family friend, Eliud, the leader of the Nazareth Essenes, confirm that the timing of His advent had indeed been affected in just that manner.[4]

According to Sister Emmerich's visions, Jesus' mother was descended from Essenes, and this played a key role in the history of Salvation. In the early times, Essene women who intended to marry first consulted with the Prophet, the spiritual head of their denomination, who lived on Mt. Horeb. In his possession were three extraordinary relics: a dalmatic or scapular which had been worn by Moses, covering the breast and shoulders; a part of the "Blessing" which had been contained in the Ark of the Covenant, and which had come to them when the Ark fell into enemy hands; and the rod of Aaron.[5] When the Prophet prayed in the cave of Elias on Mt. Horeb, vested like the high priest and holding this rod, he was divinely instructed with regard to the female ancestry of the Messiah, and in turn advised which suitor should be married in order to assist in His coming.

Emorun (the grandmother of St. Anne), her daughter Ismeria, and Ismeria's daughter Anne all cooperated by marrying men divinely chosen for them by inspiration, thereby making possible the birth of the Blessed Virgin Mary, the chosen vessel of the Promise. *Notwith-*

*standing this background, Jesus was not an Essene, according to Sister Emmerich:*

"*Jesus had no particular communication with the Essenians, although there was some similarity between His customs and theirs.*[6] *With a great many of them He had no more to do than with other pious and kindly disposed people. He was intimate with several of the married Essenians who were friends of the Holy Family. As this sect never disputed with Jesus, He never had cause to speak against them, and they are not mentioned in the Gospels, because He had nothing wherewith to censure them as He had in others. He was silent also on the great good found among them, since, if He had touched upon it, the Pharisees would have immediately declared that He Himself belonged to that sect.* Some of the most enlightened among them in Jesus' time joined the disciples. Others later on entered the Community in which by their own long practice they gave new impetus to the spirit of renunciation and a well ordered life and laid the foundation for the Christian life both eremitical and cloistered."[7]

## Opposition from the Sanhedrin

Even before the public ministry of Jesus, religious affairs in Israel had been set to boiling by John the Baptist. Members of the Sanhedrin were pleased that he censured Herod for his adulterous conduct, and they were in favor of people repenting of their sins and even of *pagans* being baptized as a token of their reform (though they did not approve of this being done for Jews). What was unacceptable to them was that John was proceeding without authorization from themselves. By acting on his own, he was arrogating to himself a rank superior to theirs—the status of a Prophet of God. And the public overwhelmingly accepted him as such!

Not only was John a loose cannon, he had the temerity to publicly call the authorities a "brood of vipers," even as Jesus Himself was to do later. And if all that were not bad enough, John was proclaiming the advent of the Messiah, eventually in terms that fit Jesus.

Jesus they had forgotten about, since nothing further had been heard from Him after His appearance in the Temple at age twelve. Now, Jesus too had sprung up from obscurity, refusing to acknowledge their authority, and claiming that both John and He had a calling from God. *Jesus demanded of the Jewish people something that they already were under an obligation to do: love the Lord their God with all their heart, soul, strength and mind, and their neighbor as themselves. But, and this was a very big "but," He also asked them to believe in Him and what He was teaching them.*

*Though the people and the authorities did not hear Him say so directly, at least not during the early stages of His ministry, they understood His veiled allusions as implying that He was the Messiah—an idea which most of them found utterly preposterous. More than that, He was prophesying that the Law was about to be fulfilled—meaning that all the hundreds of elaborate rules which the Pharisees had designed to guide daily life while maintaining purity would be obsolesced—and the Temple, the most holy place for Jews to worship God, would be destroyed! That would bring an end to their own status, power and livelihood.* Understandably, the high priests and individual members of the Pharisee and Sadducee sects considered ways to eliminate the danger they perceived from Jesus.

According to Sister Emmerich's visions, their hostile actions included intimidating the common people so that some were reluctant to come to hear Him or even present themselves to be cured by Him. However, so many needed the physical healing which only He could provide, and so great was the hunger of the poor to hear the Good News preached to them, that the Pharisees and Sadducees were unable to prevent Jesus from exercising His ministry throughout the country and, on a limited number of occasions, even in Jerusalem itself.

Did the four Evangelists gave unfairly tendentious portrayals of Pharisees and Sadducees as generally being enemies of Jesus and the Kingdom of God? Some scholars think they did; one even speculated that St. Matthew put "gross caricatures" of them into the mouth of Jesus, "to delegitimate rival Jewish leaders and to legitimate himself and his group as the true leaders of Israel, the accurate interpreters of the Bible and the authentic messengers of God's will."[8] However, the four Gospels are mutually consistent in their general view of the Pharisees and Sadducees, and the visions of Sister Emmerich support the judgment of Jesus, reported by St. Matthew, that many members of those sects were "whitewashed tombs which appear beautiful on the outside, but inside are full of dead men's bones and every kind of filth."

The hypocrisy of these Pharisees can be contrasted with the purity of the Law as Jesus expounded it on the subject of tithing. The Gospels of Matthew and Luke reported that Jesus chastised the practices of the Pharisees in these words: "Woe to you Pharisees! You pay tithes on mint and rue and all the garden plants, while neglecting justice and the love of God. These are the things you should practice, without omitting the others." While Jesus taught His disciples about justice and the love of God, He did not diminish the obligation of tithing. Indeed, according to Sister Emmerich, He told them that: "God had ordered that a tithe be made to the Temple in order to remind men that they did not have the ownership of anything, but only the use thereof. Therefore, even with regard to vegetables and green things, a tithe should be rendered by abstaining from their use."

The events described below in this chapter, seen in her visions, were some of the major confrontations between Jesus and the Pharisees which occurred during the two year period from the first Pasch of His ministry right through to Holy Week, in chronological order. (The next chapter will explore certain of His prophecies and predictions, including that of the coming destruction of the Temple.)

### Mercy and Menaces Mingled in Capernaum

Early in His ministry, Jesus had preached comfortingly in Capernaum on the mercy of God and the coming of the Messiah. As visioned by Sister Emmerich, Jesus spoke of the Prophet Elijah praying on Mt. Carmel for rain to relieve the parched land—and of the tiny cloud which finally appeared to him and grew until it watered the country.[9] *Jesus explained the cloud "as a symbol of the present and the rain as an image of the coming of the Messiah whose teaching should spread everywhere and bear new life to all. Whoever thirsted should now drink, and whoever had prepared his field, should now receive rain."* That was then. At this later point in His ministry, He delivered to the citizens of Capernaum a very different message, which Sister Emmerich described at length:

"He read from the beginning of the Fifth Book of Moses down to the account of the murmuring of the Children of Israel. He spoke of the ingratitude of their fathers, of the mercy of God toward them, and of the nearness of the Kingdom, warning them to beware of acting as their fathers had done. He explained all the errors and crooked ways of their fathers by a comparison with their own erroneous notions, drawing a parallel between the Promised Land of those far-off times and the Kingdom now so near.

"Then He read the first chapter of Isaiah, which He interpreted as referring to the present. He spoke of crime and its punishment, of their long waiting for a Prophet, and of how they would treat Him now that they had Him. He cited the various animals all of which knew their master although they, His hearers, knew Him not. He spoke of the One that longed to help them, picturing to them the woeful appearance He would present in consequence of their outrages upon Him, also of the punishment in store for Jerusalem, and of the small number of the elect when all this would take place. The Lord would, nevertheless, multiply them while the wicked would be destroyed. He called upon them to be converted, saying that even were they all covered with blood, if they cried to God and turned from their evil ways, they would become clean."[10]

### Did the Pharisees Have Any Rational Grievances About Jesus?

We know that the Pharisees everywhere attacked Jesus for His failure to follow their prescriptions as to ritual purity—a complaint which we have no sympathy for. Did they have any rational grievances about Him? Sister Emmerich saw that the Pharisees met with the magistrates in Capernaum to voice their complaints: "They said: 'What commotion, what agitation this Man creates! Peace is no longer found in the land! The people leave their daily avocations and follow His menacing speeches. He is constantly talking of His Father, but is He not from Nazareth? Is He not the Son of a poor carpenter? Whence comes it that He has so great assurance and audacity? Upon what does He rest His titles? He heals on the Sabbath, thus disturbing its peace! He forgives sins! Is His power from On High? Has He some secret arts? How has He become so familiar with the Scriptures, so ready in explaining them? Was He not reared in the school of Nazareth? Perhaps He is connected in some way with foreigners, with a strange nation! He is always speaking of the approaching establishment of a kingdom, of the nearness of the Messiah, of the destruction of Jerusalem.

"'Joseph, His father, was of illustrious birth; but perhaps He is not Joseph's Son, or He may be the supposititious Child of some other, of some powerful man who wants to get a foothold in our country, and thus become master in Judea. He must have some great protector, some secret resources upon which to count, else He could never be so bold, so audacious, He would never act with such disregard of legitimate authority and established customs, just as if He had a perfect right to do so. He absents Himself for long periods at a time. Where and among whom is He then? Whence has He His knowledge and His skill in working miracles? What must we do about Him?' And so they went on discharging their wrath and interchanging conjectures."

*If we were to read those cavils and complaints with truly neutral eyes, we might see that there actually were some rational (albeit misguided) concerns expressed about Jesus and His preaching:*

- ~ People were laying aside their work to attend instructions given by Jesus;
- ~ He disturbed the peace of the Sabbath;

~ He displayed supernatural powers—which might come from the Devil;

~ He was predicting the destruction of Jerusalem;

~ He might be acting in league with a foreign power, which would ultimately work to the detriment of the people.

Fortunately, on this occasion in Capernaum, the Centurion Zorobabel was in attendance. He exerted a calming influence with this advice: "If His power is from God, He will certainly triumph; but if not, He will come to naught. So long as He cures our sick and labors to make us better, we have reason to love Him and to thank Him who sent Him." (A few years later, the revered rabbi Gamaliel gave almost identical guidance to the Sanhedrin, when it was trying to figure out how to punish the Apostles for continuing to spread the name of Jesus after His death.[11])

### The Attempt to Kill Jesus in His Hometown

There was no similarly calming voice in the crowd that tried to kill Jesus in Nazareth. St. Luke described the poignant scene, which began with Jesus reading from the scroll of Isaiah to an admiring congregation, and ended up with Him miraculously slipping away from a villainous mob in order to save His life, after His preaching had punctured their pride. Sister Emmerich saw the events in detail, including the reason why Jesus worked few cures there—which was that the people who brought forward their sick acted not out of compassion, but from a desire to see whether Jesus could work miracles, as He had reputedly done elsewhere. Thus, they were tempting Him, as Satan had done on Mt. Quarantania.

On the first day, even before the Sabbath had begun, He read the "Spirit of the Lord is upon me" passage from Isaiah[12] and applied it to Himself. They all marveled at His speech on that day, and even had vain thoughts because such a prophet had come from their city.

However, it was different the next morning. When He resumed, He taught from Deuteronomy 4:2, that nothing must be added to the Commandments, and He severely reproached the Pharisees with their additions to the Law, laying burdens on the poor. At this the Pharisees murmured among themselves. Worse was in store for them in the afternoon, when He spoke of their depravity and the punishment in store for them if they did not reform. As set forth in St. Luke's Gospel, He explained His refusal to work miracles for them, and referred to the miracles which Elijah and Elisha worked for non-Israelites. They became furious enough to stand up, hoot at Him, and conspire to kill Him:

"Outside the door, He found Himself surrounded by about twenty angry Pharisees who laid hands on Him, saying: 'Come on up with us to a height from which Thou canst advance some more of Thy doctrines! There we can answer Thee as Thy teaching ought to be answered.' Jesus told them to take their hands off Him, that He would go with them. They surrounded Him like a guard, the crowd following.

"The moment the Sabbath ended, jeers and insults arose on all sides. They raged and hooted, each trying to outdo his neighbor in the number and quality of his scoffing attacks upon Jesus. 'We will answer Thee!' they cried. 'Thou shalt go to the widow of Sarepta [Zarephath]! Thou shalt cleanse Naaman the Syrian! Art Thou Elijah? and art Thou going to drive up to heaven? Well, we'll show Thee a good starting-place! Who art Thou? Why didst Thou not bring Thy followers with Thee? Ah, Thou wast afraid. Was it not here that Thou, like Thy poor parents, gained Thy daily bread? And now that Thou hast whereon to live, wilt Thou turn us to scorn! But we will listen to Thee! Thou shalt speak in the open air before all the people, and we will answer Thee!' and thus shouting and raging they led Jesus up the mountain. . . . They reached a lofty spur which on the northern side overlooked a marshy pool, and on the south formed a rocky projection over a steep precipice. It was from this point they were in the habit of precipitating malefactors. Here they intended once more to call Jesus to account, and then to hurl Him down.

"They were not far from the scene of action when Jesus, who had been led as a prisoner among them, stood still, while they continued their way mocking and jeering. At that instant I saw two tall figures of light near Jesus, who took a few steps back through the hotly pursuing crowd, reached the city wall on the mountain ridge of Nazareth, and followed it till He came to the gate by which He had entered the evening before. . . . All on a sudden, they found Jesus no more among them. The cry was raised: 'Halt! Where is He? Halt!' The crowd came rushing on, the Pharisees pressed back upon them, the narrow path became a scene of confusion and uproar. They laid hold of one another, they squabbled and shouted, they ran to all the ravines, and poked their torches into the caves, thinking that He had hidden therein. . . . Quiet was not restored until long after Jesus had left the city, and then they set guards upon and around the whole mountain. Returning to the city, the Pharisees said: 'Now we have seen what He is—a magician. The devil has helped Him. He will soon spring up again in some other place, and throw all around Him into confusion.'"

## A Fate Worse Than Befell Sodom and Gomorrah

Jesus was not deterred by the attempt to kill Him in Nazareth, although His relatives felt intimidated and feared for His safety, going so far as to urge Him to live elsewhere, perhaps even across the Jordan. But, He knew that His "hour" had not yet come, and He continued on His way.

This was the scene Sister Emmerich saw in Gabara, after he warned the people that it would go worse for them than it had for Sodom and Gomorrah if they rejected the salvation He offered: "Some of the Pharisees, taking advantage of a pause, stepped up to Him with the question. 'Then, will this mountain, this city, yes, even the whole country, be swallowed up along with us all? And could there happen something still worse?' Jesus answered: 'The stones of Sodom were swallowed up, but not all the souls, for these latter knew not of the Promise, nor had they the Law and the Prophets.' . . . He reminded them that they were a chosen race whom God had formed into one nation, that they had received instruction and warnings, the Promises and their realization, that if they rejected them and persevered in their incredulity, not the rocks, the mountains (for they obeyed the Lord), but their own stony heart, their own soul, would be hurled into the abyss. And thus would their lot be more grievous than that of Sodom."[13]

## Jesus is Accused of Black Magic

The enemies of Jesus could not deny the supernatural character of many of His actions—but that did not force them to recognize His authority, for they used this fact against Him, citing His acts as proof that He was in league with the Devil. It is worth reading one of these calumnies, reported by Sister Emmerich, to understand how the common people may have been misled by the slanders uttered against Jesus, especially since they were uttered by people of superior standing who were thought to be better informed about such matters.

The background circumstance was the deliverance from demonic possession and the cure of a blind and dumb man who had been greatly abused by sorcerers from Gergesa, being dragged around the Decapolis and forced through spells to perform feats of strength, before he was led into the area of Capernaum. Jesus' good deed was maliciously misrepresented to the crowd by a Pharisee: "Jesus, he said, had now a powerful spirit in league with Him. If not, why had He not long ago delivered that furious demoniac? Why, if He were the Son of God, was He not able to banish the demons from the land of Gergesa, without going there in person? No! He was obliged first to go into that country, and conclude an agreement with the chief of the Gergesean demons. He had to make a bargain with that demon prince and give him the swine as his booty, for although inferior to Beelzebub,[14] that prince was still of some consequence. And now since He had freed that man at Gergesa, He had, by virtue of the same agreement, delivered the one here in Capernaum through the power of Beelzebub."

## Accusations Written on a Wall

Jesus everywhere had to deal with such detractors. According to Sister Emmerich, in the town of Saphet, near Beth-anath, Jesus was able to quell criticism by threatening to expose publicly the crimes of the ringleaders, who were diverting funds which had been donated for the support of widows and orphans: "Jesus, to their exceedingly great terror, began to write on the wall of the house, and in letters that they alone could decipher, their secret sins and transgressions. Then He asked them whether they wanted the writing to remain upon the wall and become publicly known, or whether, effacing it, they would permit Him to continue His work in peace. The Pharisees were thoroughly frightened. They rubbed out the writing and slunk away, leaving Jesus to continue His cures."[15]

## Taunts About His Origins

A common form of attack upon Jesus was to taunt Him about His supposedly humble origins. Such sniping was especially severe in Nazareth, where the people thought they knew Him well. Following a severe sermon, the local Pharisees hooted at Him, joined by a stranger who shouted out: "'Who, then, art Thou? Hast Thou forgotten that only some years before Thy father's death, Thou didst help him to put up partitions in my house?' Still Jesus deigned no answer. Then the Pharisees all began to shout: 'Answer! Is it good manners not to answer an honorable man?' At these words, Jesus addressed His bold questioner in terms like the following: 'I did indeed work on wood belonging to thee. At the same time, I cast a glance upon thee, and I grieved at not being able to free thee from the hard rind of thine own heart. Thou hast now proved thyself to be what I then suspected. Thou shalt have no part in My Kingdom, although I have helped thee to build up thy dwelling-place upon earth.'" It was here that Jesus commented, as noted in all the Gospels, that "nowhere is a Prophet without honor, excepting in his own city, in his own house, among his own relatives."

### "Oh Generation of Vipers!"

Jesus uttered His harshest denunciation of the Pharisees in Capernaum. On this particular occasion, they were sitting in the synagogue, hoping to see or hear something which they could complain about to the Sanhedrin. They anticipated that He might heal a man with a withered hand, and they posed to Him the question as to whether it was lawful to heal on the Sabbath. They had asked it numerous times before—and they got the same answer, with Jesus using the same simile of rescuing an animal from a pit on the Sabbath. Following that, Jesus took hold of the man's arm, and straightened his crooked fingers. The congregation responded with thanksgiving at this, and again when they saw Him expel a devil from a possessed man. The Pharisees by now were completely infuriated and, according to Sister Emmerich, they attacked Jesus with the charge: "He has a devil! He drives out one devil by the help of another!" Jesus responded with equally harsh language: "Who among you can convict Me of sin? If the tree is good, so too is the fruit good, if the tree is evil, so also is the fruit evil, for by the fruit the tree is known. Oh generation of vipers, how can you speak good things, whereas you are evil! Out of the abundance of the heart the mouth speaketh."

### An End to Temple Sacrifices

One morning during the Feast of the second Pasch, when the Temple was open for the reception of thanksgiving offerings and for the conduct of services, Jesus mounted to the great teacher's chair in the court before the sanctuary, but the Pharisees were determined to prevent Him from teaching. And so, they barraged Him with questions and charges, including His failure to offer sacrifice and His profanation of the Sabbath. In her visions, Sister Emmerich heard Jesus turn their charges back on themselves: "Of sacrifice, He said again that the Son of Man was Himself a Sacrifice, and that they dishonored the sacrifice by their covetousness and their slanders against their fellow men. God, Jesus went on to say, did not desire burnt offerings, but contrite hearts;[16] their sacrifices would come to an end, but the Sabbath would continue to exist. It would indeed exist, but for man's utility, for man's salvation. The Sabbath was made for man, and not man for the Sabbath."

### The Parable of Lazarus the Beggar

The Pharisees next argued with Jesus over the parable of the rich man and Lazarus, the beggar, related in the Gospel of Luke. The Pharisees were especially furious because the rich man had been a well known member of their sect who had died a frightful death. They tried to ridicule Him, asking how He could know the facts of what went on in hell with the rich man. But Jesus persisted in expounding upon the story, applying the sins of the rich man, in his neglect of Lazarus, to themselves, and "reproaching them with their avarice, their cruelty to the poor, their self-satisfied observance of empty forms and customs, along with their total want of charity."

## God Speaks About Jesus in the Temple

Just before His Passion, when the Pharisees saw Jesus teaching in the Temple, they raised a tumult and sent for a guard to arrest Him on the spot. Then occurred a great miracle, as mentioned by St. John. It was a theophany—a manifestation of God—like those at His Baptism and Transfiguration, but this one took place where the leaders of the religious establishment could experience it for themselves. According to Sister Emmerich: "When the uproar was at its height, Jesus looked up to heaven and said: 'Father, render testimony to Thy Son!' Instantly a dark cloud covered the heavens, a loud noise like a thunderclap resounded, and I heard a piercing voice proclaiming through the edifice, 'This is My beloved Son in whom I take my delight!' Jesus' enemies were utterly dumbfounded, and gazed upward in terror." The disciples closed ranks around Him, and the crowd made way for them as they left.

## Jesus Confronts the Sadducees

A further word about the persecution of Jesus by the religious establishment needs to be said here, because almost all of the confrontations recorded in the Gospels and by Sister Emmerich concern the Pharisee sect. The Sadducees were also important in the religious life of the Jews, but we know them only from the reports of their enemies and it is hard to be certain of the truth. The Sadducees were the party of the aristocracy, and while they appear to have been suppressed by Herod the Great, the survivors may have formed an alliance with Herod Antipas and the Roman authorities, and thus held very significant power in Jerusalem during the period of Jesus' ministry. It is very possible that Caiaphas, the High Priest at the time of Jesus' trial, was a Sadducee, and that he was one of a series of seven Sadducee High Priests. There were severe theological differences between the Pharisees and the Sadducees, particularly in that the latter denied the validity of Tradition and the many regulations for purity laid down by the Pharisees, and also denied the life of the soul after death (and hence denied resurrection and eternal reward or punishment).[17]

In the Gospels, we read about Jesus interacting separately with the Sadducees only in regard to their hypothetical question about the marital status in the afterlife of a woman who died after having had seven husbands. Sister Emmerich had a vision of a very sharp interchange between Jesus and the Sadducees in a wholly different context. It happened in Ataroth, where the Sadducees had solicited Jesus to come and cure a sick man, promising to believe in Him if He did so. Jesus, of course, knew their deceit, for the man was already dead:

"The corpse presented quite a fine appearance, for they had opened and embalmed it, the better to deceive Jesus. But Jesus said: 'This man is dead and dead he will remain.' They replied that he was only in a trance, and if he was indeed dead, he had only just now died. *Jesus responded: 'He denied the resurrection of the dead, therefore he will not now arise! Ye have filled him with spices, but behold, with what spices! Uncover his breast!' Thereupon I saw one of them raise the skin like a lid from the dead man's breast, when there broke forth a swarm of worms, squirming and straining to get out. The Sadducees were furious, for Jesus rehearsed aloud and openly all the dead man's sins and delinquencies, saying that these were the worms of his bad conscience, which he had in life covered up, but which were now gnawing at his heart.* He reproached them with their deceit and evil design, and spoke very severely of the Sadducees and of the judgment that would fall upon Jerusalem and upon all that would not accept salvation. They hurried the corpse back again into the house. The scene was one of frightful alarm and confusion. As Jesus with the disciples was going to the gate of the city, the excited rabble cast stones after them."

---

[1] Previously, little had been known about this group, other than what was written by the Jewish historians Josephus and Philo, and by the Roman historian Pliny. For an analysis of the doctrines of the people at Qumran and of the place of the Essenes in Judaism, *see* the entry for "Essenes" in *The Anchor Bible Dictionary* 2:619; David Flusser, *The Spiritual History of the Dead Sea Sect* (Tel Aviv: MOD Books 1989). Flusser applied the ancient historical commentaries to them because he assumed, perhaps incorrectly, that the Qumran community was Essene and, moreover, was representative of the sect as a whole. Recently, a number of archaeologists have become skeptical that the inhabitants were Essenes, and they have questioned whether the library pertained to the settlement itself or was brought there only in its final years to escape the turmoil in Jerusalem. *See, e.g.*, Alan D. Crown & Lena Cansdale, "Qumran: Was It An Essene Settlement?," *Biblical Archaeology Review* (Sept/Oct 1994)(concluding

that the inhabitants were not Essenes); John N. Wilford, "Debate Erupts Over Authors of the Dead Sea Scrolls," *N.Y. Times*, Dec. 24, 2002, p. D1.

[2] *The Anchor Bible Dictionary* entry for "Essenes" (2:620), notes that the word 'Essenes' could be derived from the Aramaic word equivalent to the Hebrew 'hasid', suggesting a connection with the Book of Maccabees.

[3] *See* the entry for "Essene Gate" in *The Anchor Bible Dictionary* 2:618.

[4] Though mankind had no *power* to delay (or accelerate) the coming of God—in this case through His Incarnation—yet God was willing to allow His timetable to be affected by human actions. Recall that it was God's plan that the Chosen People, having been led out of slavery in Egypt, would occupy the land flowing with milk and honey. However, when they let themselves be discouraged by the report of a scouting party, and did not trust that God would deliver the inhabitants into their hands, God punished them by causing them to wander in the desert for forty years before entering the Promised Land. (Nb 13:1–33; 14:1–38.) Thus, the actions of the people were allowed to change God's timetable.

[5] *See* Ex chs. 7–8.

[6] Both Meier and Charlesworth have summarized the similarities and differences between the teachings of Jesus and those of the *Qumran* Essenes. *See* John P. Meier, *A Marginal Jew* 3: 488–532; James H. Charlesworth, *Jesus and the Dead Sea Scrolls* 9–37. While Charlesworth correctly concluded that Jesus was not an Essenian, his conclusion that Jesus "was probably influenced in minor ways by the Essenians" (*ibid.* at 38) is based on the questionable assumption that Jesus could have been influenced in what He taught or how He acted, by any sectarian doctrine or religious customs.

[7] With regard to the Essenes, Sister Emmerich related that: "a great many among them who belonged, not to the fruits of the tree, but to the dry wood, isolated themselves in their observances and degenerated into a sect. This sect was afterward imbued with all kinds of heathenish subtleties, and became the mother of many heresies in the early days of the Church." The published transcriptions of Sister Emmerich's visions do not identify the "dry wood" of the Essenian sect; however, given the doctrines of the Qumran community and its self-imposed isolation, it is conceivable that they were the people she referred to. And see Gabriele Boccaccini, *Beyond the Essene Hypothesis* (Eerdmans 1998)(Qumranites were schismatics).

Sister Emmerich did not see Jesus visit the Qumran community even though He traveled throughout the entire country, including the area around the Dead Sea. This fact fits nicely with the results of the study of the Dead Sea scrolls, for nothing has been found in them linking Jesus to the Qumran community. *See* James H. Charlesworth, *Jesus and the Dead Sea Scrolls*, xxxv. A few scholars identified a very tiny fragment of a Dead Sea scroll as coming from the Gospel of Mark. *See* Carsten P. Thiede, "Greek Qumran Fragment 7Q5: Possibilities and Impossibilities." http://www.members.aol.com/egweimi/7q5.htm. However, most scholars rejected that claim, *see, e.g.,* Peter W. Flint, "That's No Gospel, It's Enoch!," *Bible Review* (April 2003) 37; Graham Stanton, "A Gospel Among the Scrolls?," *Bible Review* (December 1995) 36.

[8] *See* Anthony J. Saldarini, "Understanding Matthew's Vitriol," *Bible Review* (April 1997) 32, 34, 36.

[9] 1 Ki 18:41-46.

[10] Is 1:18.

[11] Acts 5:34-39.

[12] Is 61:1.

[13] From the Gospels, one can readily see that Jesus cried woe to several towns and threatened them with the fate of Sodom and Gomorrah. (Mt 10:14-15; Mt. 11:23-24; Lk 10:12) But what Jesus did in this teaching was different and more wonderful, distinguishing between the rocks and the souls in the towns. According to this teaching: in the past, all the rocks of Sodom had been destroyed, but not all the souls, because some of them were ignorant of the Promise; in contrast, in the future woe, all the rocks will not be destroyed, but the souls will be, for they know the Promise and reject it. This lesson was put in a literary form frequently used in the Psalms to make contrasts between pairs of ideas, namely the form of a *chiasmus*—which can be diagrammed like the letter X. *See, e.g.,* Mitchell Dahood, *The Anchor Bible—Psalms* 1:120-21 (Psalm 19). Jesus' Jewish listeners would have instantly appreciated His wordplay: the idea at the top left of the cross would be "stones destroyed," and that at the top right would be "stones spared."; the idea at the bottom right of the cross would be "souls spared," while at the bottom left would be "souls destroyed."

[14] It is somewhat unclear who Beelzebub was thought to be at that time, though commentators often equate him with Satan. One scholar has suggested that he was "the Canaanite god Baal, reduced from deific grandeur to a malevolent spirit." *See* Bradley L. Stein, "Who the Devil is Beelzebul?," *Bible Review* (Feb. 1997) 42, 45.

[15] *Cf.* Jn 7:53-8:11, when Jesus was confronted with the woman caught in adultery, and wrote with His finger on the ground. Raymond E. Brown suggested that Jesus was just making meaningless lines on the ground to show His lack of interest in, or disgust with, the zeal of the accusers. *See* John P. Meier, *A Marginal Jew* 1:269 (quoting Brown). But, Jesus' apparent indifference would not have caused the Pharisees to turn away, given that they were there to trap Him.

[16] *Cf.* Ps 40:7-8.

[17] *See* the entry for "Sadducees" in *The Anchor Bible Dictionary* 5:892; John P. Meier, *A Marginal Jew* 3:294-98, 389-411.

# Chapter Ten

## *What Did Jesus Look and Sound Like?*

There are probably more artistic representations of Jesus throughout the world than of anyone else who ever lived[1]—yet there is considerable variation among them, for we have not a single eyewitness description of what he looked like. The Evangelists, who were inspired by the Holy Spirit to report what He said and did, apparently received no such prompting to describe His appearance, for they gave us no hint as to how tall He was, what color His hair and eyes were, whether He had a beard, and so forth. However, from the visions of Sister Emmerich, we do have this picture of Him during His ministry:

"Jesus was taller than the Apostles. Walking or standing, His fair, grave face rose above them. His step was firm, His bearing erect. He was neither thin nor stout. . . . By the journeys and fatigue of His later years, His cheeks below the eyes and the bridge of His nose were somewhat tanned. His chest, high and broad, was free from hair, unlike that of John the Baptist, which was like a skin quite covered with hair. Jesus had broad shoulders and strong, muscular arms. His thighs also were provided with powerful, well marked sinews, and His knees were large and strong, like those of a man that had traveled much on foot and knelt long in prayer. His limbs were long, the muscles of the calves strongly developed by frequent journeying and climbing of mountains. His feet were very beautiful and perfect in form, though from walking barefoot over rough roads the soles were covered with great welts. His hands too were beautiful, his fingers long and tapering. Though not effeminate, they were not like those of a man accustomed to hard work. His neck was not short, though firm and muscular.

"His head was beautifully proportioned, and not too large, His forehead, high and frank, His whole face a pure and perfect oval. His hair, not exceedingly thick, and of a golden brown, was parted in the middle and fell in soft tresses down His neck. His beard, which was rather short, was pointed and parted on His chin."

As for what He sounded like, Sister Emmerich, who heard Him speak in her visions, had this to say: "His words and the tone of His voice were like living, deeply penetrating streams of light. He spoke with extraordinary calmness and power, and never very rapidly, excepting sometimes when talking with the Pharisees. At such times, His words were like sharp arrows and His voice less gentle. The tone of His ordinary voice was an agreeable tenor, perfectly pure in sound, without its counterpart in that of any human being. He could, without raising it, be distinctly heard above a great clamor."

A pleasing, but human, appearance was not all that people sometimes saw, again according to Sister Emmerich. When Jesus celebrated the first Passover of His public ministry in Jerusalem, in all the hustle and bustle of the festival *Jesus at times stood out, even to people who were not looking for Him, because His face glowed as if it were somehow illuminated.* While this may strike the reader as bizarre, students of the Old Testament will recall that the face of Moses, after he met with God, glowed so brightly that the people had to shield their eyes.[2]

There were three things that Jesus did at that first Paschal celebration which caused Him to be noticed. The first was that He awakened His listeners to some notable past events which they had not connected Him with:

"He drew their attention to man's indifference respecting the completion of the time marked by the Prophets. 'It was fulfilled thirty years ago, and yet who thinks of it excepting a few devout, simple minded people? Who now recalls the fact that three Kings, like an army from the East, followed a star with childlike faith seeking a newborn King of the Jews, whom they found in a poor child of poor parents? Three days did they spend with these poor people! Had their coming been to the child of a distinguished prince, it would not have been so easily forgotten!' Jesus however did not say that He Himself was that Child."

He also reminded them that "'It is now about eighteen years ago since a little *bachir* (by which Jesus must have meant a young scholar) argued most wonderfully with the Doctors of the Law who in consequence were filled with wrath against the Child.' And then He related to them the teachings of the little *bachir*." Those who had disputed with Him on that occasion in the Temple must have felt their anger returning at the thought of how they had been publicly embarrassed by the young Jesus.

Second, He made some apocalyptic remarks in the Temple. In figurative language, "He told them that the time was approaching when the symbolical Paschal lamb would give place to the reality; then would the Temple and its services come to an end. ... When they questioned Him as to how He knew that, He answered that His Father had told Him, but He did not say who that Father was."

And third and most important, it was during that first Pasch, that one of the most dramatic incidents reported in the Gospels occurred: Jesus cleansed the Temple.

### The Pious People Approve of Jesus Cleansing the Temple

Jesus had a major confrontation with the moneychangers and vendors in the Temple, reported by St. John. (A second, apparently minor, incident occurred immediately after Jesus' triumphal entry into Jerusalem on Palm Sunday of Holy Week, as reported by Sts. Matthew, Mark and Luke.) Sister Emmerich saw the incident at the first Pasch as unfolding in three separate episodes of increasing severity and tumult because Jesus' first, courteous warning failed to have a lasting effect. He acted twice on the day before the Paschal supper was eaten; the third time was on the day after:

"When Jesus with all His disciples went to the Temple, He found there ranged around the court of the suppliants, dealers in green herbs, birds, and all kinds of eatables. In a kindly and friendly manner, He accosted them and bade them retire with their goods to the court of the Gentiles. He admonished them gently of the impropriety of taking up a position where the bleating of the lambs, and the noise of the other cattle would disturb the recollection of the worshippers. With the help of the disciples, He assisted the dealers to remove their tables to the places that He pointed out to them.

"When Jesus again [that day] went up to the Temple with His disciples, He admonished the dealers a second time to withdraw. Since all the passages on account of the immolation of the Paschal lamb soon to take place were open, many had again crowded up to the court of the suppliants. Jesus bade them withdraw, and shoved their tables away. He acted with more vehemence than on the last occasion. The disciples opened a way for Him through the crowd. Some of the dealers became furious. With violent gesticulations of head and hands, they resisted Him, and then it was that Jesus, stretching out His hand, pushed back one of the tables. They were powerless against Him, the place was soon emptied, and all things carried to the exterior court.

"Then Jesus addressed to them words of warning. He said that twice He had admonished them to remove their goods, and that if He found them there again, He would treat them still more severely. The most insolent insulted Him with: 'What will the Galilean, the Scholar of Nazareth, dare to do? We are not afraid of Him.' These taunts began at the moment of their removal. Many were standing around looking at Jesus in amazement. *The devout Jews approved His action and praised Him in His absence. They also cried out: 'The Prophet of Nazareth!'*

"Jesus and His disciples spent the night in prayer and with but little sleep at Lazarus's on Mount Zion. The disciples from Galilee slept in the wings of the building. At daybreak they went up to the Temple, which was lighted by numerous lamps, and to which the people were already flocking from all parts with their offerings. Jesus took His stand in one of the courts with His disciples, and there taught. A crowd of venders had again pressed into the court of the suppliants and even into that of the women. They were scarcely two steps from the worshippers. As they still came crowding in, Jesus bade the newcomers to keep back, and those that had already taken their position to withdraw.

"But they resisted, and called upon the guard near by for help. The latter, not venturing to act of themselves, reported what was taking place to the Sanhedrin. Jesus meantime persisted in His command to the venders to withdraw. When they boldly refused, He drew from the folds of His robe a cord of twisted reeds or slender willow branches and pushed up the ring that held the end confined, whereupon one half of it opened out into numerous threads like a discipline. With this He rushed upon the venders, overthrew their tables, and drove back those that resisted, while the disciples, pressing on right and left, shoved His opponents away.

"And now came a crowd of priests from the Sanhedrin and summoned Jesus to say who had authorized Him to behave so in that place. Jesus answered that, although the Holy Mystery had been taken away from the Temple, yet it had not ceased to be a sacred place and one to which the prayer of so many just was directed. It was not a place for usury, fraud, and for low and noisy traffic. Jesus having alleged the commands of His Father, they asked Him who was His Father. He answered that He had no time then to explain that point to men and even if He did they would not understand, saying which He turned away from them and continued His chase of the vendors.

"*Two companies of soldiers now arrived on the spot, but the priests did not dare to take action against Jesus. They themselves were ashamed of having tolerated such an abuse. The crowd gathered around declared Jesus in the right, and the soldiers even lent a hand to remove the vendors' stands and to clear away the overturned tables and wares.* Jesus and the disciples drove the vendors to the exterior court, but those that were modestly selling doves, little rolls, and other needful refreshments in the recesses of the wall around the inner court, He did not molest. After that He and His followers went to the court of Israel. It may have been between seven and eight in the morning when all this took place."

No doubt Jesus did want the moneychangers out, and His Father's house restored as a house of prayer. But, there was another crucial dynamic to what Jesus did. The Pharisees had elevated their rules about ritual cleansings to a point where they almost seemed as important as the Ten Commandments. His unvarying response to the constant reproaches of the Pharisees was that they were blind fools for cleansing the outside, but not the inside—of themselves and their vessels—for inside, there was rot and corruption. *At the first Pasch, He embarked on an offensive right in heart of their territory, the Temple itself. And, as Sister Emmerich was careful to note, the "devout Jews" approved of what Jesus had done! He gave the Pharisees an example of what He meant by driving out the corruption inside—which put them to shame in front of all the people, for they themselves should have done it. Thus, He exposed them as hypocrites—which is exactly the charge He had brought against them in His discourses.*

## Murmuring of the Chosen People Against the Kingdom

After the first Pasch, Jesus resumed His itinerant ministry. In His travels, He arrived at Beth-haggan, south of Jezreel, on the day of a fast marking the murmuring of the Israelites against God and Moses. The next day He taught in the synagogue, giving the congregation a very full message, predicting the destruction of the Temple and Jerusalem, and invoking the Sign of Jonah. Sister Emmerich recounted it as follows:

"He spoke of the murmuring of the Children of Israel in the desert, saying that they would have taken a much shorter way to the Promised Land, had they kept the Commandments that God gave them on Sinai, but on account of their sins, they were obliged to wander, and they that murmured died in the desert. And *so too would they among His present hearers wander in the desert and die therein, if they murmured against the Kingdom that was now at hand and with it the final mercy of God. Their life had been an image of that wandering in the desert, but they should now go by the shortest way to the promised Kingdom of God, which would be pointed out to them.* He referred also to the dissatisfaction of the Children of Israel with the Judgeship of Samuel, their clamoring after a king, and their receiving one in Saul.

"Now when the Prophecy was fulfilled, when on account of their impiety the scepter had passed from Judah, they were again sighing for a king and for the reestablishment of the kingdom. *God would send them a King, their true King, Just as the lord of the vineyard had sent his own son after his servants had been murdered by the unfaithful vinedressers. But in the same way would they too expel their King and put him to death. He also explained those verses of the Psalms that speak of the cornerstone rejected by the builders, applying them to the son of the lord of the vineyard, and spoke of the punishment that would fall upon Jerusalem. The Temple, He said, would not exist much longer, and Jerusalem itself would soon be unrecognizable.*"

### Jesus Speaks of the Sign of Jonah

"There were twelve obstinate Pharisees at this instruction, and when it was over they disputed with Jesus. They pointed to a roll of parchment, and asked what was meant by Jonah's lying three days in the whale's belly. Jesus answered: 'In like manner will your King, the Messiah, lie three days in the grave, descend into Abraham's bosom, and then rise again.'[3] They laughed at that."

### Jesus Rails Against False Interpreters of Scripture

In Arumah, on the occasion of the feast for the dedication of Solomon's Temple, Jesus reminded His audience that God had told Solomon that He would destroy the Temple if the people fell away from Him.[4] *Jesus went on to say that the evil of the present generation was so great that the Temple would be destroyed if they were not converted. The Pharisees argued that God had never made such a threat—it was a figment of Solomon's imagination, to which Jesus retorted strongly in words which might be applicable to many biblical scholars today:*

"*He spoke to them . . . of distorting and corrupting the eternal truths, of the history and chronology of ancient, heathen nations, the Egyptians, for instance. He demanded of the Pharisees how they could venture to reproach these pagans, they themselves being even then in so miserable a condition, since what had been handed over to them as something so peculiarly theirs, something so sacred, the Word of the Almighty upon which His covenant with their holy Temple was founded, they could whimsically and capriciously reject as imaginations and fables. He affirmed and repeated God's promises to Solomon, and told them that in consequence of their false interpretations and sinful explanations, Yahweh's menaces were about to be fulfilled, for when faith in His most holy promises was wavering, the foundation of His Temple, also began to totter. He said: 'Yes, the Temple will be overturned and destroyed, because ye do not believe in the promises, because ye do not know that which is holy, because ye treat it as a thing profane! You yourselves are laboring at its downfall. No part of it shall escape destruction. It will go to pieces on account of your sins!'"*

### Jesus Himself as the Suffering Servant

One of the main Scriptural texts used by Jesus in His preaching was the Book of Isaiah, and He specifically identified Himself as the Suffering Servant. Sister Emmerich recounted such a teaching of Jesus in the synagogue of Capernaum. He read from Isaiah 49:14-15 and 22-23, assuring the people that God had not forgotten them, and that the time had come for the Lord to gather the nations into His sanctuary. However, while the gentiles would be converted, God would snatch from the perverted synagogue her children. Jesus explained Isaiah 50:1 as applying to the destruction of Jerusalem, since it would not receive the kingdom of grace.

*With regard to the words of Isaiah 50:4-7, about the maltreatment of the suffering servant, He explicitly linked them to how He had already been persecuted and would continue to be in the future.* He went on in that vein: "He spoke of the ill-treatment He had received at Nazareth, saying: 'Let him who can condemn Me, come forward!' His enemies, He said, would grow old and come to naught in their vain teachings, the Judge would come upon them. The godly would hear His voice, while the ignorant, the unenlightened should call to God and hope in Him. The Day of Judgment would come, and they that had kindled the fire would go to ruin. [Isaiah 50:11] This passage also Jesus explained of the destruction of the Jewish people and Jerusalem."

The next day was the Sabbath. The synagogue was packed and surrounded with people who could see Him from the court, the steps, and the flat roofs of the enclosing buildings. Even before He taught, He expelled an unclean spirit from a demoniac, as reported by St. Mark and St. Luke. Jesus again took the text of His sermon from Isaiah, saying that the prophecies were fulfilled and the time was near.

*They had longed after the Messiah, He said, but when He came they would not receive Him because of their erroneous notions of Him.*

Then taking the signs of the coming of the Prophet for whose accomplishment they always sighed, those signs that were still read from the Scriptures in their synagogues and for which they prayed, He proved that they had all been fulfilled. He said: "The lame shall walk, the blind see, the deaf hear. Is there not something of this now? What mean these gatherings of the gentiles to hear instruction? What do the possessed cry out? Why are the demons expelled? Why do the cured praise God? Do not the wicked persecute Him? Do not spies surround Him? But they will cast out and kill the Son of the Lord of the vineyard, and how shall it be with them? If ye will not receive salvation, yet shall it not be lost. Ye can not prevent its being given to the poor, the sick, to sinners and publicans, to the penitent, and even to the gentiles in whose favor it shall be taken from you." Such was the substance of Jesus' discourse. He added: "That John whom they have imprisoned ye acknowledge to be a Prophet! Go to him in his prison and ask him for whom did he prepare the ways and of whom did he bear witness?"

Jesus gave a similar instruction in Bezek, west of the Bethel Hills, preaching on the themes of the offered redemption and the coming rejection of the Messiah—who He said plainly was Himself—and the woe to befall those who rejected His message. Some of His discourse can be found in the Gospels of Matthew and Luke, but Sister Emmerich gave a much more complete account:

"Jesus recounted all that He had done, all the miracles He had wrought since His baptism, the persecution He had undergone at Jerusalem and Nazareth, the contempt He had endured, the spying and scornful laughter of the Pharisees. He alluded to the miracle at Cana, to the healing of the blind, the dumb, the deaf, the lame, and to the raising from the dead of the daughter of Jairus of Phasael [not the same man as Jairus the synagogue leader in Capernaum]. Pointing in the direction of Phasael, He said: 'It is not very far from here. Go and ask whether I say the truth!'"

## A Messiah According to Each One's Own Ideas

"He continued: 'Ye have seen and known John. He proclaimed himself the precursor of the Messiah, the preparer of His ways! Was John an effeminate man, one given to the softness and delicacy of high life? Was he not rather reared in the wilderness? Did he dwell in palaces? Did he eat of costly dishes? Did he wear fine clothing? Did he make use of flattering words?—but he called himself the precursor—then did not the servant wear the livery of his Lord? Would a king, a rich, a glorious, a powerful king such as ye expect your Messiah to be, have such a precursor? *And yet ye have the Redeemer in your midst, and ye will not recognize Him. He is not such as your pride would have Him. He is not such as ye are yourselves, therefore ye will not acknowledge Him!'*

"Jesus then turned to Deuteronomy 18:18-19: 'I will raise them up a prophet out of the midst of their brethren . . . and he that will not hear his words, which he shall speak in my name, I will be the revenger,' and He delivered a powerful discourse upon these texts. No one dared oppose a word to His teaching. *He said: 'John lived solitary in the desert. He mingled not with men, and ye blamed the life he led. I go from place to place, I teach, I heal, and that too ye blame! What kind of a Messiah do ye want? Each one would like to have a Messiah according to his own ideas!*

"'Ye resemble children running in the streets. Each makes for himself the instrument he likes best. One brings forth low, bass notes from the horn he has twisted out of bark, and another screeches high on his flute of reeds.' Then Jesus named all kinds of playthings used by children, saying that His hearers were like the owners of those toys. Each wanted to sing upon his own note, each was pleased with his own toy alone."

### Grace Will Triumph Over Law

Jesus taught on the ending of the rule of the Law in the synagogue of Daberath, at the foot of Mount Tabor. The text of the day was Genesis 25:19-34, about Jacob and Esau. He taught that the strife between Esau and Jacob prefigured that between the Law and Grace: "Jesus applied the details connected with the birth of the two brothers to His own time. Esau and Jacob struggled in their mother's womb, thus did the synagogue struggle against the piously disposed. The Law was harsh and severe, the firstborn like Esau, but it had sold its birthright to Jacob for a mess of pottage, for the redolent odors arising from all kinds of unimportant usages and exterior ceremonies. Jacob, who had now received the Blessing, would become a great nation whom Esau would have to serve." Thus, grace would triumph over the Law.

### The Last Chance for Israel

*And, as to grace, Jesus warned that the Jewish people were now being offered their final chance to receive it as a nation.* He delivered this profound message on a visit to Shiloh, where it was the custom that during the Festival of Tabernacles, a Doctor of the Law would deliver a sermon chastising the people: *"He spoke of the mercy of God toward His people, of Israel's revolts and turpitude, of the chastisements awaiting Jerusalem, of the destruction of the Temple, of the present time of grace, the last that would be offered them. He said that if the Jews rejected this last grace, never to the end of time should they as a nation receive another, and that a much more frightful chastisement should fall upon Jerusalem than it had ever yet experienced.* The whole discourse was calculated to inspire fear. All listened silent and terrified, for Jesus very clearly signified, as He explained the Prophecies, that He Himself was the One who was to bring salvation."

---

[1] *See, e.g.,* Marcelle Auclair, *Christ's Image* (New York: Tudor Publishing 1961); Frederick Buechner, *The Faces of Jesus* (New York: Stearn/Harper & Row 1989). For those who believe it to be authentic, the Shroud of Turin provides significant information about Jesus' face and build.

[2] Ex 34:29-30.

[3] The fact that Jesus used the Book of Jonah for purposes of instruction did not necessarily mean that He vouched for its factual verity. A modern story of a seaman found in the belly of a whale proved to be fictitious. *See* Edward B. Davis, "A Whale of a Tale: Fundamentalist Fish Stories," 43 *Perspectives in Science and Christian Faith* (1991). http://www.asa3.org. (accessed October 2003).

[4] 1 Ki 9:6-8.

# CHAPTER ELEVEN

## The Multiplications of the Loaves

Jesus explicitly offered His hearers the choice of life or death. And, He made them this promise: If they chose life, Jesus would give them His own flesh and blood, preserving them to life everlasting. *The proof that His apparently ordinary and finite body could be transformed into real food and multiplied to feed every one of His followers lay precisely in His feedings of the great multitudes who lacked provisions, by using only a few loaves of bread and some fish.*

That is why the Gospel stories of Jesus' multiplication of loaves and fishes have always been of great importance to Catholics, although many Protestants, who deny the Real Presence, have rejected the historicity of these miracles. A Protestant pastor living two hundred years ago suggested that Jesus did not really multiply anything—rather, the miracle was that Jesus persuaded the people listening to Him to share the food they had brought with them. This idea was recently embroidered by a Catholic pastor in a nationwide magazine,[1] so it needs to be understood that such a fiction is truly subversive of the Faith.

*While on other occasions Jesus did encourage His hearers to share food with the needy, to suggest that the miracles of the loaves and fishes were simply ones of human generosity, is to deny the clear words of the Gospels as to what happened, and eliminate a support for the doctrine of the Real Presence, which is central to Catholic theology.*[2]

Sister Emmerich had a number of visions of Jesus' multiplication miracles, two of which took place on a terraced mountain northeast of the Sea of Galilee, where Jesus several times taught on the Beatitudes and the Our Father. By the end of one such afternoon, the people were hungry, as they had not thought to bring food with them. Sister Emmerich saw the scene unfold as all four Evangelists recorded it, but she recounted far more details.

Jesus had the people seat themselves in groups below Him, and had flat baskets of woven bark brought to Him, along with two fish, which had been roasted and split lengthwise, five loaves of bread, which had been scored into sections for ease of breaking, and a couple of honeycombs. The food was spread upon a cloth and Jesus first cut the long and narrow loaves, and then the fish, crosswise, with a bone knife.

"After that He took one of the loaves in His hands, raised it on high and prayed. He did the same with one of the fish. . . . Three of the disciples were at His side. Jesus now blessed the bread, the fish, and the honey, and began to break the cross-sections into pieces, and these again into smaller portions. Every portion immediately increased to the original size of the loaf, and on its surface appeared as before the dividing lines. Jesus then broke the new loaves into portions sufficiently large to satisfy a man, and gave with each a piece of fish. Saturnin, who was at His side, laid the piece of fish upon the portion of bread, and a young disciple of the Baptist, a shepherd's son, who later on became a Bishop, laid upon each a small quantity of honey. There was no perceptible diminution in the fish, and the honeycomb appeared to increase. Thaddeus laid the portions of bread upon which were the fish and honey in the flat baskets, which were then borne away to those in most need."

Sister Emmerich related that the feeding of the multitude by the disciples, which took two hours, was accomplished in an orderly way— and the crowd did indeed understand that they had witnessed a great miracle. As mentioned by St. John, when the people saw this sign, they acknowledged among themselves that Jesus was the Promised One, and as He left they raised the cry, "He is our king!"

### Jesus as the "Bread of Life"

According to Sister Emmerich's visions, it was at this point in His ministry that Jesus taught the multitudes at length about the Bread of Life which He would give them. Not only did Sister Emmerich hear these teachings from His own lips, she saw that they were brought up against Him—as *false teachings*—when He was hauled before Annas and then Caiaphas for trial during His Passion.

The locales of the Bread of Life discourses were, primarily, Peter's house, where thousands of people had gathered, and also the synagogue of Capernaum, and a spot outside of the town when Jesus was alone with His disciples for the denouement of His public

addresses. The words which were set down by St. John in the form
of one very long but continuous dialogue between Jesus and His
listeners, including Pharisees and some of His disciples, were heard
by Sister Emmerich too, albeit spread out over two days. Many were
said first at Peter's house, but then repeated in the synagogue, as Jesus
kept being questioned about what He had said earlier.

She recounted that: "As Jesus was teaching in the synagogue upon
the lesson of the Sabbath, some of His hearers interrupted Him with
the question: 'How canst Thou call Thyself the Bread of Life come
down from heaven, since every one knows whence Thou art?' To
which Jesus answered by repeating all that He had already said on that
subject." After much back and forth between the Pharisees and Jesus,
He continued with His instruction on the Bread of Life. "He said,
'The bread that I will give, is My flesh for the life of the world.' At
these words, murmurs and whispers ran through the crowd: 'How can
He give us His flesh to eat?' Jesus continued and taught at length as
the Gospel records: 'Except you eat the flesh of the Son of Man and
drink His blood, you shall not have life in You.'" And when they asked
Him *when* He would give them that food, He told them a precise date,
somewhat more than a year in the future.

Such teachings were hard for the disciples to fathom, and a
number of those who had come over to Him from John the Baptist
now left. But, Jesus knew this would happen and, as reported by St.
John, He exclaimed that "No man can come to Me, unless it be given
him by My Father." When Jesus was alone with His Apostles, He
asked them whether they, too, were going to leave Him, drawing the
response from Peter that they would not, for they believed Jesus had
"the words of eternal life."

In the same location northeast of the Sea where He had
performed the first recorded multiplication of loaves and fishes, Jesus
did so again, to feed the 4,000 people assembled there, as related by
Sts. Matthew and Mark. This occasion was memorable for the crowd
not only because of the miracle itself, but also because of the openness
of His discourse and the maledictions He uttered.

Sister Emmerich related that: "He spoke very plainly of His being
the Messiah, of the persecutions that awaited Him, and of His
approaching imprisonment. But on that day, He said, those mountains
would quake and that rock (here He pointed to the stone ledge)
whereon He had announced the truth they had refused to receive,
would split asunder. Then He cried woe to Capernaum, to Chorazin,
and to many other places of that region. On the day of His arrest they
should all become conscious of having rejected salvation.

"He spoke of the happiness of this region to which He had broken the Bread of Life, but added that the strangers passing through had carried away with them that happiness. The children of the house threw that Bread under the table, while the stranger, the little whelps, as the Syrophoenician had called them, gathered up the crumbs which were sufficient to vivify and enliven whole towns and districts. Jesus then took leave of the people. He implored them once more to do penance and amend their life, repeated His menaces in the most forcible language, and informed them that this was the last time He would teach in those parts."

## Jesus as the Sacrificial Lamb

Sister Emmerich saw that Jesus was conscious from the very beginning of His ministry of the bitter end He would meet, and the benefits to mankind that would flow therefrom. The following are two of those visions. The first was of Jesus in the synagogue of Regaba, in the land of Bashan, northeast of the Sea of Galilee: "The Pharisees began a violent dispute with Jesus, again bringing forward their charge that He drove out the devil through the power of Beelzebub. *Jesus called them children of the father of lies, and told them that God no longer desired bloody sacrifices. I heard Him speaking of the Blood of the Lamb, of the innocent blood that they would soon pour out, and of which the blood of animals was only a symbol. With the Sacrifice of the Lamb, He continued, their religious rites would come to an end. All they that believed in the Sacrifice of the Lamb would be reconciled to God, but they to whom He was addressing Himself should, as the murderers of the Lamb, be condemned."*

An even more significant, though obscure, prophecy was uttered in Chorazin, the next town He went to: "In spite of the violent attacks of the Pharisees, Jesus spoke in prophetic terms of His future Passion. He alluded to their repeated sacrifices and expiations, notwithstanding which they still remained full of sins and abomination. *Then He spoke of the goat which at the Feast of Atonement was driven from Jerusalem into the desert with the sins of the people laid upon it. He said very significantly (and yet they did not understand Him) that the time was drawing near when in the same way they would drive out an innocent Man, One that loved them, One that had done everything for them, One that truly bore their sins. They would drive Him out, He said, and murder Him amid the clash of arms.* At these words, a great din and jeering shouts arose among the Pharisees."

Sister Emmerich also provided this description of the scapegoating ritual which was conducted by the High Priest on the holiest day of the Jewish calendar: "I saw too the celebration of the Feast of Atonement in Jerusalem, the numerous purifications of the High Priest, his arduous preparations and mortification, the sacrifices, the sprinkling of blood, the burning of incense, also the scapegoat, and the casting of lots for the two goats. One was for sacrifice, the other was chased away into the desert with something containing fire tied to its tail. It ran wildly through the wilderness, and at last plunged down a precipice. This desert, which was once traversed by David, commenced above the Mount of Olives."

The visions of Sister Emmerich, quoted above, showing that Jesus clearly foresaw and accepted His fate as the price of our salvation, are in accord with the teachings of the Catholic Church that:

Jesus' violent death was not the result of chance in an unfortunate coincidence of circumstances, but is part of the mystery of God's plan. . . .

The Scriptures had foretold this divine plan of salvation through the putting to death of "the righteous one, my Servant" as a mystery of universal redemption, that is as the ransom that would free men from the slavery of sin. . . . Indeed Jesus himself explained the meaning of his life and death in the light of God's suffering Servant. . . .

Christ's whole life expresses his mission: "to serve and to give his life as a ransom for many."[3]

The Catholic Church also teaches that Jesus specifically predicted His own resurrection on the third day—not at the end of the world— and that He did so not merely in private with His disciples at the Transfiguration,[4] but also publicly, when He declared that no sign would be given to the people of His age except the "sign of Jonah, explicitly describing the rising of the Messiah after three days in the grave."[5] Sister Emmerich related that on the latter occasion, He predicted the number of weeks which would elapse before the sign occurred.

The confusion and surprise of the disciples when He arose does not disprove the authenticity of the passages in which He predicted those events in advance: recall that both St. Mark and St. Luke expressly stated that the disciples had not understood when He predicted His Resurrection, but were afraid to question Him about it.

[1] *See* Charles Faso, "Catch the Dream," *U.S. Catholic* (October 1994) 38, 39. This suggestion had already been made in the 19th century by Heinrich Paulus, a German pastor. *See* Charlotte Allen, *The Human Christ—The Search for the Historical Jesus* 138–39.

[2] The Catholic Church teaches that "The miracles of the multiplication of the loaves, when the Lord says the blessing, breaks and distributes the loaves through the disciples to feed the multitude, prefigure the superabundance of this unique bread of his Eucharist." *See Catechism of the Catholic Church* § 1335.

[3] *See ibid.* § 599, § 601, and § 608 (quoting Mk 10:45).

[4] *See ibid.* §§ 554–55.

[5] *See ibid.* § 994.

# CHAPTER TWELVE

## Mission to Jews in the Diaspora

Jesus cast His net far beyond the Jews living in Israel itself. According to the visions of Sister Emmerich, He traveled to Cyprus to urge the Jews in the Diaspora (those who had been scattered outside Israel by exile) to return and join His followers. The fact that this trip was not recorded by the Evangelists is not surprising since Sister Emmerich did not see any of them accompanying Him there, and He took along only one Apostle, James the Lesser, and a few disciples.

Jesus went there aboard a ship with Jews returning to Cyprus from the Passover celebration in Jerusalem, the second of His ministry. He was cordially welcomed on Cyprus and He taught in the synagogues there much as He had on the mainland, with little opposition from the Pharisees. Sister Emmerich recounted an instruction on sacrifice, based on the Books of Leviticus and Ezekiel, but evolving into the new teachings of Jesus Himself:

*"He spoke of the offering of a pure heart. He said that sacrifices multiplied a thousand times could no more be of any avail, for one must purify his soul and offer his passions as a holocaust.[1] Without rejecting anything, without condemning or abolishing any of the prescriptions of the Mosaic Law, He explained it according to its real signification, thus making it appear far more beautiful and worthy of reverence.* Jesus, at the same time, prepared His hearers for baptism and exhorted to penance, for the time was near."*

In Salamis, Jesus was summoned to meet the Roman proconsul at his palace by the open square. To the surprise of the populace, the Roman official showed respect for Jesus by coming down the steps to meet Him and bowing low before Him. The proconsul led Him up to the balcony and then propounded an unending string of questions, centering on who He was and what His mission was—but all done earnestly and respectfully. Jesus answered him in vague terms, except that He said explicitly that His kingdom was not of this world.

At the communal well by the square, Jesus spoke about the waters of baptism and the regeneration of mankind. From time to time, there and elsewhere on Cyprus, Jesus and His disciples held baptismal services, using the local water to which some drops had been added of water from the Jordan carried thence in a leather bottle.

As He traveled throughout the island, He taught the reapers in the fields, the shepherds in the pastures, the miners by their caves, and the bee keepers by their apiaries, using the same similes and parables as He had in Israel. He frequently spoke against the sin of idolatry, because the Jewish people had intermingled freely with the pagans on Cyprus, with a consequent diminution of the Jewish faith. Sister Emmerich described the Jews there as being rich and comfortable, thanks to their lucrative commercial dealings with the natives, and the fact that they were not oppressed by the Roman administration. However, the pagan women who converted to Judaism and married Jewish men did so for mercenary reasons and did not keep the faith alive in their households.

Jesus did not simply counsel the Jews to avoid such alliances; rather He strongly urged them to change their lives and emigrate to Israel. Sister Emmerich recounted one discourse as follows:

"He told His audience that God would not abandon them that call upon Him. He ended by dilating on their attachment to their houses and possessions, and exhorted them, if they put faith in His teaching, to forsake the great occasion of sin in which they were living among the pagans, and, among those of their own belief, practice truth in the Promised Land. Judea, He said, was large enough to harbor and support them, although at first they might have to live under tents. *It was better to give up all than to lose their soul on account of their idolatry, that is, their worship of their fine houses and possessions, better to give up all than to sin through love of their own convenience. That the Kingdom of God might come to them, it was necessary that they should go to meet it.* They should not put their trust in their dwellings in a pleasant land, solid and magnificent though they might be, for the hand of God would fall suddenly upon them, scattering them in all directions, and overturning their mansions."

Jesus gave an even more severe and explicit discourse on the occasion of His departure from the island:

"He spoke again of the approach of the Kingdom and of the obligation to go to meet it, of His own departure, and of the short time remaining to Him, of the bitter consummation of His labors, and of the necessity they were under of following Him and laboring with Him. . . . *Referring to the country in which they lived where every-*

*thing was so pleasant and the conveniences of life so many, Jesus compared it after all to an ornamented tomb whose interior was full of filth and corruption.*

"Then He bade them reflect upon their own interior, and see what lay concealed under their beautiful exterior. *He touched upon their usury, their avarice, their desire of gain which led them to communicate so freely with the pagans, their violent attachment to earthly possessions, their sanctimoniousness; and He again told them that all the magnificence and worldly conveniences that they saw around them would one day be destroyed, that the time would come in which no Israelite would there be found living.*"

The result was that many Jews, and also some pagans, heeded His injunction and emigrated to Israel, bringing with them their wealth, which was later used in founding Christian communities after Jesus' death. Jesus was pleased with those He had been able to save, and propounded a new parable from His experience on Cyprus:

"Jesus walked in the garden with His disciples and related the parable of a fisherman that went out to sea to fish, and took five hundred and seventy fishes. He told them that an experienced fisherman would put into pure water the good fish found in bad, that like Elijah, he would purify the springs and wells, that he would remove good fish from bad water, where the fish of prey would devour them, and that he would make for them new spawning ponds in better water. . . . The Cypriotes who had followed Jesus could not restrain their tears when they heard Him speak of the laborious task of transporting the fish from bad to good water. Jesus mentioned clearly and precisely the number 'five hundred and seventy good fish' that had been saved, and said that that was indeed enough to pay for the labor."

To save the "good fish," Jesus gave specific instructions as to where they should settle in Israel. They were told to go to Lazarus, John Mark, or others friends of Jesus for assistance, and the Blessed Virgin Mary also aided them in beginning life anew.[2] Sister Emmerich related that there was "a tacit understanding, an interior agreement" between Jesus and His Mother, to the effect that she would take His followers into her heart, and become their spiritual mother, an obligation which she earnestly fulfilled.

### Mission to the Samaritans

Another major example of Jesus' outreach to those not in the mainstream of the Jewish religion was His dealings with the Samaritans. Jesus repeatedly stressed that He had come for the lost sheep of the House of Israel, but His disciples and most others in Israel no longer thought of the Samaritans as such, although the Samaritan territory was that of their ancestors from the tribes of Ephraim and Manasseh, sandwiched between the Jewish territories of Galilee on the north and Judea on the south.

The two peoples held themselves apart and there was a very strong antipathy between them. This had led the Jews to destroy the Samaritan sanctuary on Mt. Garizim, and their religious capital, Shechem, a hundred years before Jesus was born. The same spirit of hostility was exhibited by James and John, when Jesus traveled through Samaritan territory and the people would not receive Him. According to St. Luke's Gospel, Jesus' Apostles asked Him: "Lord, do you want us to call down fire from heaven to consume them?" Even today, we have a negative stereotype of them, namely, that they were degenerate Jews, a people with a bastard religion which synthesized the worship of Yahweh and pagan polytheism.[3]

Jesus was at pains not only to bring about the salvation of the Samaritan people, but to use His efforts for their salvation to open the minds of His disciples to the all-inclusive nature of His Kingdom. By His teachings, Jesus showed that good could be found even among the Samaritans. Indeed, His most famous parable about love for one's neighbor—the Parable of the Good Samaritan reported by St. Luke— showed that a member of that despised group had better taken to heart the injunction to love one's neighbor than had two paradigm members of the Jewish religion, a priest and a Levite. Moreover, He once called His disciples' attention to the fact that out of ten lepers He had healed in a group, the only one to return and pay Him homage was a Samaritan, referred to by Jesus as "this foreigner."

The famous encounter between Jesus and the Samaritan woman, related by St. John, came about at Jacob's well,[4] a spot revered by both Samaritans and Jews. The deep well there was enclosed in a roomy, octangular spring house, which in turn was encircled by an open arched gallery. A pump raised the water so that it would fill basins for travelers to wash, and to water their animals. As recorded in St. John's Gospel, Jesus had sent the disciples who accompanied Him—Andrew, James the Greater and Saturnin—into Sychar to obtain food, and He was alone when the Samaritan woman, Dina by name, came to draw water.

According to the visions of Sister Emmerich, Dina was a beautiful woman, about 30 years old, born of the marriage between a Jewish mother and a pagan father. She had had five husbands; some had died, others had been turned out by her new lovers. She was then living with a rich merchant, who had moved with her to Sychar from Syria. *Also according to Sister Emmerich, while Dina was indeed a real person, she was also a "type," meaning that she stood in a representative capacity for all of Samaria, just as Christ stood as a representative for those subsequently to be resurrected.* That is not an easy concept to grasp, but it is perfectly illustrated by what Sister Emmerich related of the meeting. Sister Emmerich did not merely see sights and hear sounds—she was given to understand the mystical significance of events. The following paragraphs were her effort to retell that ineffable experience (the narrative picks up after Jesus told Dina that He could supply her with "living water" and she asked Him to do so):

"Jesus at the Well of Jacob thirsted after the chosen souls of Samaria, in order to refresh them with the living waters from which they had cut themselves off. *It was that portion of the rebellious sect still open to salvation that here thirsted after this living water and, in a certain way, reached out an open hand to receive it. Samaria spoke through Dina: 'Give me, Oh Lord, the Blessing of the Promise! Help me to obtain the living water from which I may receive more consolation than from this temporal Well of Jacob, through which alone we still have communication with the Jews.'*

"When Dina had thus spoken, Jesus said to her: 'Go home, call thy husband, and come back hither!' and I heard Him give the command twice, because it was not to instruct her alone that He had come. *In this command the Redeemer addressed the whole sect: 'Samaria, call hither him to whom thou belongest, him who by a holy contract is lawfully bound to thee.'*

"Dina replied to the Lord: 'I have no husband!' *Samaria confessed to the Bridegroom of souls that she had no contract, that she belonged to no one.*

"Jesus replied: 'Thou hast said well, for thou hast had five husbands, and he with whom thou now livest is not thy husband. Thou hast spoken truly.' *In these words the Messiah said to the sect: 'Samaria, thou speakest the truth. Thou hast been espoused to the idols of five different nations, and thy present alliance with God is no marriage contract.' (These words of Jesus referred to the five different pagan colonies with their idolatry, placed by the King of the Assyrians in Samaria after the greater part of its inhabitants had been led into the Babylonian Captivity. What remained of the original people of God in Samaria, had become mixed up with the heathens and their idol-worship.)*

"Here Dina, lowering her eyes and hanging her head, answered: 'Sir, I see that Thou art a Prophet,' and she drew down her veil. *The Samaritan sect recognized the divine mission of the Lord, and confessed its own guilt.*

"As if *Dina understood the prophetic meaning of Jesus' words 'and he with whom thou livest is not thy husband,' that is, thy actual connection with the true God is imperfect and illegal, the religion of the Samaritans has by sin and self-will been separated from God's covenant with Jacob;* as if she felt the deep significance of these words, she pointed toward the south, to the temple not far off on Mount Garizim, and said questioningly: 'Our Fathers adored on that mountain, and you say that Jerusalem is the place where men must adore?'

"Jesus replied with the words: 'Woman! believe Me, the hour cometh when neither in Garizim nor in Jerusalem wilt thou adore the Father.' *In this reply He meant to say, 'Samaria, the hour cometh when neither here nor in the sanctuary of the Temple will God be adored, because He walks in the midst of you,'* and He continued: 'You adore that which you know not, but we adore that which we know, for salvation is of the Jews.' *Here He related to her a similitude of the wild, unfruitful suckers of trees, which shoot forth into wood and foliage, but produce no fruit. It was as if He had said to the sect: 'Samaria, thou hast no security in thy worship, Thou hast no union, no sacrament, no pledge of alliance, no Ark of the Covenant, no fruit. The Jews, from whom the Messiah will be born, have all these things, the Promise, and its fulfillment.'*

"And again Jesus said: 'But the hour cometh and now is when the true adorers will adore the Father in spirit and in truth, for the Father wills such to adore Him. God is a spirit, and they that adore Him must adore Him in spirit, and in truth.' *By these words the Redeemer meant: 'Samaria, the hour cometh, yea, it now is, when the Father by true adorers will be adored in the Holy Ghost and in the Son, who is the Way and the Truth.'*

"Dina replied: 'I know that the Messiah cometh. When He is come, He will tell us all things.' *In these words here at the Well of Jacob, spoke that portion of the Samaritan sect, which might lay some legitimate claim to the Promise:* 'I hope for, I believe in the coming of the Messiah. He will help us.'

"Jesus responded: 'I am He, I who now speak to thee!' *By this He said to all Samaria that would be converted: 'Samaria! I came to Jacob's Well athirst for thee, thou water of this well. And when thou didst give Me to drink, I promised thee living water that would never*

*let thee thirst again. And thou didst, hoping and believing, make
known to Me thy longing for this water. Behold, I reward thee, for
thou hast allayed My thirst after thee by thy desire after Me! Samaria,
I am the Fountain of living water. I who now speak to thee, am the
Messiah.'"*

We know from the Gospel of John that Dina, deeply touched by
Jesus' words, ran back to Sychar, spread the news that the Messiah had
appeared to her, and returned with some of her neighbors. (Sister
Emmerich also saw in her visions that so great was Jesus' effect on
Dina that she resolved to separate from her consort and to consecrate
her wealth to the work of the future Church.) From an initial posture
of hostility toward Jesus simply because He was a Jew, the woman had
been led step by step to an acceptance of Him as the Messiah. And
not only did she show how even a Samaritan could accept salvation,
she showed how a Samaritan could be the "good ground" which would
yield a hundred-fold return when seeded!

While Jesus was addressing the Samaritans gathered by Dina, a
number of the disciples who had been off in other directions appeared.
The latter were displeased to see the Lord treating the Samaritans with
consideration, for if it had been left up to them, He would have had
nothing to do with the sect. In part, they were afraid that if His
communication with the Samaritans became known to the Jews, they
themselves would be the object of derision.

Jesus took the disciples out of the city, and gave them a lecture
on the ready harvest, even in Samaria, and the need for them to act
as harvesters: "'Ye disciples are called to the harvest, though ye have
not sown. Others have sown, namely, the Prophets and John and I
Myself. He that reapeth, receiveth wages and gathereth fruit for
eternal life, that both He that soweth and he that reapeth may rejoice
together.'" It is no wonder then, that after His resurrection, Jesus
explicitly directed His disciples to be His witnesses in Samaria, as in
Jerusalem and Judea.[5]

## Mission to the Gentiles

At the presentation of the infant Jesus in the Temple, Simeon had
prophesied that Jesus would be "a revealing light to the gentiles," and
so He was! Some of the pagans he saved were right at hand in Israel,
one being the Centurion Cornelius. Sister Emmerich had visions of
the healing of the centurion's slave, an act mentioned by Sts. Matthew
and Luke.[6] She related that the Blessed Virgin Mary had interceded
with Her Son because Cornelius was a good man, who had built the
Jews of Capernaum their synagogue. Upon being told that Jesus was

on His way to his sick slave, Cornelius went out to see Him, but also sent ahead a messenger with words expressing Cornelius' recognition of his own unworthiness and his faith that Jesus could heal his servant at a distance, simply by giving orders to those under His command— which Jesus promptly did. By the time of Jesus' Passion, Cornelius and his family had received baptism, and he was instructing pagan youths in his new faith. Sister Emmerich had a vision of him doing this, and making a confession to them about the cure of his slave the year before: "He told them that through shame of the idols that were in his house, and because it was just the time at which the pagan carnival was celebrated, he had begged Jesus, the Son of God, not to enter into his idolatrous household."

Sister Emmerich also saw that immediately after the miracle, Cornelius proposed to offer a sacrifice of burnt offerings. *"But Jesus replied that it would be better for him to invite his enemies in order to reconcile them one with another; his friends, that he might lead them to the truth; and the poor, that he might recreate and entertain them with the food he had destined for sacrifice, for God no longer delighted in burnt offerings."*

One of the memorable stories in the Gospels about faith in Jesus centered around a pagan, known as the Syrophoenician woman. Sister Emmerich placed the locale as being Dan, in northern Israel due east of Tyre. Jesus was teaching there in the garden of a Nazirite family, when the Syrophoenician woman, from a distance, and very humbly, solicited His help. Sts. Matthew and Mark related that she finally worked up the courage to come up and prostrate herself before Him, begging a cure for her possessed daughter. When Jesus rejected her plea with the words, "It is not good to take the bread of the children and to cast it to the dogs," instead of taking offense or being discouraged, she responded with words of great faith: "Yea, Lord! for the whelps also eat of the crumbs that fall from the table of their masters." Jesus thereupon relented and exorcised the demon from a distance.

Sister Emmerich saw that scene, but also something more than what is to be found in the Gospels. According to her visions, the woman was crippled on one side. Jesus asked her if she did not want a cure for herself, but she said that she was not worthy and asked help only for her daughter. As we would expect, Jesus responded to her humility and self-sacrifice by healing her. And, there was a sequel the next day: the woman returned with one of her relatives, who was deaf and dumb, and partly paralyzed, and Jesus healed him too. Whereupon the cured man began to utter prophecies to the crowd, as to the ruin of the unbelieving Jews and the consequent benefits to the pagans, in words which echoed the dialogue of the previous day: "'The food that ye, the children of the house, reject, we outcasts shall gather up. We shall live upon it, and give thanks. The fruit of the crumbs that we gather up will be to us what you allow to go to waste of the Bread of Heaven.'" The phrase "Bread of Heaven" is one which he must have spoken under inspiration, for that is what the body of Christ was later to become (and be known as), in the form of consecrated hosts.

At the Syrophoenician woman's invitation, Jesus and the disciples traveled into pagan territory, to visit her at Ornithopolis. There, she showered them with costly gifts, for she was a very rich widow, and Jesus put them to use in relief of the poor Jews of that city. *Jesus gave an instruction in a Jewish school, where He taught that the saying "Our fathers have eaten sour grapes, and the teeth of the children are on edge,"⁷ was no longer in force. Instead, He said, "every one that abides by the Word of God announced by Me, that does penance and receives baptism, no longer bears the sins of his father."*

Jesus' major "mission" to the gentiles was a trip He kept secret from all His followers. Jesus' raising of Lazarus had prompted some of the religious authorities to plot to kill Him, and He significantly lowered His public presence. According to Sister Emmerich's visions, Jesus left the territory of Israel for close to three months, journeying to the lands of the Three Kings, then to Egypt, and finally back into Israel. This lengthy journey was not noted or even hinted at in the Gospels (or in any of the apocrypha) because none of the Apostles, and none of His disciples as of that date, attended Him. Instead, he deliberately took with Him only three teenage assistants, who were descendants of one of the Three Kings. Their ancestors had come in the caravan for His birth, and had thereafter remained and intermarried with the shepherds of Bethlehem, becoming Jews.

He told the Apostles only that He would be traveling, and arranged to meet them upon His return at Jacob's Well in Sychar. In the meantime, they too were to go off on missions. Sister Emmerich noted that the mission assigned to Matthew was to teach in his own home, and endure the contempt of his former colleagues who would not convert.

*At Jesus' last stop among Jews, in Kedar, the people there could not understand why He would leave them to go among the star-worshipping heathens, but He told them that He had friends among those who had attended His birth, and He wanted to invite them into the vineyard and Kingdom of His Father.* Jesus, with his three young attendants, journeyed into the land of the Three Kings along the Tigris and Euphrates Rivers, going as far east as Ur. Wherever He went, the people were enthralled with His teachings and begged Him to stay with them.

Two of the Three Kings, Mensor and Theokeno, were still living, only Seir having died since His birth. They asked whether it was time for them to pull up stakes (they lived in tents) and follow Him back to Israel, but He told them it was not. He described to them the bitter fate which He was soon to meet—a fate which they could not fathom because they regarded Him as divine. He explained that He was also man, and as man, He could truly suffer.

*His hosts told Him about a dove which frequently perched on Seir's tomb, and they asked what that signified. Jesus said that the dove signified that Seir had been baptized with the baptism of desire.* They too wanted to be part of His kingdom, but He told them that they were not yet ready for baptism, for they still held to heathenish practices in their worship. While they knew something about the Promise, and His own role in salvation history, they were largely in ignorance, and He could not prepare them adequately in the time He had to spend with them. Therefore, He told them that He would send His helpers in three years; Sister Emmerich said that Thomas and Thaddeus were the Apostles who carried out the work of their conversion.

He gave many instructions not only about the true God and the true faith, but about how they should live. He pointed out that they devoted more care to their sick animals than to their sick fellow men. He denounced their idolatry, and commanded the destruction of the idols they worshipped, with the metals to be melted down and given to the poor. He deliberately performed almost no miracles; and when they asked Him why He did not, He explained that He wanted their faith to be based on what He had to say.

When Jesus left the land of the Three Kings, He traveled westward across Arabia, to Heliopolis, in Egypt, where He had lived as a child. The purpose of His visit there was to teach and console those who had been friendly to the Holy Family while they were in exile. This journey was like a "bookend" to the one He undertook at the beginning of His ministry, to bring the Good News to people who had helped the Holy Family at His birth and on their flight. Finally, only three months before His Passion, He returned to Jewish territory, and gave the three young men accompanying Him strict instructions, which they honored, to keep secret everything they had seen on the trip.[8]

[1] *Cf.* Heb 10:5–9; Ps 40:7–8.

[2] According to Sister Emmerich, many of the emigrés lived in caves at first and then established over the caves the city of Eleutheropolis, west of Hebron. She also related that, in the attacks on Christians by Jews, which began at the time of the stoning of Stephen, the Christians took refuge in the caves; Joses Barsabas, a son of Mary Cleophas (by her second husband, Sabas), who had become the first bishop of the city, was crucified on a tree.

[3] For a general discussion of the problem, *see* John P. Meier, *A Marginal Jew* 3: 532–42.

[4] *See* the entry for "Jacob's Well" in *The Anchor Bible Dictionary* 3:608. The location was just east of Sychar, in between Mt. Ebal to the north and Mt. Garizim to the south.

[5] Acts 1:8.

[6] Mt 8:5–13; Lk 7:1–10. The same incident is recorded slightly differently in the Gospels of both Matthew and Luke. Sister Emmerich's visions are in accord with the latter account, in that the declaration of faith was carried to Jesus by a messenger on the Centurion's behalf.

[7] Ezk 18:2.

[8] One of them begged to be allowed to write down the details of the trip, which Jesus acceded to, provided it was done after Jesus' death and the writing was given to John. Sister Emmerich thought she saw it still in existence, though she did not say where it was.

# CHAPTER THIRTEEN

### *Why Was Peter Reluctant to Be a Disciple?*

Following the Wedding at Cana, one might have expected that Jesus would proceed to call His Apostles, and have them accompany Him throughout His public ministry, but Sister Emmerich's visions place their call later, well after the first Passover He celebrated with them. In the meantime, various of them joined with Him on one journey or another, and then went back to their occupations. One day, when some of the disciples with Him caught sight of Peter, James and John out fishing on the Sea of Galilee, they asked Jesus to summon them, but He refused, saying: "I have not yet called them. They, and especially Peter, carry on a large business upon which many depend for subsistence. I have told them to continue it, and in the meantime hold themselves in readiness for My call."

Peter's business, which operated out of the fishing town of Bethsaida, was substantial. He had a license to fish a certain area of the Sea of Galilee, and he owned a number of boats, some of which he had built, together with Andrew. The small boats held about ten men; others were considerably larger, with galleries around the masts, and floating barrels on either side, to prevent the vessel from being overturned in a storm. When not being used for fishing, the boats transported caravans across the Sea. According to Sister Emmerich, Peter employed other fishermen and pagan slaves.

Peter had been reluctant to travel with Jesus, complaining that he had not been paying enough attention to his own business, and had to return to work to take care of his family. Peter was married, and though he had no children by his wife, through her he had a stepdaughter and stepsons. His mother-in-law, who lived with them, was so sickly that she could not walk without leaning on the walls. According to Sister Emmerich, apart from the financial consideration, Peter held back because "he was always of the opinion that life with the Master was too high for him, he could not understand it. He believed in Jesus, he saw His miracles, he shared freely his substance with the other disciples, he did willingly all that was enjoined upon him, but yet he felt unfit for such a vocation. He thought himself too simple, too unworthy. . . . Sometimes also it was very vexatious to him to find himself the object of such railleries as, 'He is only a poor fisherman, and yet look at him going around with the Prophet! And his house is a perfect rendezvous for fanatics and seditious persons. See how he neglects his business!' All this made it a struggle for Peter since, though full of faith and love, he was not at that time so enthusiastic, so zealous as Andrew and the other disciples."

Eventually, Jesus came to Bethsaida. There He cured Peter's mother-in-law, as reported in the Synoptic Gospels, and again instructed Peter and His other chief followers on discipleship. Sister Emmerich related that: "He spoke principally of the fact that they would soon give up their present occupations and follow Him. Peter became quite timid and anxious. He fell on his knees before Jesus, begging Him to reflect upon his ignorance and weakness, and not to insist on his undertaking anything so important, that he was entirely unworthy, and quite unable to instruct others. Jesus replied that His disciples should have no worldly solicitude, that He who gave health to the sick would provide for their subsistence and furnish them with ability for what they had to do. All were perfectly satisfied, excepting Peter who, in his humility and simplicity, could not comprehend how he was for the future to be, not a fisherman, but a teacher of men."

### How Did Jesus Come to Choose Judas Iscariot?

While Peter had no thought of joining Jesus for a reward, such was not the case with Judas Iscariot. Jesus encountered Judas in Meroz (a city mentioned in the Bible but not yet located by archaeologists). Meroz had been substantially isolated from the rest of the country; the Jews who settled there had intermarried with the Shechemites, and the inhabitants had a reputation for faithlessness and perfidy. The chief employment of the townspeople was leather tanning, which they carried on near Iscariot (hence Judas' name), a small town and marshy region to the west, where a little stream flowed through a ravine. In their synagogue, Jesus taught the parable of the buried talents, likening the inhabitants to the slothful servant who had received only one talent of silver, which he should have put out at interest instead of burying it pending his master's return from a trip.

Jesus then repaired to an inn outside of town with His disciples. Those present included Bartholomew, who had received an interior call from Jesus, Simon Zelotes, Jude Thaddeus and Philip. At the request of Judas Iscariot, some of them spoke to Jesus about him and his desire to be of service. Jesus looked to be troubled, and told them that He would have to think about that.

According to Sister Emmerich, Judas was the illegitimate son of an army officer and a woman who was a public dancer and singer. Judas lived with his uncle, and helped him in his tanning business. He was then 25 years old, neat and well dressed in appearance; his hair was black, his beard reddish, and he was of middle height. Sister Emmerich had this to say about his character and motives:

"He was affable in address, obliging, and fond of making himself important. He talked with an air of confidence of the great or of persons renowned for holiness, affecting familiarity with such when he found himself among those that did not know him. But if any one who knew better convicted him of untruth, he retired confused. *He was avaricious of honors, distinctions, and money. He was always in pursuit of good luck, always longing for fame, rank, a high position, wealth, though not seeing clearly how all this was to come to him. The appearance of Jesus in public greatly encouraged him to hope for a realization of his dreams. The disciples were provided for, the wealthy Lazarus took part with Jesus of whom every one thought that He was about to establish a kingdom, He was spoken of on all sides as a King, as the Messiah, as the Prophet of Nazareth. His miracles and wisdom were on every tongue. Judas consequently conceived a great desire to be numbered as His disciple and to share His greatness which, he thought, was to be that of this world*. . . . With all his cleverness, courteousness, and obligingness, there was a shade of darkness, of sadness in the expression of his countenance proceeding from his avarice, his ambition, his secret envy of even the virtues of others."

The next day, when Judas Iscariot was introduced to Jesus, he bowed and asked if he could join Jesus' group. Sister Emmerich related that: "Jesus replied sweetly and in words full of prophetic meaning: 'Thou mayest have a place among My disciples, unless thou dost prefer to leave it to another.' These were His words or at least their purport. I felt that Jesus was prophesying of Matthias, who was to fill Judas's place among the Twelve,[1] and alluding also to His own betrayal."

According to the Gospel of John, at the Last Supper Jesus told His Apostles: "It was not you who chose me, but I who chose you." Why would Jesus, knowing that Judas would betray Him, choose such a man? The Apostle Thomas did not foresee the treachery of Judas, but he did not like him, and when Thomas himself became a disciple, he asked Jesus almost the same question—why did you pick *him*? *The answer which Sister Emmerich heard Jesus give Thomas was that "from eternity it was decreed by God for Judas, like all the others, to be of the number of His disciples."* Jesus had picked Judas knowing full well what it would entail, because that was His Father's will for Him.

## The Calling of Levi (Matthew)

Jesus traveled to the northeast corner of the Sea of Galilee, to call a customs collector there by the name of Levi. We know him as an Apostle and Evangelist under the new name Jesus gave him—Matthew. Sister Emmerich saw the events as follows:

"When Matthew from the top of a little eminence beheld Jesus and the disciples coming toward him, he became confused and withdrew into his private office. But Jesus continued to approach, and from the opposite side of the road called him. Then came Matthew hurrying out, prostrated with his face on the ground before Jesus, protesting that he did not esteem himself worthy that Jesus should speak with him. But Jesus said: 'Matthew, arise, and follow Me!' Then Matthew arose saying that he would instantly and joyfully abandon all things and follow Him. He accompanied Jesus back to where the disciples were standing, who saluted him and extended to him their hands. Thaddeus, Simon, and James the Lesser were particularly rejoiced at his coming. They and Matthew were half-brothers."

Matthew's ready acceptance of the call might seem surprising, since he was not only a publican, but a married man as well, with four children. But, he had once met Jesus on the road, and had subsequently received John's baptism. Both he and his wife were overjoyed at this development, and Matthew made arrangements to give up his customs position.

## The Calling of Zacchaeus

Another noted calling of a disciple was that of Zacchaeus, in the third year of Jesus' ministry. According to Sister Emmerich, it began as set forth in Luke's Gospel, with Jesus summoning the publican down from his perch in the tree which he had climbed to get a better look as Jesus passed by. When Jesus went to dine at Zacchaeus' house, "Jesus related the parable of the fig tree in the vineyard which for three years bore no fruit, and for which the vinedresser implored one more year of indulgence. When uttering this parable, Jesus addressed the Apostles as the vineyard, of Himself He spoke as the owner, and of Zacchaeus as the fig tree.

"It was now three years since the relatives of the last named had abandoned their dishonorable calling and followed Jesus, while he all this time had still carried on the same business, on which account he was looked upon with special contempt by the disciples. But Jesus had cast upon him a look of mercy when He called him down from the tree. *Jesus spoke also of the sterile trees that produce many leaves, but no fruit. The leaves, He said, are exterior works. They make a great rustling, but soon pass away leaving no seed of good. But the fruits are that interior, efficacious reality in faith and action, with their capability of reproduction, and the prolongation of the tree's life stored away in the kernel.* It seems to me that Jesus in calling Zacchaeus down from the tree, did the same as to engage him to renounce the noise and bustle of the crowd, for Zacchaeus was like the ripe fruit which now detached itself from the tree that for three years had stood unfruitful in the vineyard."

At a later time, Jesus held up Zacchaeus as a role model for the people, telling them about his climbing up the fig tree and leaving all to follow Him. Jesus contrasted that incident with one He had witnessed in the Temple, where a Pharisee had boasted "I thank God that I am not like the publican," whereas a publican, striking his breast, had prayed, "Lord, be merciful to me, a poor sinner!"

## What Great Role Did the Holy Women Play in Jesus' Ministry?

Just as the Apostles were called, so were the "Holy Women," a group of women, headed by the Blessed Virgin Mary, who frequented His discourses and provided material support for His work. The piety and formality with which they, including His Mother, dealt with Him can be seen from Sister Emmerich's description of a meeting, as follows:

"After He had washed and let down His robe, Jesus entered the large apartment in which several little alcoves were cut off by curtains. Mary, her head veiled and humbly inclined, stretched out to Him her hand when He had first proffered His, and He graciously, though gravely, saluted her. The other women stood veiled forming a semicircle in the rear. I have indeed seen Jesus when alone with Mary, in order to console and strengthen her, press her to His breast while conversing with her. But Mary herself, since His going forth to teach, treated Him as one would treat a saint, a Prophet; or as a mother might treat her son were he a Pope, a Bishop, or a King. Still, there was something much more noble, more holy in Mary's demeanor, though marked at the same time with indescribable simplicity. She never embraced Him now, but only extended her hand when He offered His."

Each of the Evangelists recorded pious acts of the Holy Women, but they failed to describe the important role the ladies played in making the logistic arrangements which were necessary to feed and shelter Jesus and His disciples as they constantly traveled throughout the country. In the early days, Jesus, together with a few followers, could be accommodated at various dwellings owned by Lazarus and also at public dwellings. However, as His retinue grew, and as He was progressively denied access to public accommodations on the orders of the Pharisees, it was necessary that a concerted effort be made to line up lodgings and provisions on His route.

Following John's imprisonment, Jesus went down quietly to Bethania, where he could stay in Lazarus' castle without attracting attention. This is Sister Emmerich's account of what was accomplished when Jesus met with the Holy Women there:

"The Holy Women had heard with sorrow what hardships Jesus and His followers had had to endure upon their journeys, and that Jesus especially, on His last hurried journey to Tyre, had suffered such want; they had heard of His having to soften the hard crusts, which Saturnin had begged on the way, in order to be able to eat them. They had therefore offered to establish inns and furnish them with all that was necessary.

"Jesus accepted their offer, and came hither to make with them the necessary arrangements. *As He now declared that He would henceforth publicly teach everywhere, Lazarus and the women again offered to establish inns, especially since the Jews in the cities around Jerusalem, instigated by the Pharisees, would furnish nothing to Him and His disciples.* They also begged the Lord to signify to them the principal stopping-places on His journeys and the number of His disciples, that they might know how many inns would be needed and what quantity of provisions to supply.

"Jesus replied by giving them the route of His future journeys, also the stopping-places, and the probable number of disciples. *It was decided that about fifteen inns should be made ready and entrusted to the care of confidential persons, some of them relatives either of*

*Lazarus or of the Holy Family. They were scattered throughout the whole country with the exception of the district of Cabul toward Tyre and Sidon.* The Holy Women then consulted together as to what district each should see to and what share each should take in the new establishments, to supply furniture, covers, clothes, sandals, etc., to provide for washing and repairing, and to attend to the furnishing of bread and other necessaries." As one might have expected, Martha was in her element with this work!

### Secret Disciples

Other vital services unrecorded by the authors of the Gospels were provided by secret disciples of Jesus. In particular, while the Gospels describe the critical assistance rendered by Nicodemus and Joseph of Arimathea in connection with Jesus' burial, they fail to mention that (as seen by Sister Emmerich), the two had been secret disciples of His since the first Passover of His public ministry. Moreover, she heard them pledge fidelity to Him and acknowledge that they regarded Him as more than human, while, for His part, Jesus enjoined secrecy on them.

### Unwanted Disciples

While Jesus was slowly choosing His Apostles and disciples, many of the wrong sort sought to attach themselves to Him. These were the people who regarded Him as a sage who could make them wise, or even as a future king who would give them choice positions in His kingdom. Sister Emmerich saw Jesus rebuff would-be disciples whom He knew were unfit for the task (the exception being Judas Iscariot). These included three rich young men of Nazareth, whose parents thought that He would be glad to tutor them for pay, and a rich young man of Samaria, who thought that Jesus was about to found an earthly kingdom. The second meeting between Jesus and the latter, from which the young man walked away dejected because he did not want to give up his earthly possessions, was recorded in the Gospels of Matthew and Mark.

Jesus did not always explain to a would-be disciple why he was being rejected. The young man who asked to be allowed to "bury his father" did not understand why this request was refused with the response "Let the dead bury the dead!," as recorded in the Gospels of Matthew and Luke. He complained publicly about his rejection, and the Pharisees reproached Jesus—How, they asked him, could one dead man bury another? "Jesus answered by saying that . . . whoever follows not His teachings and believes not in Him, has in himself not life, but death. Such were the dispositions of this young man. He had wished to come to terms with his aged father concerning his inheritance and put the latter upon a pension; he had clung to the dead inheritance, and consequently he could have no share in the Kingdom of Jesus and eternal life."

¹ Acts 1:15–26.

# CHAPTER FOURTEEN

## *The Disciples Experience Trials*

The visions of Sister Emmerich support the inference which one might draw from the Gospels themselves, that Jesus' disciples, and even His Apostles, were often more of a burden than a help to Him. For the most part, the work they did was simply to act as an advance party, spreading out to announce His forthcoming appearance for a public teaching, or gathering the sick to be healed. In trying to control the crowds, they pushed away women bringing their children for a blessing—until He rebuked them. When He empowered them to heal and expel demons themselves, they came back from their journeys exulting and boasting of what they had accomplished, again to His displeasure.

Sister Emmerich related that "the disciples had much to endure, and it was often very hard for them. On reaching a town or village and announcing the coming of Jesus, they often heard the scornful words: 'What! is He coming again! What does He want? Whence comes He? Has He not been forbidden to preach?' and they laughed at them, derided and insulted them. There were indeed a few that rejoiced to hear of Jesus coming, but they were very few. No one ventured to attack Jesus Himself, but wherever He taught surrounded by His disciples or proceeded along the street followed by them, the crowd shouted after them. They stopped the disciples and plied them with impertinent questions, pretending that they had misunderstood or only half-comprehended His severe words, and demanding an explanation."

At the beginning, if the disciples were questioned as to the meaning of Jesus' instructions, they pretended that they did not know either. And, they let their discouragement show.

Despite everything He said privately to them, as well as what they heard in His public discourses, and despite all His miracles performed before their eyes, they never grasped what kind of a king He was, or how His kingdom was to be accomplished, and they were constantly wondering what the payoff for themselves would be. "They thought to themselves: 'Now we have left all things, and what have we for it but all this tumult and embarrassment? Of what kind of a kingdom is He always speaking? Will He really gain it?' These were their thoughts. . . . John alone acted with the simplicity of a child. He was perfectly obedient and free from constraint."

*As Sister Emmerich remarked: "It was indeed touching to think that Jesus knew all their thoughts, and yet acted as if wholly ignorant of them.* He changed nothing in His manner, but calmly, sweetly, and earnestly went on with His work."

The trials of the first few months were minor in the scheme of things. Worse was in store following the first Passover of Jesus' public ministry, when He appeared in Jerusalem. Sister Emmerich recounted that the immense crowds which started to appear for baptism by Jesus served to goad the Pharisees into taking action against Him. Letters were sent out to the elders in synagogues throughout the country, directing them to take Jesus and His disciples into custody, with the latter to be punished on the spot and Jesus to be brought to Jerusalem. Jesus Himself was not captured, perhaps because He was traveling through Samaria to pagan country, and then to the far north, around Lake Merom (Lake Huleh). However, many of the disciples who went in other directions were hauled before assemblies of Pharisees, mistreated, and interrogated about Jesus and His doctrines.

## Jesus Praises His Disciples

Jesus told His disciples about persecutions to come, and said: "If the Pharisees, the Sadducees, or the Herodians should love or praise ye, it would be a sign that ye had wandered from My teachings and were no longer My disciples." In contrast, He variously described the "sign" He wanted them to be. At one point, He called them the "salt of the earth," destined to enliven and preserve others, and warned them not to lose their savor. At another point, He told them that they were "the light of the world," as was related by St. Matthew. Even more approvingly, He called them family, in the incident set forth in the Synoptic Gospels, when Jesus asked the rhetorical question, "Who is my mother?" "During several days they had had on account of their great labors, no regular hours for meals. Now when Jesus went on instructing, Mary taking with her some relatives in order not to go through the crowd alone, approached with the intention of speaking to Him and begging Him to come and partake of some food. But it was impossible for her to make her way through the crowd, and so her request was passed from onto to, another, until it reached a man standing near Jesus. He was one of the spies of the Pharisees.

"As Jesus had several times made mention of His Heavenly Father, the spy, not without a secret sneer, said to Him: 'Behold Thy Mother and Thy brethren stand without seeking Thee.' But Jesus looking at him, said: 'Who is My Mother, and who are My brethren?' Then grouping The Twelve and placing the disciples near them, He extended His hand over the former with the words: 'Behold My Mother!' and then over the latter, saying: 'And these are My brethren, who hear the word of God and do it. For whosoever shall do the will of My Father who is in heaven, he is My brother, My sister, and My Mother.' Then He went on with His discourse, but sent His disciples in turn to take what food they needed."

### Jesus Commissions His Disciples

According to Sister Emmerich, Jesus had taken great pains in teaching His followers, to make sure that they not only understood His doctrines, but that they memorized the right words with which to explain them. When He taught them the Lord's Prayer, he dwelled at length on each of the petitions, used examples such as the child who asks its father for an egg and surely will not receive a scorpion, and drilled them until they could repeat His words exactly. This method of teaching was well designed to preserve the integrity of His proclamations when He was not with them.

Now, it was time for the Apostles and disciples to go forth alone, proclaiming what they had learned. But first, in order to strengthen them, Jesus held several "commissioning" ceremonies with them, at which He imparted special powers and gave them detailed instructions on their forthcoming missions. For example, on one of these occasions, Jesus took the Twelve Apostles and 30 disciples, and went to a mountain top several miles from Capernaum, for the purpose of instructing them privately on their vocation. Sister Emmerich's visions provide more details of this gathering than are recorded in the Synoptic Gospels:

"He said ... they should proclaim the advent of the Kingdom, that the last chance for doing penance had arrived, that the end of John's life was very near. They should baptize, impose hands, and expel demons. He taught them how they should conduct themselves in discussions, how recognize true from false friends, and how confound the latter. He told them that now none should be greater than the others. In the various places to which their mission called them, they should go among the pious, should live poorly and humbly, and be burdensome to none.

"He told them also how to separate and how again to unite. Two Apostles and some disciples should journey together, while some other disciples should go on ahead to gather together the people and announce the coming of the former. The Apostles, He said, should carry with them little flasks of oil, which He taught them how to consecrate and how to use in effecting cures. Then He gave them all the other instructions recorded in the Gospels on the occasion of their mission. He made allusion to no special danger in store for them, but said only: 'Today ye will everywhere be welcomed, but a time will come wherein they will persecute you!' After that, the Apostles knelt down in a circle around Jesus as He prayed and laid His hands upon the head of each; the disciples He only blessed. Then they embraced and separated."

On another occasion, Jesus led the Apostles and 72 disciples high up the mountain northeast of the Sea, where He had taught the Beatitudes to crowds. He gave the directions set forth in the Gospels of Matthew and Luke, including a command to go only to the lost sheep of the house of Israel, and to proclaim that "The reign of God is at hand!" *Sister Emmerich related that: "Jesus drew a definitive line between the Apostles and the disciples, the former of whom were set over the latter. To them He said that they should send and call the disciples as He Himself sent and called them, namely, the Apostles. This they were empowered to do by virtue of their own mission."*

## Jesus Strengthens the Apostles With Miracles

Jesus attempted to strengthen His Apostles and disciples in yet another profound way. That was through working major miracles which were for their eyes only—these were miracles showing His command over the forces of nature. A key example, reported in the Synoptic Gospels, came on the very day when the Apostles had received their final call. They were with Jesus in a boat out in the middle of the Sea of Galilee, when a violent storm arose, terrifying the Apostles. They awoke Jesus, who instantly stilled the storm with a command, leaving them to ponder what His true nature might be. While they could not reach the right conclusion before His Resurrection, after their eyes had been fully opened, they could regard this event as verifying the words of His which St. John recorded: "I and the Father are one," and "Before Abraham was, I AM."

A second "nature miracle" was a catch of fish. That doesn't sound impressive, but it was such a gargantuan catch that the experienced fishermen were awestruck by it, recognizing that it had come about supernaturally. The background was that ill people and travelers had been coming to Peter's houses in Capernaum and in Bethsaida for attention and food, while Jesus was in the vicinity giving His instructions. As the supplies had run low, Jesus had authorized the Apostles who were traveling with Him to return to their boats for a day, while He continued to teach the crowds along the seashore. At night, the fishermen came back empty handed. Jesus instructed Peter to go out again and fish, using Peter's large boat. This annoyed Peter, for he had been fishing for hours without results and he knew that there were no fish to be caught. However, he acceded to Jesus' command, and the boat put out to sea. When the crew tried to raise their net, they could not, so full was it of fish. They dragged the net to shallower water where the could scoop the fish into smaller nets and casks that floated attached to the sides of the vessel, and they got help from the men in Zebedee's boat.

Sister Emmerich's report is in accord with the account of St. Luke, regarding the impact which this event had on Peter in particular:

*"They were actually terrified at sight of the draft of fishes. Never before had such a thing happened to them. Peter was confounded. He felt that they had never yet sufficiently appreciated Jesus. He felt how vain were all the cares they had hitherto bestowed upon their fishing, how fruitlessly they had labored notwithstanding their trouble and here, at a word from Him, they had caught at one draft more than they had ever done in months together. When the net was relieved of part of its weight, they rowed to the shore, dragged it out of the water, and gazed awestruck at the multitude of fish it still contained. Jesus was standing on the shore. Peter, humbled and confused, fell at His feet and said: 'Lord, depart from me, for I am a sinful man!' But Jesus said: 'Fear not, Peter! From henceforth thou shalt catch men!' Peter however was quite overcome by sadness at sight of his own unworthiness and vain solicitude for the things of this life."*

A third "nature miracle" occurred when Jesus walked on top of the Sea of Galilee. Sts. Matthew, Mark and John related that one night, as the Apostles were out in a boat, Jesus, who had remained on the shore to pray, came to them, walking across the water as if it were dry land. Some commentators seem especially embarrassed by this miracle because it seems to them that it was more like a magic trick— a miracle not done for the purpose of accomplishing a worthy end. One point which they overlook is that a significant part of the incident was how Peter responded. In his enthusiasm, Peter tried to accomplish the same feat, walking out to meet Jesus—but failed when his fear rose and his faith faltered. Sister Emmerich had this to say about the event:

"Jesus allowed Peter to come to Him on the water in order to humble him, for He knew very well that he was going to sink. Peter was very fiery and strong in believing, and in his zeal he wanted to give a testimony of his faith to Jesus and the disciples. *By his sinking, he was preserved from pride.* The others had not sufficient confidence to wish to follow his example and, while wondering at Peter's faith, they could see that although it excelled their own it was not yet what it ought to be."

## Peter's Profession of Faith

It was after that incident, and a few days before the second Pasch of Jesus' ministry, that the notable event of Peter's profession of faith in Jesus occurred. Sister Emmerich's visions contain many details of the setting near Caesarea Philippi, and what was said, in addition to what the Synoptic Gospels set forth. The twelve Apostles were in a circle around Jesus, with the disciples around them in turn. When Jesus asked: "Who do *men* say that I am?," various conjectures were voiced. And when Jesus asked: "And *you*, for whom do *you* take me?," Peter responded, "Thou are the Christ, the Son of the living God!" St. Matthew reported Jesus' reply as: "Blessed are you, Simon Bar-Jona! For flesh and blood has not revealed this to you, but my Father who is in heaven. And I tell you, you are Peter, and on this rock I will build my church, and the powers of death shall not prevail against it. I will give you the keys of the kingdom of heaven, and whatever you bind on earth shall be bound in heaven, and whatever you loose on earth shall be loosed in heaven."

Sister Emmerich recounted that: "Jesus made this response in a manner both solemn and prophetic. He appeared to be shining with light, and was raised some distance above the ground. Peter, in the same spirit in which he had confessed to the Godhead, received Jesus' words in their full signification. He was deeply impressed by them. . . . *The other Apostles did not fully comprehend, and still formed to themselves earthly ideas. They thought that Jesus intended to bestow upon Peter the office of High Priest in His Kingdom, and James told John, as they walked together, that very probably they themselves would receive places next after Peter.*

"Peter, still profoundly impressed by Jesus' words relative to the power of the Keys, drew near to Him on the way to ask for information upon some points not clear to him. He was so full of faith and ardor that he fancied his work was to begin right away for the conditions, namely, the Passion of Christ and the descent of the Holy Ghost, were as yet unknown to him. He asked therefore whether in this or that case also he could absolve from sin, and made some remarks upon publicans and those guilty of open adultery. Jesus set his mind at ease by telling him that he would later on know all things clearly, that they would be very different from what he expected, and that a new Law would be substituted for the old.

"As they proceeded on their journey, Jesus began to enlighten His Apostles upon what was in store for them. They should now go to Jerusalem, eat the Paschal lamb with Lazarus, after which they might expect many labors, much weariness and persecution. He mentioned in general terms many circumstances of His future: namely, His raising of one of their best friends from the dead, which fact was to give rise to such fury among His enemies that He would be obliged to flee; and their going again after another year to the Feast, at which time one of them would betray Him. He told them moreover that He would be maltreated, scourged, mocked, and shamefully put to death; that He must die for the sins of men, but that on the third day He would rise again. He told them all this in detail and proved it from the Prophets. His manner was very grave, but full of love.

"Peter was so distressed at the thought of Jesus' being maltreated and put to death that, following Him, he spoke to Him in private, disputing with Him and exclaiming against such suffering, such treatment. No, he said, that should not be. He would rather die himself than suffer such a thing to happen! 'Far be it from Thee, Lord! This shall not be unto Thee!' he exclaimed. But Jesus turned to him gravely and said with warmth: 'Go behind Me, Satan! Thou art a scandal unto Me! Thou savorest not the things that are of God, but the things that are of men!' and then walked on.

"Peter struck with fear, began to turn over in his mind why it was that Jesus a short time before had said not from flesh and blood but by a revelation from God he (Peter) had declared Him to be the Christ; but now He called him Satan and, because he had protested against His sufferings, He reproached him with speaking not according to God, but according to human desires and considerations. Comparing Jesus' words of praise with those of His reproof, Peter became more humble and looked upon Him with greater faith and admiration. He was nevertheless very much afflicted since he became thereby only the more convinced of the reality of the sufferings awaiting Jesus."

Jesus reproved Peter on yet another occasion, though this time it was for excessive zeal which brought on the sin of pride. The Apostles and disciples were making their reports to Jesus of the results of their missions without Jesus. According to Sister Emmerich, "Peter began eagerly to tell of the different kinds of possessed that had fallen in his way, his manner of treating them, and how Satan had retired before him when commanded in the Name of Jesus. . . . Once more, he was all fire and zeal. He said that in the land of the Gergeseans, he had encountered a couple of possessed whom several others were unable to free from the demon. . . . But he, Peter, had easily expelled the devils; they had instantly submitted to him. . . . Jesus reproved Peter for his too great warmth, as well as all the others that had, either in thought or word, yielded to a spirit of boasting. They should, He said, act and work in His name and by Him, in humility and faith, never harboring the thought that one could do more than another. He said (as reported by St. Luke): 'Behold, I have given you power to tread upon serpents and scorpions and upon all the might of the enemy, and nothing shall hurt you. But yet rejoice not in this that spirits are subject to you, but rejoice in this that your names are written in heaven.'"

## The Transfiguration

The pinnacle of Jesus' self-revelation to the Apostles, prior to the Resurrection, was His Transfiguration on Mount Tabor, an event witnessed by Peter, James and John, which the Church teaches was a historical reality.[1] Only a small part of the event that Sister Emmerich saw has been preserved in the Synoptic Gospels. According to her, the four climbed the mountain slowly, with Jesus stopping to explain many mysteries to them and lead them in the Lord's Prayer and the Psalms. When night fell, Jesus became bright, and the Apostles saw angels hovering around Him.

"Jesus began again His instructions and along with the angelic apparitions flowed alternate streams of delicious perfumes, of celestial delights and contentment over the Apostles. Jesus meantime continued to shine with ever increasing splendor, until He became as if transparent. The circle around them was so lighted up in the darkness of night that each little plant could be distinguished on the green sod as if in clear daylight. The three Apostles were so penetrated, so ravished that, when the light reached a certain degree, they covered their head, prostrated on the ground, and there remained lying. . . .

"The Apostles lay, ravished in ecstasy rather than in sleep, prostrate on their face. Then I saw three shining figures approaching Jesus in the light. Their coming appeared perfectly natural. It was like that of one who steps from the darkness of night into a place brilliantly illuminated. Two of them appeared in a more definite form, a form more like the corporeal. They addressed Jesus and conversed with Him. They were Moses and Elijah. The third apparition spoke no word. It was more ethereal, more spiritual. That was Malachi." (The latter was not mentioned in the Gospel accounts.)

"I heard Moses and Elijah greet Jesus, and I heard Him speaking to them of His Passion and of Redemption. . . . Jesus spoke with them of all the sufferings He had endured up to the present, and of all that still awaited Him. . . .

"The disciples raised their head, gazed long upon the glory of Jesus, and beheld Moses, Elijah, and Malachi. When in describing His Passion, Jesus came to His exaltation on the Cross, He extended His arms at the words: 'So shall the Son of Man be lifted up!' His face was turned toward the south, He was entirely penetrated with light, and His robe flashed with a bluish white gleam. He, the Prophets, and the three Apostles—all were raised above the earth."

Peter, under the sway of the vision of the Prophets, proposed building tabernacles for them and Jesus, but the Prophets vanished. It was then that an even more awesome vision took place. Sister Emmerich related that: "A cloud of white light descended upon them, like the morning dew floating over the meadows. I saw the heavens open above Jesus and the vision of the Most Holy Trinity, God the Father seated on a throne. He looked like an aged priest, and at His feet were crowds of angels and celestial figures. A stream of light descended upon Jesus, and the Apostles heard above them, like a sweet, gentle sighing, a voice pronouncing the words: 'This is My beloved Son in whom I am Well pleased. Hear ye Him!' Fear and trembling fell upon them. Overcome by the sense of their own human weakness and the glory they beheld, they cast themselves face downward on the earth. They trembled in the presence of Jesus, in whose favor they had just heard the testimony of His Heavenly Father."

As they descended the mountain in the light of dawn, Jesus told them that He had arranged the visions to strengthen their faith against the day when they would see Him maltreated by evildoers and apparently powerless, for then it would be their job to strengthen their weaker brethren.

---

[1] See the *Catechism of the Catholic Church* §§ 554–56, 568; Pope John Paul II, "On the Most Holy Rosary," Apostolic Letter (Oct. 16, 2002)(the Transfiguration is the "mystery of light par excellence" of the Rosary). See 32 *Origins* (October 31, 2002)345,350. http://www.petersnet/research/retrieve_full.cfm?RecNum=4466.

# Chapter Fifteen

## *Why Did John the Baptist Have to Decrease?*

We know from the Gospel of John that John the Baptist contrasted himself to Jesus with these words: "He must increase, while I must decrease." We may well wonder, was it necessary for John not only to "decrease," but to get out of the way completely? Could he not have become a disciple, or even an Apostle of Jesus?

Neither John nor Jesus suggested any such course of action, because there were two great obstacles. The first was the recalcitrance of John's own disciples: their pride in John (and in being *his* disciples) was so great that it blinded them to the acts of Jesus, and it deafened them to the voice not only of Jesus, but of John himself, who did all he could to facilitate a transfer of their loyalty to Jesus.

The other obvious obstacle to John's becoming an Apostle was the effort of the Pharisees to play John and Jesus off against one another. John had enormous charisma—to some it appeared even more compelling than that of Jesus. Indeed, Sister Emmerich heard Jesus tell His disciples that John "is pure as an angel," and, the Gospels record that Jesus said: "I solemnly assure you, history has not known a man born of woman greater than John the Baptizer." As long as John was on the stage, there would have remained questions, which were asked repeatedly, as to whose baptism was preferable, and who had the better claim to be followed. John's great humility precluded him from upstaging His Lord by remaining on the scene.

A great multitude had assembled from Jerusalem, Judea and Arabia, where John was baptizing, near Ainon, on the east bank, in view of the Jordan. Even King Herod, together with his paramour, Herodias, had journeyed there. As related by Sister Emmerich, John knew that the time of his arrest was near, and He gave this message under inspiration, as if taking leave of those who had looked to him:

"He had announced Jesus more clearly than ever. He was now coming, he said, consequently he himself should retire and they should go to Jesus. He, John, was soon to be apprehended. They were, he continued addressing his audience, a hard and indocile people. They should recall how he had come at first and prepared the ways for the Lord. He had built bridges, made footpaths, cleared away stones, arranged baptismal pools, and conducted thither the water. *He had a difficult task, struggling against stony earth, hard rocks, and knotty wood. And these labors he had had to continue toward a people stubborn, obdurate, and unpolished. But they whom he had stirred up, should now go to the Lord, to the well-beloved Son of the Father. They whom He received, would be truly received; they whom He rejected, should indeed be rejected.* He was coming now to teach, to baptize, to perfect what he himself had prepared. Then turning toward Herod, John earnestly reproached him several times before the people for his scandalous connection. Herod, who both reverenced and feared him, was inwardly furious, though preserving a cool exterior."

### John is Arrested by Herod

After the crowd and John's disciples departed, Herod's soldiers surrounded John's tent and arrested him. John was forced to march all night, arriving at Hesebon (northeast of Mt. Nebo), where he was put in a prison tower. Once the people of the town learned that John was there, they repeatedly gathered, only to be dispersed by the soldiers. *Meanwhile, John was crying out in a loud voice, through the cracks in the walls, telling the people to turn to Jesus, the straps of whose sandals he was unworthy to loose.* His guards later led him down to Machaerus, Herod's fortress built on a steep mountain on the east side of the Dead Sea. While in a prison vault underground there, John was allowed to receive a few of his disciples at a time, talking with them through a grating. John instructed them to continue baptizing at Ainon until Jesus came to take over that mission.

In Capernaum, Jesus was joined by some disciples of John the Baptist, who brought news that their master had been imprisoned by Herod. In discussing this event, the disciples were highly indignant at this development, but Jesus reproved them, telling them John had to be removed from the scene so that He could do His work. In private, Jesus conversed with His Mother about John's imprisonment and the growing menace to Himself.

### Jesus Comforts His Mother

*Sister Emmerich related that the Blessed Virgin Mary "was weeping at the thought of His exposing Himself to danger by going to Jerusalem. He comforted her, telling her that she must not be anxious, that He would accomplish His mission, and that the sorrowful days had not yet come. He encouraged her to persevere in prayer, and exhorted the others to refrain from all comments and judgments upon John's imprisonment and the action of the Pharisees against Himself, for such proceedings on their part would only increase the danger, that the Pharisees' manner of acting was permitted by Divine Providence, though thereby they were working out their own destruction."*

### What Was John's Final Witness to Jesus?

When people coming to Ainon for baptism learned that John had been imprisoned, they continued on to Herod's fortress, crying out for him to be released, and even throwing stones at the palace. In view of the tumult, and the reports that the Herodians had brought back of Jesus, Herod determined to hold an examination of John. He was summoned from the dungeon for interrogation in the presence of Herodias, and assembled Pharisees, Sadducees and Herodians. Herod wanted to know just who Jesus was, since He called Himself the son of a king, and whether He had come to take over Herod's kingship. Sister Emmerich heard John give this witness to Jesus:

"He declared that he himself was only to prepare His ways; that compared with Him, he was nobody; that never had there been a man, not even among the Prophets, like unto Jesus, and never would there be one; that He was the Son of the Father; that He was the Christ, the King of Kings, the Savior, the Restorer of the Kingdom; that no power was superior to His; that He was the Lamb of God who was to bear the sins of the world, etc. So spoke John of Jesus, crying in a loud voice, calling himself His precursor, the preparer of His ways, His most insignificant servant. It was evident that his words were inspired. His whole bearing was stamped with the supernatural, so much so that Herod, becoming terrified, stopped his ears."

Herod offered John his freedom if he would recognize Herod's union with Herodias as lawful, whereupon John launched into a tirade against Herod's debauchery. John's denunciation was all the more poignant because the people everywhere were discussing the beheading of some adulterers in Jerusalem, and contrasting their fate with Herod's. The result was that John was banished to a cell which had no communication with the outside world.

That left Jesus to deal with. Herod sent a group of Pharisees to warn Jesus that He should limit Himself to Upper Galilee and the eastern side of the Sea, outside of Herod's jurisdiction, or else He might be imprisoned like John! The warning did not silence Jesus. In the town of Jetabatha, Jesus preached a condemnatory sermon in the presence of the Herodians. This was a group of people, particularly numerous east of the Jordan, who were secret enemies of the Romans; they were in league with the Sadducees plotting a revolution in favor of Herod. Sister Emmerich heard Jesus denounce them as hypocrites, laying snares for Him. And He strongly attacked both Herod Antipas, and Herod's late father (Herod the Great), charging them with numerous crimes ranging from the massacre of the Holy Innocents, to Herod's adultery and imprisonment of John the Baptist.

John's confinement did not keep him from continuing to announce the advent of the Messiah. Several of John's chief disciples arrived in Capernaum with a message from the Baptist written on parchment. It consisted of two copies of the instruction given by their master at a public audience in an open square of the castle of Machaerus, in front of Herod and Herodias. One copy was given to the Pharisees assembled at the synagogue; the other was read to the crowd by John's disciples. Sister Emmerich summarized John's oration, which could be viewed as his final testament, as follows:

"He himself, he said, was sent only to prepare the ways for Him [Jesus]. He had never announced another than Jesus; but, stubborn as they were, the people would not acknowledge Him. Had they then forgotten, he asked, what he had told them of Him? He would recall it to them clearly once more, for his own end was not far distant! At these last words, the whole assembly was moved, and many of John's disciples wept. Herod grew uneasy and embarrassed, for he had by no means resolved upon John's death, while his concubine dissembled her feelings as best she could.

*"John continued zealously to speak. He recounted the wonders that took place at Jesus' baptism and declared Him the Beloved Son of God announced by the Prophets. His doctrine was the same as His Father's. What He did the Father also did, and no one can go to the Father excepting by Him, that is, by Jesus.* And so he went on, refuting at length the reproaches of the Pharisees against Him, and especially that of His healing on the Sabbath-day. Every one, he said, should keep holy the Sabbath, but the Pharisees profaned it, since they did not follow the teachings of Jesus, the teachings of the Son of Him who had instituted the Sabbath.

*"John said many things of a similar nature, and proclaimed Jesus the One outside of whom no salvation could be found. Whoever believed not in Him and followed not His doctrine, would be condemned. He exhorted his disciples to turn to Jesus, not to remain*

*standing blindly near Him on the threshold, but to enter into the Temple itself."*

Notwithstanding that moving and conclusive attestation by John, some of his disciples who had brought the messages to Capernaum expressed indignation that Jesus had not come to John's aid. Sister Emmerich related that many followers of John were narrow minded and jealous. They could see no kingdom being established by Jesus, and at the same time they were scandalized by the behavior of His disciples. But, not all of John's disciples were intractable. Two of them, seeing the miracles that Jesus was performing, declared that they now believed all that John had said of Him, and they asked Him whether He would soon establish His kingdom and go to Machaerus release John. Jesus did not give them the answer they were hoping for. He told them that He would fulfill His mission, but that even John himself did not expect Him to go to Herod's castle on John's behalf.

### The Beheading of John the Baptist

Herod had been keeping John alive, thinking possibly of releasing John as part of his birthday celebration. That was before the lascivious dance of Salome, which Sister Emmerich saw in her visions:

"Herod was seated on his throne surrounded by some of his most intimate associates, who were Herodians. Salome appeared with some of her dancing companions clothed in a light, transparent robe. Her hair was interwoven in part with pearls and precious stones, while another part floated around her in curls. She wore a crown and formed the central figure in the group of dancers. The dance consisted of a constant bowing, a gentle swaying and turning. The whole person seemed to be destitute of bones. Scarcely had one position been assumed, when it glided into another. The dancers held wreaths and scarves in their hands, which waved and twined around one another. The whole performance gave expression to the most shameful passions, and in it Salome excelled all her companions. I saw the devil at her side as if bending and twisting all her limbs in order to produce that abominable effect. Herod was perfectly ravished, perfectly entranced by the changing attitudes."

As reported in the Gospels of Matthew and Mark, Herod was so enchanted by the girl's dance that he promised to give her anything she wished, and, prompted by her mother, she asked for the head of John the Baptist on a platter. While Herod regretted his promise, he was not about to break it. According to Sister Emmerich's visions, John was not beheaded with a sword, as might have been expected.

The means used, and the despicable actions of Herodias toward the severed head, were as follows:

"Salome waited in the entrance hall of the vast and intricate dungeonhouse. With her was a maidservant who gave the executioner a dish wrapped in a red cloth. The latter addressed John: 'Herod the King sends me to bring thy head on the dish to his daughter Salome.' John allowed him little time to explain. He remained kneeling, and bowing his head toward him, he said: 'I know why thou hast come. Thou art my guest, one for whom I have long waited. *Didst thou know what thou art about to do, thou wouldst not do it.* I am ready.' Then he turned his head away and continued his prayer before the stone in front of which he always prayed kneeling.

"The executioner beheaded him with a machine, which I can compare to nothing but a fox trap. An iron ring was laid on his shoulders. This ring was provided with two sharp blades, which, being closed around the throat with a sudden pressure given by the executioner, in the twinkling of an eye severed the head from the trunk. John still remained in a kneeling posture. *The head bounded to the earth, and a triple stream of blood springing up from the body sprinkled both the head and body of the saint, as if baptizing him in his own blood.*[1] The executioner's servant raised the head by the hair, insulted it, and laid it on the dish which his master held. The latter presented it to the expectant Salome.

"Salome held the dish timidly at arm's length before her, her head still laden with its ornaments turned away in disgust. Thus she traversed the solitary passages that led up to a kind of vaulted kitchen under the castle of Herodias. Here she was met by her mother, who raised the cover from the holy head which she loaded with insult and abuse. Then taking a sharp skewer from a certain part of the wall where many such instruments were sticking, with it she pierced the tongue, the cheeks, and the eyes. After that, looking more like a demon than a human being, she hurled it from her and kicked it with her foot through a round opening down into a pit into which the offal and refuse of the kitchen were swept. Then did that infamous woman together with her daughter return to the noise and wicked revelry of the feast, as if nothing had happened."

## Jesus Assists at the Burial of John

Jesus was, of course, aware of what had happened to John. He was then preaching in Hebron, and He and His followers assembled at the home of one of John's relatives in nearby Yatta. Jesus sorrowfully told them that John had been executed. Further, they would be able to retrieve his body after Herod left Machaerus, but John's head had been abused and thrown in a sewer. Jesus wept with them in their grief, and He helped John's relatives prepare a burial place for John in a vault by his father.

When Herod left his fortress, John's disciples were admitted and were allowed to embalm the body and remove it for burial. At the vault, the headless torso presented a heartrending sight. After it was again anointed with myrrh and sweet spices, the body was rewrapped and laid in its compartment. According to Sister Emmerich, the Essenians who were present then held a religious service, honoring John "not only as one of their own,[2] but as one of the Prophets promised to them." The altar had a representation of a Paschal lamb on it, and the priest, under inspiration, alluded to the lamb and to a prophetic vision which John had had, concerning the Paschal Lamb, Jesus as the Lamb of God, and His Passion. Thus, the last words said about John were in keeping with his mission of announcing the way of the Lord.

Retrieving the head of John the Baptist from the sewer posed a real problem. But, several months later, when the castle was being cleaned out in preparation for adding to its defenses, some women from Yatta and Jerusalem were able to bribe their way to access the partially emptied sewer. Finding the bloody relic, they reverently took it back and had it embalmed and laid with John's body in his tomb.

---

[1] Despite Jesus' high praise for John, He also said that "the least born into the kingdom of God is greater than he." That was because John had not been "born into the kingdom"—he had not yet been baptized. It was only later that, as Jesus foretold to John when Jesus was baptized, John received the baptism of blood and baptism of desire. The doctrines of baptism of blood and baptism of desire are set forth in the *Catechism of the Catholic Church* §§ 1258–60.

[2] Scholars have tried to deduce whether John the Baptist was an Essene. *See, e.g.*, Otto Betz, "Was John the Baptist an Essene?," *Bible Review* (Dec. 1990) 18. According to Sister Emmerich, John's mother was the offspring of a marriage directed by the Essenian Prophet, but she did not relate whether the marriage of Elizabeth and Zachary was similarly arranged. In any event, John the Baptist had a mission which set him apart from any religious group, including the Essenes, and he clearly was not the "Teacher of Righteousness" looked up to by the Qumran community.

# CHAPTER SIXTEEN

*Hosanna to the Son of David!*
*Blessed is he who comes in the name of the Lord!*
*Hosanna in the highest!*

### The Messiah Enters Jerusalem

The time had come for Jesus to enter Jerusalem in a way deliberately evoking expectations that He was coming as the long-awaited Messiah.

All the Apostles, disciples and close friends were summoned to participate, and Jesus instructed two of His trusted disciples to prepare the route. This was to be a little used road from Bethphage, less than a mile northeast of Jerusalem. It was their duty to open hedges and remove barriers, also to tie up the little animal which He would ride upon for His triumphal entry into the city.

In Bethphage, where the ass waited covered with trappings and a side-saddle, Jesus donned a flowing, white woolen robe, with a girdle and stole. Disciples walked on either side of Him and behind, followed by the Blessed Virgin Mary and the other Holy Women. Up in front, Jesus had Peter walk first, followed by pairs of Apostles bearing palm branches, with those destined for the most remote missions preceding the others. Right before Jesus came John and James the Lesser.

The crowds were shouting out His praises and singing psalms! People took off garments and threw them in His path! In places, Jesus rode under arches which had been formed with the top branches of small trees transplanted earlier that day for the occasion. And it seemed that everyone was waving a palm branch. In return, He took this last opportunity to extend His mercy to those who sought it: Sister Emmerich saw Jesus repeatedly dismount to heal the ill and injured by the road.

St. Luke recounted that, when some priests stepped out and brought the procession to a halt with a challenge to Jesus, He refused to rebuke His disciples for chanting Messianic psalms, and said that if He did so, the very stones would cry out. At the same time, we know from St. Luke's Gospel that Jesus could not rejoice that finally He was receiving the homage due the Messiah—for He well knew what lay ahead, and en route, Jesus wept over the approaching fate of Jerusalem, and the many who would soon abandon Him.[1]

Indeed, Sister Emmerich saw that, in the days immediately before this triumphal procession, Jesus had given a number of discourses in the Temple itself predicting His bitter end. He touched upon the near fulfillment of His mission, His Passion, and His death. He exposed the deep corruption and guilt of mankind, and explained that without His Passion no man could be justified. *He prophesied that He must suffer and suffer exceedingly in order to satisfy Divine justice, and spoke of the grief awaiting His Blessed Mother.*

## Final Teachings and Actions Before the Passover

The day following His entrance into Jerusalem, He cleansed the Temple once again of illicit vendors, and He cursed a fruitless fig tree, that it should wither, saying that the same would happen to those who would not acknowledge Him. Peter expressed amazement the next morning when he saw the tree already withered, but Jesus told him: "If ye believe, ye shall do still more wonderful things. Yea, at your word mountains will cast themselves into the sea."

It was at this time that Judas went to Caiaphas' palace to discuss betraying Jesus. Sister Emmerich heard Jesus many times during His ministry predict that one of His Apostles would betray Him, without either naming the one or commenting further. However, at this time, she saw Him return to the subject more pointedly, after a meal with the Apostles, disciples and Holy Women at Lazarus' home. Peter vehemently denied that any of the Apostles could betray Him, drawing a strong rebuke:

"Jesus replied with more warmth than I ever before saw in Him, more even than had appeared when He said to Peter: 'Get thee behind Me, Satan!' He said that without His grace, without prayer, they would all fall away, that the hour would come in which they would all abandon Him. There was only one among them, He continued, who wavered not, and yet he too would flee, though he would come back again. By these words, Jesus meant John who, at the moment of Jesus' arrest, fled leaving his mantle behind him. All became very much troubled, excepting Judas who, while Jesus was talking, put on a friendly, smiling, and insinuating air."

Next, Jesus brought up the subject of the Holy Spirit and what was to come: "When they asked Jesus about the Kingdom that was to come to them, His answer was inexpressibly kind. He told them that another Spirit would come upon them and then only would they understand all things. He had to go to the Father and send them the Spirit which proceeded from the Father and Himself. . . . Then He spoke of troublous times to come, when all would have to suffer like a woman in the pains of childbirth, of the beauty of the human soul created to the likeness of God, and He showed how glorious a thing it is to save a soul and lead it home to heaven. He recalled to them how many times they had misunderstood Him, and His own forbearance with them; in like manner should they, He said, treat with sinners after His departure."

On the next day, Jesus spent the morning in the Temple, seated in the priest's chair by the money box which had been set up to receive offerings from those who wished to purify themselves for the feast. Jesus remarked that a poor widow had given more than all the others, for her coins were all that she had to buy food with that day. He met her outside, and told her that her son would be joining His followers.

After the time for offerings had past, Jesus taught in the portico of the Temple. *When approached by the Pharisees, He prophesied that they would not have a peaceful Pasch that year, for the blood of the Prophets whom they murdered should fall upon their head, and the Prophets themselves would rise from their graves. As for the beauty of the Temple, which one of the disciples exclaimed about, Jesus told them that one stone would not be left on another.*

*Jesus now spoke out boldly to all hearers in the Temple itself about His mission on earth—and even about what would happen after His death:* "He called Himself in plain terms the Salvation of mankind, and said that He had come to put an end to the domination of sin over man. Sin began in a garden, and in a garden it should end, for it would be in a garden that His enemies would seize Him. He reproached His hearers with the fact of their already wanting to kill Him after the raising of Lazarus, and said that He had kept Himself at a distance, that all things might be fulfilled. . . . He told them also how they would treat Him and put Him to death with assassins, and yet they would not be satisfied, they would not be able to effect anything against Him after His death. He once more made mention of the murdered just who would arise again; yes, He even pointed out the spot in which their resurrection would take place. But as for the Pharisees, He continued, in fear and anguish they would see their designs against Him frustrated."

In the days of Holy Week immediately before the Last Supper, Jesus addressed several discourses only to His followers, although they were given in the Temple itself. The following were some of His key points, as Sister Emmerich recounted them:

~ "The disciples had questioned Him upon the reunion after death of friends and married people. Jesus said that there was a twofold union in marriage: the union of flesh and blood which death cuts asunder, and they that were so bound would not find themselves together after death; and the union of soul, which would outlive death. They should not, He continued, be disquieted as to whether they would be alone or together in the other world. *They that had been united in union of soul in this life, would form but one body in the next.*"

~ "He spoke also of the Bridegroom and named the Church His affianced. Of the martyrdom of the body, He said that it was not to be feared, since that of the soul was the more frightful. . . ."

~ "The obligation of perfect continence, Jesus exposed to the Apostles by way of interrogation. He asked, for instance, 'Could you do such and such a thing at the same time?' and He spoke of a sacrifice that had to be offered, all which led to perfect continence as a conclusion. He adduced as examples Abraham and the other Patriarchs who before offering sacrifice, always purified themselves and observed a long continence."

~ "When He spoke of Baptism and the other Sacraments, He said that He would send to them the Holy Ghost who by His Baptism, would make them all children of Redemption. They should after His death baptize at the Pool of Bethesda all that would come and ask for it. If a great number presented themselves, they should lay their hands upon their shoulders, two and two, and baptize them there under the stream of the pump, or jet. As formerly the angel, so now would the Holy Ghost come upon the baptized as soon as His Blood should have been shed, and even before they themselves had received the Holy Spirit."

~ He spoke to them all about the end of the world and of the signs that would precede it. A man enlightened by God would have visions on that subject. By these words, Jesus referred to John's revelations, and He Himself made use of several similar illustrations. He spoke, for instance, of those that would be marked with the sign on their forehead, and said that the fountain of living water which flowed from Calvary's mount would at the end of the world appear to be almost entirely poisoned, though all the good waters would finally be gathered into the Valley of Jehoshaphat."

~ "He spoke of truth and the necessity of acting out what they, the Apostles, taught. He Himself, He said, was now about to fulfill it. It is not enough to believe, one must practice one's faith."

~ *"He would give over to them, would leave to them all that He possessed. Money and property He had not, but He would bequeath to them His strength and power. He would establish with them a union which should be still more intimate than that which united them to Him, and which should last till the end of time. He would also bind them to one another as the members of one body."*

~ *"He said to the Apostles with Him that, when He should have departed from them, they should seek Him in the noonday. Peter, always so bold, asked what that meant, 'in the noonday.' Then I heard Jesus saying: 'At noon the sun is directly above us and there is no shadow. At morn and eve shadows follow the light, and at midnight darkness prevails. Seek Me, therefore, in the full noonday light. And you shall find Me in your own heart, provided no shadow obscures its light.'"*

### Jesus Begins to Take Leave, as Judas Plots to Betray Him

Finally, He started to take leave of His followers. He told them He would never again enter the Temple in His body. The Apostles and disciples all threw themselves on the ground and wept—all except for Judas. On the day before the Last Supper, Jesus spoke with His Apostles in the morning, commanding them to make notes of what He was predicting about the future, including their own flight. *His most touching prophecy concerned the Blessed Virgin Mary—out of compassion, she would suffer with Him all the cruel torture of His death, and with Him she would die His bitter death.* In the afternoon, according to Sister Emmerich, He instructed about sixty of His disciples at a special afternoon repast, again mentioning His forthcoming betrayal:

"One, He said, that had been on intimate terms with Him, one that owed Him a great debt of gratitude, was about to sell Him to the Pharisees. He would not even set a price upon Him, but would merely ask: 'What will ye give me for Him?' If the Pharisees, were buying a slave, it would be at a fixed price, but He would be sold for whatever they chose to give. The traitor would sell Him for less than the cost of a slave!"

That evening, at a dinner in the public house of Simon the (cured) Leper, Mary Magdalene rose from her place among the Holy Women and anointed Jesus for the last time, with the costliest perfumes, which she had purchased with her remaining money. Sister Emmerich saw the scene, exactly as three of the Evangelists had described it, albeit she saw the event as taking place about two weeks after His triumphal entry into Jerusalem, and not the day before that event, as St. John recounted it. This anointing of Jesus was followed immediately by Judas sealing his bargain with the Pharisees. Sister Emmerich saw Judas being helped along on his evil course by the Devil himself. As Jesus had predicted, Judas asked what they would give for Jesus, and accepted their offer of thirty silver pieces; he promised them that the next day he would supply the details of his plot.

## Arrangements for the Last Supper

St. Mark and St. Luke briefly recounted an incident whereby Peter and John made arrangements with an unnamed stranger for Jesus and His followers to celebrate the final Passover of Jesus' earthly life. Sister Emmerich's visions provide information which demystify the event. The man whom they encountered in Jerusalem turned out to be Heli, the brother-in-law of the late Zachary, father to John the Baptist. It was Heli's charitable custom at the time for the Pasch to rent a banquet hall and make provision to feed strangers who had no friends in the city. For this purpose he had already hired the extremely large dining hall of the Cenacle, part of a complex of buildings owned by Nicodemus and Joseph of Arimathea on Mt. Zion.

The Cenacle itself was a long building surrounded by a colonnade and divided into three parts. Sister Emmerich related something of the history of the building: The Ark of the Covenant had once been housed there, and King David and his officers had used it; at a later time, hidden there in an underground vault, Malachias had written his prophecies. In Jesus' times, the Cenacle was being used primarily as a warehouse for tombstones and building stones, and as a place where the cutting was done of stone from Joseph's quarry in his home town. For the occasion, the Cenacle had been emptied of its statutes and tombstones, the walls had been decorated with tapestries, with the aperture in the ceiling being covered with transparent blue gauze.

Jesus had given Peter and John many instructions for preparations in addition to lining up the dining hall, and they hurried throughout the city. They went to the home of the late Simeon, for one of his sons was to procure four lambs for the dinner, and also to the home of Seraphia—soon to be renamed Veronica for her role in the Passion.

According to Sister Emmerich, she had long known the Holy Family; when as a boy Jesus had remained in Jerusalem, it was she who had supplied Him with food. Now, she gave Peter and John the chalice to be used in instituting the Blessed Sacrament.

### Jesus' Mother Asks to Die With Him

Jesus, meanwhile, had a task which only He could perform, and it was a very distressing one: He had to meet with His Mother to prepare her to see Him being tortured and executed as a criminal. According to Sister Emmerich's visions, *"When Jesus made known to the Blessed Virgin what was about to happen to Him, she besought Him in touching terms to let her die with Him.* But He exhorted her to bear her grief more calmly than the other women, telling her at the same time that He would rise again, and He named the spot upon which He would appear to her. This time she did not shed so many tears, though she was sad beyond expression and there was something awe-inspiring in her deep gravity. Like a devoted son, Jesus thanked her for all her love. He embraced her with His right arm and pressed her to His breast. He told her that He would celebrate His Last Supper with her in spirit, and named the hour at which she should receive His Body and Blood."

### The Last Supper

Just before the Last Supper, one of the four lambs to be eaten was actually slaughtered in the Cenacle (the other three were killed at the Temple), in an impressive ceremony described by Sister Emmerich. Simeon's son, a Levite, assisted at it:

"The Apostles and disciples were present chanting the 118th Psalm [Hymn of Thanksgiving].[2] Jesus spoke of a new period then beginning, and said that the sacrifice of Moses and the signification of the Paschal lamb were about to be fulfilled, that on this account the lamb was to be immolated as formerly in Egypt, and that now in reality were they to go forth from the house of bondage.

"The lamb was then bound, its back to a little board, with a cord passed around the body. It reminded me of Jesus bound to the pillar. Simeon's son held the lamb's head up, and Jesus stuck it in the neck with a knife, which He then handed to Simeon's son that he might complete the slaughter. Jesus appeared timid in wounding the lamb, as if it cost Him pain. His movement was quick, His manner grave. The blood was caught in a basin, and the attendants brought a branch of hyssop, which Jesus dipped into it. *Then stepping to the door of the hall, He signed the two posts and the lock with the blood, and* stuck the bloody branch above the lintel. He then uttered some solemn words, saying among other thing: 'The destroying angel shall pass by here. Without fear or anxiety, ye shall adore in this place when I, the true Paschal Lamb, shall have been immolated. A new era, a new sacrifice are now about to begin, and they will last till the end of the world.'" Finally, Jesus consecrated the Cenacle as a place for worship.

The picture of the Last Supper painted in the Synoptic Gospels is explicitly that of a Seder—a ritual meal held by Jews to celebrate the Passover. The Gospel of John, however, is somewhat unclear on this point, in that John placed the Last Supper on the evening *before* Passover (with Jesus' trial being on the morning of the Passover ceremonies), and he did not refer to the ceremony itself. Because of this apparent contradiction, some biblical scholars have expressed doubt that the Last Supper was really a Seder.[3] The visions of Sister Emmerich, however, show that indeed it was, with Jesus presiding over the traditional meal and the men standing in traveling clothes, staff in hand, chanting and eating their lamb, unleavened bread, garlic and herbs in haste. There were three separate groups of men (the women ate in a side-court): Jesus and the Twelve Apostles ate in the main hall; Nathanael and twelve disciples were in a room on the side, while Heliachim (a son of Cleophas and Mary Heli) ate with twelve more disciples in another room.

*Sister Emmerich's visions provide a convincing explanation of how the Synoptic Gospels can be harmonized perfectly with that of St. John: Jesus was killed before the night of the Passover, but He and His Apostles had already celebrated the Passover meal. At the trial of Jesus before Caiaphas, when Jesus was accused of having eaten the Paschal lamb ahead of time, and Caiaphas demanded that Nicodemus and Joseph of Arimathea explain why they had allowed that irregularity to occur in their building, they responded by proving that there was an ancient privilege which Galileans had of celebrating the Pasch one day early. This custom had grown up in order to spread out the crowds attending Temple ceremonies and traveling the roads from and to Galilee.*

*Moreover, Sister Emmerich's visions answer the objection that the Last Supper as portrayed by St. John was not a Seder meal, but instead was a wholly new ceremony. She saw three separate events following one after another: the traditional Seder meal; the washing of the feet; and then the farewell love-fest ceremony at which Jesus instituted the Blessed Sacrament. St. John, while mentioning a meal, described only the latter two events.*

*Jesus Gives a Final Example of Loving Service*

According to Sister Emmerich, immediately after the Paschal meal but before the foot washing ceremony, Jesus gave the Apostles a solemn instruction on penance, the knowledge and confession of sin, contrition, and justification. The Apostles—with the exception of Judas—acknowledged their sins.

Jesus then went into another room, where He adjusted His clothing and tied a towel around His waist, leaving an end hanging down. John and James the Lesser obtained water in a leather bottle, and a basin. Sister Emmerich saw that, meanwhile, the other Apostles rekindled their running dispute as to who among them should have the first place, "for as the Lord had expressly announced that He was about to leave them and that His Kingdom was near, they were strengthened anew in their idea, that He had somewhere a secret force in reserve, and that He would achieve some earthly triumph at the very last moment." When He rejoined them, Jesus once again chastised them for this way of thinking, and began to wash their feet, with James the Lesser pouring water as needed into the basin which John held.

*According to Sister Emmerich, "during the whole of the Paschal Supper, the Lord's demeanor was most touching and gracious, and at this humble washing of his Apostles' feet, He was full of love. He did not perform it as if it were a were ceremony, but like a sacred act of love springing straight from the heart. By it He wanted to give expression to the love that burned within.* When He came to Peter, the latter through humility objected. He said: 'Lord, dost Thou wash my feet?' And the Lord answered: 'What I do, thou knowest not now, but thou shalt know hereafter.'

"And it appeared to me that He said to him in private: 'Simon, thou hast deserved that My Father should reveal to thee who I am, whence I came, and whither I go. Thou alone hast known and confessed it, therefore I will build My Church upon thee, and the gates of hell shall not prevail against it. My power shall continue with thy successors till the end of the world.' Here Jesus pointed to Peter while saying to the others: 'Peter shall be My representative with you when I shall have gone from among you. He shall direct you and make known to you your mission.'"

When He came to Judas, Jesus made a last effort to break through the rind around his heart—even telling him the He knew Judas was a traitor, but Judas pretended not to hear.

[1] This exact duality is captured in the Palm Sunday liturgy of the Catholic Church. This begins with the congregation carrying palm branches in a triumphant procession into the church, but it turns somber when a Gospel account of Christ's Passion is read in the Mass itself.

[2] This Psalm begins "Give thanks to Yahweh for he is good, for his kindness is eternal," and contains the verse "The stone the builders rejected became the cornerstone."

[3] See John P. Meier, A Marginal Jew 1:390–401; Jonathan Klawans, "Was Jesus' Last Supper a Seder?," Bible Review (October 2001) 24; Baruch M. Bokser, "Was the Last Supper a Passover Seder?," Bible Review (Summer 1987)24. In an attempt to answer the timing objection, one scholar theorized that Jesus was following a solar calendar, rather than the traditional lunar calendar. See, e.g., the entry for "Calendars" in The Anchor Bible Dictionary 1:810, 820; Paolo Sacchi, "Recovering Jesus' Formative Background," and Rainer Riesner, "Jesus, the Primitive Community, and the Essene Quarter of Jerusalem," both in Jesus and the Dead Sea Scrolls (James H. Charlesworth, ed.) 128–29, and 217–18. The problem with this hypothesis is that it would leave a very large gap in the Evangelists' account of the events between the Last Supper and the Crucifixion.

# CHAPTER SEVENTEEN

## *The Holy Grail*

The quest to find the "Holy Grail"—the vessel which Jesus first used to transform wine into His Blood—has inspired countless works of fiction over the centuries.[1] These range from the sublime—Malory's romance *Le Morte d'Arthur* and Wagner's music drama *Parsifal*—to the ridiculous (the movie *Indiana Jones and The Last Crusade*) and even the blasphemous (the novel, *The DaVinci Code*). While the vessel would be a priceless relic, it was not described at the time, and searchers have not known what to look for. However, a very clear description of the Holy Grail, along with its prior history, was given by Sister Emmerich, from her visions of the ceremony which Jesus presided over on the night of the Last Supper. According to her:

"The large chalice consisted of the cup and the foot, which latter must have been added at a later period, for it was of different material. The cup was pear-shaped, and of a brownish, highly polished metal overlaid with gold. It had two small handles, by which it could be raised when its contents rendered it tolerably heavy. The foot was elaborately wrought of dark virgin gold, the edge encircled by a serpent. It was ornamented with a little bunch of grapes, and enriched with precious stones.

"Melchizedek[2] brought it . . . to the land of Canaan when he began to mark off settlements on the site afterward occupied by Jerusalem. He had used it at the Sacrifice of bread and wine offered in Abraham's presence, and he afterward gave it to him. This same chalice was even in Noah's possession. It stood in the upper part of the ark. Moses also had it in his keeping." "This chalice was a very wonderful and mysterious vessel that had lain in the Temple for a long time. . . . It was stowed away in a chest along with other objects no longer of use, and when discovered was sold to some antiquaries. The chalice and all the vessels belonging to it were afterward bought by Seraphia."[3]

### How Was the Holy Eucharist Celebrated for the First Time?

Sister Emmerich also had detailed visions of how the Holy Grail was used in the institution of the "Eucharist" (meaning, *thanksgiving*)—the central one of the seven sacraments of the Catholic Church. Her accounts reconcile and greatly supplement the accounts in the Synoptic Gospels, which are surprisingly terse in relating a matter of such great interest and significance.

Directly following the washing of the Apostle's feet, a table in the middle of the dining hall was covered with a red cloth and, on top, a transparent white one. Peter and John carried in the special chalice they had brought from Seraphia's house and put it on the table. Jesus then stood between Peter and John and prayed over the uncovered chalice. He began to explain the Eucharist to the Apostles, and also the ceremonies that were to accompany it. He laid on a plate before Him Passover loaves, blessed them, elevated the plate of bread with both hands, raised His eyes toward heaven, prayed, offered, set the plate down on the table, and covered it.

At Jesus' direction, Peter poured wine into the chalice, and John poured in water after He had blessed it. Jesus then added a little more water from the small spoon, blessed the chalice, raised it on high, praying and offering, and set it down again. After that Jesus washed his hands in water poured over them, and had the Apostles do likewise. Sister Emmerich's description of the ceremony continued as follows:

*"In profound recollection and prayer, Jesus next broke the bread into several morsels and laid them one over another on the plate. With the tip of His finger, He broke off a scrap from the first morsel and let it fall into the chalice. . . . Again Jesus prayed and taught. His words glowing with fire and light, came forth from His mouth and entered into all the Apostles, excepting Judas. He took the plate with the morsels of bread and said, 'Take and eat. This is My Body which is given for you.' While saying these words, He stretched forth His right hand over it, as if giving a blessing, and as He did so, a brilliant light emanated from Him. His words were luminous as also the Bread, which as a body of light entered the mouth of the Apostles. It was as if Jesus Himself flowed into them. I saw all of them penetrated with light, bathed in light. Judas alone was in darkness."*

Peter was the first to receive the Eucharistic host, followed by the other Apostles.[4] *"Jesus next raised the chalice by its two handles to a level with His face, and pronounced into it the words of consecration. While doing so, He was wholly transfigured and as it were, transpar-*

ent. *He was as if passing over into what He was giving. He caused Peter and John to drink from the chalice while yet in His hands, and then He set it down. With the little spoon, John removed some of the Sacred Blood from the chalice to the small cups, which Peter handed to the Apostles who, two by two, drank from the same cup."* As a last part of the ceremony, Jesus reserved what remained of the consecrated bread and wine, now His Body and Blood, so that they could be used after the Resurrection, and cleansed the vessels.

*In her visions, Sister Emmerich saw that during the institution of the Blessed Sacrament, the Apostles, at Jesus' command, were making notes on little parchment rolls. The ceremony which she described as taking place after the Last Supper is identical in substance with the ceremony Catholics still observe at Mass today.*[5] This celebration of the Eucharist is the center of the spiritual life of the Catholic Church as a whole and its members as individuals.[6] As Pope John Paul II stated in a recent Encyclical: "The Eucharist, as Christ's saving presence in the community of the faithful and its spiritual food, is the most precious possession which the Church can have in her journey through history."[7]

*From the beginning, the Church has consistently taught that bread and wine, when consecrated by an ordained priest, truly become the Body and Blood of Jesus—that is, He is really, and not merely symbolically, present in them.*[8] As St. Paul asked rhetorically: "Is not the cup of blessing we bless a sharing in the blood of Christ? And is not the bread we break a sharing in the body of Christ?"[9]

Sister Emmerich saw that even before Jesus had concluded the ceremony, Judas left, without prayer or thanksgiving, hurried on his way by devils. She also saw the following additional actions of Jesus and the Apostles, which were not reported in the Gospels:

"Jesus now gave to the Apostles an instruction full of mystery. He told them how they were to preserve the Blessed Sacrament in memory of Him until the end of the world, taught them the necessary forms for making use of and communicating It, and in what manner they were by degrees to teach and publish the Mystery. He told them likewise when they were to receive what remained of the consecrated Species, when to give some to the Blessed Virgin, and how to consecrate It themselves after He should have sent them the Comforter."

### How Did Jesus Institute the Priesthood?

"Then He instructed them upon the priesthood, the sacred unction, and the preparation of the Chrism and the Holy Oils. . . .

Jesus taught many secret things concerning them: how to mix the ointment, what parts of the body to anoint, and upon what occasions." *"After that I saw Jesus anointing Peter and John, on whose hands at the institution of the Blessed Sacrament, He had poured the water that had flowed over His own, and who had drunk from the chalice in His hand. From the center of the table, where He was standing, Jesus stepped a little to one side and imposed hands upon Peter and John, first on their shoulders and then on their head. During this action. they joined their hands and crossed their thumbs. As they bowed low before Him (and I am not sure that they did not kneel) the Lord anointed the thumb and forefinger of each of their Hands with Chrism, and made the sign of the Cross with it on their head. He told them that this anointing would remain with them to the end of the world. James the Lesser, Andrew, James the Greater, and Bartholomew, were likewise consecrated." "I saw too that the Lord twisted crosswise over Peter's breast the narrow scarf that he wore around his neck, but that on the others He drew it across the breast over the right shoulder and under the left arm."*

The Gospel of John records in detail Jesus' prayers and very extensive discourses on topics of lasting importance immediately before He left with the Apostles for the Mount of Olives. Sister Emmerich's visions accord with Scripture. As she saw it: "He often appeared to be conversing with His Heavenly Father, and to be overflowing with love and enthusiasm. The Apostles also were full of joy and zeal. They asked questions about different things, all of which Jesus answered." The discourse was not without a jarring note, however. As reported by St. John, Jesus had to reprove Peter for the latter's boast of fidelity to Jesus, which would shortly be exposed as hollow. Before leaving the Cenacle, Jesus encountered His Mother, Mary Cleophas, and Magdalene, the latter of whom begged Him not to go to the Mount of Olives, for she had heard that He was to be arrested there. Jesus tried to comfort the women, but He left with the Apostles.

### Jesus Leads The Eleven to the Mount of Olives

Sts. Matthew and Mark each devoted eleven verses to the events between the end of the ceremonies at the Cenacle and the arrest of Jesus on the Mount of Olives; St. Luke devoted seven, and St. John none. By comparison, the visions of Sister Emmerich concerning those few hours fill *38 pages* of type, single-spaced. Her visions compellingly reinforce the Scriptural accounts with a plethora of details. She saw Jesus and eleven Apostles proceeding by a back path from Mt. Zion through the Valley of Jehoshaphat, to the Mount of Olives a half hour away. *En route, He made several significant utterances—one not recorded in the Gospels: "He said that He would one day return hither, though not poor and powerless as He then was, to judge the world. Then would men tremble with fear and cry out: 'Ye mountains, cover us!' But the disciples understood Him not. They thought . . . that from weakness and exhaustion, He was wandering in speech."* But, it seems likely that Jesus was adverting to the fact that the Valley of Jehoshaphat (whose name meant "the Valley of the Lord will judge") was the place where, according to the Book of Joel, the Lord is to gather together and judge the nations.[10]

Jesus and the Eleven arrived at the Mount of Olives, where there were two gardens. Sister Emmerich described the larger one, the Garden of Gethsemane, as a pleasure garden with fruit trees and shrubs, surrounded by a hedge. It was a place of prayer and also recreation, with enclosures made of boughs and branches. Across the road from it, and higher up the mount was the Garden of Olives. This had a different character: it was wilder, and full of olive trees, terraces and grottoes. It was to the latter that Jesus repaired, taking with Him Peter, John and James the Greater; the other eight Apostles were told to wait in the Garden of Gethsemane. Telling His companions that His soul was sorrowful, and directing them to remain and watch, Jesus moved only a few feet away from them, but out of their sight, below them in a dark grotto. There, He suffered harsh torments from a series of visions (which were, like physical realities, mystically visible to Sister Emmerich). The torments were interrupted very briefly when He would emerge to say a few words to the three Apostles, and would start again when He was alone. Sister Emmerich gave the accounts set forth below.

### The First Agony

*"I felt in a most lively manner that Jesus, in resigning Himself to the sufferings that awaited Him and sacrificing Himself to Divine justice in satisfaction for the sins of the world, caused in a certain manner His Divinity to return into the Most Holy Trinity.* This He did in order out of infinite love, in His most pure and sensitive, His most innocent and true Humanity supported by the love of His human Heart alone, to devote Himself to endure for the sins of the world the greatest excess of agony and pain. . . . He allowed those infinite sufferings in satisfaction for endless sins, like a thousand-branched tree of pain, to pierce through, to extend through all the members of His Sacred Body, all the faculties of His holy Soul. Thus,

entirely given up to His humanity, He fell on His face calling upon God in unspeakable sorrow and anguish. He saw in countless forms all the sins of the world with their innate hideousness. He took all upon Himself and offered Himself in His prayer to satisfy the justice of His Heavenly Father for all that guilt by His own sufferings.

"But Satan who, under a frightful form and with furious mockery, moved around among all this abomination, became at each moment more violently enraged against Him. He evoked before the eyes of His soul visions of the sins of men, one more frightful than the other, and constantly addressed to the Sacred Humanity of Jesus such words, as, 'What! Wilt Thou take this also upon Thyself? Art Thou ready to endure its penalty? How canst Thou satisfy for this?'

"At first Jesus knelt calmly in prayer, but after a while His soul shrank in affright from the multitude and heinousness of man's sins and ingratitude against God. So overpowering was the sadness, the agony of heart which fell upon Him that, trembling and shuddering, He prayed imploringly (as the Synoptic Gospels record): 'Abba, Father, if it be possible, remove this chalice from Me! My Father, all things are possible to Thee. Take this chalice from Me!' Then, recovering Himself, He added: 'But not what I will, but what Thou wilt.' His will and the Father's were one. But now that through love He had delivered Himself up to the weakness of His human nature, He shuddered at the thought of death."

Jesus staggered out of the grotto to where Peter, James and John lay sleeping. If Jesus had hoped to find succor from His chief Apostles, He was disappointed, for they knew not what was happening with Him nor what He wanted them to do. Despite that, He continued to have infinite patience with them, as Sister Emmerich saw: "In His spiritual dereliction, He said: 'What! Could ye not watch one hour with Me?'" (The Gospels of Matthew and Mark contain that question of His.) "John said to Him: 'Master! what has befallen Thee? Shall I call the other disciples? Shall we take to flight?' Jesus answered: "Were I to live, teach, and work miracles for thirty-three years longer, it would not suffice for the accomplishment of what I have to fulfill before this time tomorrow. Do not call the Eight! I have left them where they are, because they could not see Me in this suffering state without being scandalized at Me. They would fall into temptation, forget many things that I have said to them, and lose confidence in Me. But you who have seen the Son of Man transfigured, may also see Him in this hour of darkness and complete dereliction of soul; nevertheless watch and pray, lest ye fall into temptation, for the spirit is willing, but the flesh is weak." (The Synoptic Gospels contain the latter injunction.)

### The Second Agony

Sister Emmerich saw Jesus return to the little grotto, to continue His spiritual struggle to overcome His human fear of pain and death. *Given that it was Jesus' purpose to atone for every sin committed by mankind—future as well as past—it was necessary and appropriate that He be tormented with visions of the sins to be committed in the future by His own declared followers as the Church grew: "He saw heresies and schisms entering her fold, and the sin of Adam repeated by pride and disobedience in all forms of vanity and delusive self-righteousness. The tepidity, the malice, the wickedness of innumerable Christians; the manifold lies, the deceptive subtlety of all proud teachers; the sacrilegious crimes of all wicked priests with their frightful consequences; the abomination of desolation in the Kingdom of God upon earth, in the sanctuary of the thankless human race whom amid inexpressible sufferings, He was about to redeem with His Blood and His life."*

*Satan mounted one especially powerful temptation—the temptation not to suffer for such a wicked and ungrateful race. According to Sister Emmerich, "Jesus beheld with bitter anguish all the ingratitude, the corruption of Christendom past, present, and future. While these visions were passing before Him, the voice of the tempter of His humanity was constantly heard whispering, 'See! Canst Thou undergo such sufferings in the sight of such ingratitude?'* These words added to the mockery and the abominations that He beheld in the rapidly changing visions pressed with such violence upon Him that His most Sacred Humanity was crushed under a weight of unspeakable agony. Christ, the Son of Man, writhed in anguish and wrung His hands. As if overwhelmed, He fell repeatedly on His knees, while so violent a struggle went on between His human will and His repugnance to suffer so much for so thankless a race, that the sweat poured from Him in a stream of heavy drops of blood to the ground." At that point, Sister Emmerich saw the three Apostles arise, and Peter go to Him. But, seeing Jesus trembling and bloody, Peter retreated.

### The Third Agony

*Jesus, left alone, was then besieged by visions of the Devil in hideous forms, representing discord and abomination, especially that which was to arise in His Church.* The following are among the most mystical of Sister Emmerich's visions:

"At first I saw the serpent but seldom, but toward the last I beheld it in gigantic form, a crown upon its head. With terrible might, and leading after it immense legions of human beings from every condition of life and of every race, it prepared to attack Jesus. Armed with all kinds of engines and destructive weapons, they struggled for some moments among themselves, and then with frightful fury turned the attack upon Jesus. It was an awful spectacle. Their weapons, their swords, and spears rose and fell like flails on a boundless threshing-floor, and they raged against the Heavenly Grain of Wheat that had come upon earth to die in order to feed mankind eternally with the Bread of Life.

"I saw the offenders in immense crowds with weapons corresponding to the species of crime perpetrated by them, assailing the Lord, and striking Him to the ground. I saw irreverent sacristans of all centuries, lightminded, sinful, worthless priests offering the Holy Sacrifice and distributing the Blessed Sacrament, and multitudes of tepid and unworthy communicants. I saw countless numbers to whom the source of all blessing, the mystery of the living God, had become an oath or a curse, expressive of anger, and furious soldiers and servants of the devil who profaned the sacred vessels, who threw away the Most Blessed Sacrament, who horribly outraged It, or who dishonored It in their frightful, hellish worship of false gods.

"Side by side with these hideous, barbarous cruelties, I saw innumerable other forms of godlessness more refined and subtle, but not less atrocious. I saw many souls, owing to bad example and perfidious teachers, losing their faith in Jesus' promises to remain always in the Blessed Sacrament, and no longer humbly adoring their Savior therein present. I saw in this multitude a great many sinful teachers who became teachers of error. They first struggled against one another, and then united against Jesus in the Blessed Sacrament of His Church. I saw a great crowd of these apostate heresiarchs disdainfully rejecting the priesthood of the Church, attacking and denying Jesus Christ's presence in the Mystery of the Blessed Sacrament in the manner in which He Himself gave this Mystery to the Church, which has truly preserved It.

"I saw whole nations torn in this way from the heart of Jesus and deprived of participation in the treasures of grace left to the Church. It was frightful to behold how at first only a few separated from Christ's Church; and when, having increased to whole nations, they returned to her, they again attacked her and warred against one another on the question of what was holiest in her worship, namely, the Blessed Sacrament. But finally, I saw all who had separated from the Church plunging into infidelity, superstition, heresy, darkness, and the false philosophy of the world. Perplexed and enraged, they united in large bodies to vent their anger against the Church. They were urged on and destroyed by the serpent in the midst of them. Ah! it was as if Jesus felt Himself torn into countless shreds. The Lord saw and felt in this distressing vision the whole weight of the poisonous tree of disunion with all its branches and fruits, which will continue to rend itself asunder until the end of time when the wheat will be gathered into the barn and the chaff cast into the fire."

Sister Emmerich described seeing Jesus, following such spiritual lacerations, staggering out of the grotto. He was trembling and groaning, His hair all disheveled and his head soaked with blood. So ghastly was the spectacle He presented in the dim light that at first the Apostles did not recognize Him when they awoke. He spoke to them of the horrible death which was soon to befall Him, and He begged them to console His Mother and Magdalene. The Three did not know what to say or do; at His request, they led Him back to the grotto for His final agony there.

Meanwhile, the other Apostles were becoming terribly discouraged, thinking of their own safety and wondering what was to become of them without Him to protect them. The Blessed Virgin Mary and Magdalene were overwhelmed with grief. They prayed at the house of Mary Marcus, but then walked out into the Valley of Jehoshaphat, toward the Mount of Olives as if they could assist Jesus by being physically closer to Him.

## The Final Agony

Alone in the grotto, Jesus again prayed to have the chalice of pain and death taken from Him, but submitted Himself to the Father's will. Then, He was strengthened by a vision of the souls in Limbo, from Adam and Eve, through the Prophets, to His Mother's parents and John the Baptist. They were all longing for His coming to open the way to heaven for them. Angels also showed Him the many saints to come in the future, who would join Him in heaven.

The comforting visions soon ended and the horrors began again, as the angels showed Him all the scenes of His imminent Passion, ending with His death on the Cross. Jesus lay prostrate on the ground, sweating blood profusely. At that point, Sister Emmerich saw an angel, in priest-like robes, coming to Him, and bearing a chalice above which floated a morsel about the size of a bean, which glowed with a reddish light. The angel hovered over the place where Jesus was lying and stretched forth his hand to Him. When Jesus arose, he placed the shining morsel in His mouth and gave Him to drink from the little luminous chalice. This was the chalice of His Passion, which Jesus voluntarily accepted. The angel disappeared, while Jesus, strengthened, remained to pray in the grotto. Finally, Jesus rose again, wiped His face with a cloth, and emerged from the grotto for the last time, with a firm step.

He woke the sleeping Apostles, pointed out to them the approaching band of soldiers, and told them that He would deliver Himself into the hands of His enemies without resistance, which He did on the road that separated the Garden of Olives from the Garden of Gethsemane.[11]

## Why Did Judas Betray the Son of Man?

The Gospels fail to provide any motive for the betrayal of the Son of Man by Judas Iscariot. To fill this gap, we have the visions of Sister Emmerich, which provided her with insight into his character, as well as the details of his infernal actions. According to her: "He had always counted upon Jesus establishing a temporal kingdom in which he hoped for some brilliant and lucrative post. But as this was not forthcoming, he turned his thoughts to amassing a fortune. He saw that hardships and persecution were on the increase; and so he thought that before things came to the worst he would ingratiate himself with some of the powerful and distinguished among Jesus' enemies." "He wanted to obtain the traitor's reward and please the Pharisees by pretending to deliver Jesus into their hands, but he had never counted on things going so far, he never dreamed of Jesus' being brought to judgment and crucified. He was thinking only of the money."

That fateful Thursday evening, they paid him thirty pieces of silver, which were shaped like a tongue, pierced at one end, and strung together with a chain. Because he could feel their contempt, Judas sought to elevate himself in their eyes by pretending that money was not his motive for betraying Jesus. He offered to donate the money to the Temple treasury, but they rejected the coins as blood money. Judas then raced to the Cenacle, and came back to report that Jesus had already left there, and must be in His place of prayer on the Mount of Olives.

Judas had arranged that he would step forward and mark Jesus with a kiss, but he planned to behave as though the soldiers' arrival was coincidental. The soldiers had their own instructions to watch Judas closely, for the leaders regarded him as an untrustworthy lout who might try to escape with his money, without the mission succeeding in capturing Jesus.

## Jesus is Arrested by the High Priests' Men

Sister Emmerich described the posse which Judas led up the Mount of Olives as being composed of about twenty soldiers carrying swords and spears, and wearing uniforms very similar to those of Roman soldiers, but having been drawn from the Temple guard or the employ of the High Priests. In addition, there were four wretched pagan executioners who were appointed to drag Jesus to judgment, and half a dozen of the most vicious enemies of Jesus among the Pharisees, Sadducees and Herodians. When Jesus and the three Apostles confronted the approaching band on the road, Judas' treachery was quickly exposed: the soldiers were unwilling to let him out of their grasp.

Sister Emmerich heard Jesus asking Judas why he had come, and Judas inventing a lie about having been on a errand for Jesus. In reply, Jesus said: "Oh, how much better it would have been for thee if thou hadst never been born." Judas finally gave the agreed upon signal— kissing Jesus on the cheek—prompting Jesus to ask, as recorded by St. Luke, "Judas, would you betray the Son of Man with a kiss?"

The soldiers seized Jesus, though not before He gave two displays of supernatural power, the first in causing the soldiers—but not Judas, the executioners or the civilian guard—to fall to the ground as if they were in an epileptic fit. (Sister Emmerich explained that those who remained standing were completely in Satan's power, while the ones who were convulsed were not. The fall and rise of the latter was an omen of their later conversion to Christianity.) The second miraculous sign which Jesus gave was His healing of the ear of Malchus, the High Priest's slave, which Peter had impetuously cut off. So converted was Malchus by this that, during Jesus' Passion the next day, he ran back and forth to the Blessed Virgin Mary and those disciples he could find, to apprise them of what was happening.

---

[1] See the entry for "The Holy Grail" in The Catholic Encyclopedia. http://www.newadvent.org/cathen.

[2] Melchizedek was referred to as the king of Salem in the Book of Genesis. (Gn 14:18) Sister Emmerich understood Melchizedek to be an angel-priest rather than a human. Melchizedek was considered to be more than an ordinary man in Jewish antiquity. See George W. Buchanan, The Anchor Bible—To the Hebrews (New York: Doubleday & Co. 1972) 119; Charles A. Geischen,

*Angelomorphic Christology* (Boston: Brill 1998) 171–73 (citing, *inter alia*, 2 Enoch ch. 69–73). He was apparently regarded as angel by St. Paul, *see* Heb ch. 7 ("Without father, mother or ancestry, without beginning of days or end of life, like the Son of God he remains a priest forever."), and certain Christian sects may have heretically identified him with the Godhead, *see* Fred L. Horton, Jr., *The Melchizedek Tradition* (New York: Cambridge U. Press 1976) 108–11.

[3] As to the further history of the Holy Grail, Sister Emmerich related that "the large chalice was left to the Church of Jerusalem under the care of James the Lesser. I see it still carefully preserved somewhere. It will again come to light as it did once before. The smaller cups that stood around it were distributed among the other Churches: one to Antioch, another to Ephesus. These vessels enriched seven Churches."

[4] Sister Emmerich did not remember seeing Jesus Himself partake, but her angelic guide instructed her that it was necessary that a priest-celebrant do so.

[5] At least as early as the middle of the second century, there was a written outline of the order of the celebration, which is still observed today. *See Catechism of the Catholic Church* § 1345. *And see* "The Didache" §§ 9–10, in 6 *Ancient Christian* Writers (New York: Paulist Press 1948); many scholars believe that it was composed during the first century, *see ibid.* 4–6.

[6] *See Catechism of the Catholic Church* §§ 1113, 1211, and 1324.

[7] *See* Pope John Paul II, "Ecclesia de Eucharistia (Encyclical)," 32 *Origins* (May 1, 2003) 753. http://www.vatican.va.holy_father/special_features/encyclicals/documents/hf_jp-ii_enc_20030417_ecclesia_eucharistia_en.html.

[8] *See Catechism of the Catholic Church* §§ 1373–81.

[9] 1 Cor 10:16.

[10] Jl ch. 4.

[11] There is no indication in Sister Emmerich's visions that Jesus was arrested in the Cave of Gethsemane, contrary to the theory of Joan E. Taylor set forth in "The Garden of Gethsemane: Not the Place of Jesus' Arrest," *Biblical Archaeology Review* (July/Aug 1995).

# CHAPTER EIGHTEEN

*Jesus is Tortured En Route to His Trial*

According to the visions of Sister Emmerich, Jesus was brutalized continuously from the time He was arrested. His hands and forearms were bound tightly to each other, a collar, with sharp points in it to wound Him, was placed over His neck, and a girdle was fixed around His waist, with ropes attached so that the executioners could pull Him wherever they pleased. The following are excerpts from her description of how He was dragged from the Mount of Olives to Mount Zion for trial:

"First went ten of the guard, then followed the executioners dragging Jesus by the ropes, next came the scoffing Pharisees, and the ten other soldiers closed the procession. . . . The executioners dragged and ill-used Jesus in the most cruel manner. They exercised upon Him all kinds of malice, and this principally from a base deference and desire to please the six officials, who were full of rage and venom against Him. They led Him along the roughest roads, over ruts and stones and mire, keeping the long ropes stretched while they themselves sought good paths. In this way Jesus had to go wherever the ropes would allow Him. His tormentors carried in their hands knotted cords with which they struck Him, as a butcher might do the animal he was leading to slaughter." John at first followed close behind, but when the guard sought to arrest him, he fled, as noted in the Gospel of Mark.

At the bridge over the Kidron River, the executioners pushed Him off the bridge, causing Him to fall on the stony bottom and injure His knees. Sister Emmerich related that: "I had not seen Jesus take anything to drink in the vehement thirst that consumed Him after His awful agony in the Garden of Olives. But when pushed into the Kidron, I saw Him drinking with difficulty and, at the same time, I heard Him murmuring that thereby was fulfilled a prophetic verse from the Psalms, which bore reference to drinking from the torrent by the way."[1] He was dragged backwards out of the river and up the bank, then forced to go across the bridge again, with His waterlogged garment impeding His steps.

"It was not yet midnight when I saw the four executioners dragging Jesus over a rugged, narrow road, along which ran only an uneven footpath. They dragged Him over sharp stones and fragments of rocks, through thorns and thistles, inhumanly hurrying Him on with curses and blows. The six brutal Pharisees were, wherever the road permitted it, always in His vicinity. Each carried in his hand a different kind of torturing stick, with which he tormented Him, thrusting Him, goading Him on, or beating Him with it.

"While the executioners were dragging Jesus, His naked feet bleeding, over sharp stones, thorns, and thistles, the scornful satirical speeches of the six Pharisees were piercing His loving Heart. It was at these moments they made use of such mockery as: 'His precursor, the Baptist, did not prepare a good way for Him here!'; or, 'The words of Malachi, I send My angel before thee, to prepare thy way, does not apply here'; or, 'Why does He not raise John from the dead that he may prepare the way for Him?' Such were the taunts uttered by these ignominious creatures and received with rude shouts of laughter. They were caught up in turn by the executioners, who were incited thus to load poor Jesus with fresh ill-usage."

The soldiers summoned reinforcements to prevent any attempt to free Jesus by the poor artisans and day laborers who lived in Ophel, a neighborhood on a walled hill south of the Temple. Many of them were His devoted followers, especially since He had healed those injured in the collapse of the tower at Siloam, and had stopped there to console the people after the death of John the Baptist. When these good people came out of their houses to see about the shouting by soldiers, they were insolently beaten back, while the soldiers jeered them, saying: "Jesus, the evildoer, your false Prophet, is about to be led in a prisoner. The High Priests will put an end to His proceedings. He will have to pay the penalty of the cross." His supporters were left behind when the procession passed beyond the gate of Ophel, went past the Pool of Bethesda, and then up a flight of steps to the house of Annas on Mount Zion.

## Jesus is Arraigned Before Annas

According to Sister Emmerich, when news came that Jesus had been apprehended, Annas, a very influential former High Priest,[2] and Caiaphas, his son-in-law and incumbent High Priest, began their work in earnest, dispatching messengers to summon those members of the Sanhedrin who were not already assembled at Caiaphas' palace.

Pharisees, Sadducees, and Herodians from all parts of the country were in Jerusalem at that time, and the High Priests now selected those whom they knew to be His most bitter enemies. These they summoned with the command to gather up evidence against Jesus and bring it to the judgment court; His enemies proceeded to do this with bribes to secure false testimony. In addition to those who were against Him simply because they were Pharisees or Scribes, there were some who had come up against Him personally, from the illicit vendors in the Temple, to impenitent sinners whom He had refused to heal, to adulterers whose victims He had turned from sin to virtue.

The city was coming alive with sounds and torch lights; as messengers ran to and fro, people came out to see what was happening, and more soldiers appeared. Except for Peter and John, the Apostles and disciples were discouraged, intimidated and silent. They wandered around valleys or hid in caves, though sometimes they returned to the city to try to get the latest news.

Sister Emmerich saw that Jesus' Mother was contemplating His torments, of which she was interiorly aware, as she walked in the Valley of Jehoshaphat. Accompanying her were Martha, Magdalene, Mary Cleophas, Mary Salome, Mary Marcus, Susanna, Johanna Chusa, Seraphia, and Salome. She was led through the Valley of Kidron and Ophel to the house of Mary Marcus. The Blessed Virgin Mary was speechless with grief, until John appeared and she could question him. He described to her all the events following his departure from the Cenacle. After that, she was conducted by back paths to Martha's house. The crowd around Mt. Zion was overwhelmingly hostile to Jesus, expressing satisfaction at the developments, and even making malicious comments about the Holy Women as they passed, because of their support for Him.

St. John alone among the Evangelists recounted the interrogation of Jesus by Annas before He was taken to Caiaphas for judgment. Jesus was dragged into a large hall which held a tribunal in the palace of Annas. There sat Annas, with twenty-eight councilors, as the head of a committee authorized to examine into false doctrines and hand over persons to be tried by the High Priest. Sister Emmerich saw this scene:

"Jesus stood before Annas pale, exhausted, silent, His head bowed, His garments wet and spattered with mud, His hands fettered, His waist bound by ropes the ends of which the archers held. Annas, that lean, old villain, with scraggy beard, was full of irony and freezing pride. He put on a half-laughing appearance, as if he knew nothing at all of what had taken place, and as if he were greatly surprised to find Jesus in the person of the prisoner brought before him. His address to Him, which however I can not reproduce in his own words, was in sense something like the following: 'Ha, look there! Jesus of Nazareth! It is Thou! Where now are Thy disciples, Thy crowds of followers? Where is Thy kingdom? . . . Thou dost wish to introduce a new doctrine. Who has given Thee authority to teach? Where hast Thou studied? Speak! What is Thy doctrine which throws everything into confusion? Speak! Speak! What is Thy doctrine?'" Jesus would not answer that question, and suggested that Annas call as witnesses those who had heard Him in public. A menial struck Jesus in the face with his armored fist, to the approval of the rabble.

*Note well exactly what allegations were made against Him in response to Annas' call for testimony:*

"'He has said,'" they cried, "'that He is a king, that God is His Father, that the Pharisees are adulterers. He stirs up the people, He heals on the Sabbath-day and by the power of the devil. The inhabitants of Ophel have gone crazy over Him, calling Him their Deliverer, their Prophet. He allows Himself to be called the Son of God. He speaks of Himself as One sent by God. He cries woe to Jerusalem, and alludes in His instructions to the destruction of the city. He observes not the fasts. He goes about with a crowd of followers. He eats with the unclean, with heathens, publicans, and sinners, and saunters around with adulteresses and women of bad character. Just now, outside the gate of Ophel, He said to a man who gave Him a drink that He would give to him the waters of eternal life and that he should never thirst again. He seduces the people with words of double meaning. He squanders the money and property of others. He tells people all kinds of lies about His kingdom and such like things.'"

*What is noteworthy about these charges is that many of them were true, and would have caused concern to pious Jews who were not convinced that He was their Messiah.*

Having heard the allegations without response by Jesus, Annas had a final sarcastic soliloquy to deliver against Jesus: "'Who art Thou? What kind of a king art Thou? What kind of an envoy art Thou? I think that Thou art only an obscure carpenter's son. Or art Thou Elijah who was taken up to heaven in a fiery chariot? They say that he is still living. Thou too canst render Thyself invisible, for Thou hast often disappeared. Or perhaps Thou art Malachias? Thou hast always vaunted Thyself upon this Prophet, and Thou didst love to apply his words to Thyself. It is also reported of him that he had no father, that he was an angel, and that he is not yet dead. What a fine opportunity for an imposter to give himself out for him! Say, what kind of a king art Thou? Thou art greater than Solomon! That too is one of Thy speeches. Come on! I shall not longer withhold from Thee the title of Thy kingdom!'"

Annas then wrote out accusations against Jesus on a strip of parchment. This he put in a hollow gourd and fastened the gourd to a reed as a mock scepter, saying: "'Here, take the scepter of Thy kingdom! In it are enclosed all Thy titles, Thy rights, and Thy honors. Carry this hence to the High Priest, that he may recognize Thy mission and Thy Kingdom, and treat Thee accordingly.'" Jesus was thereupon led to the palace of Caiaphas, passing through the well-lit street filled with mocking enemies.

### Jesus is Tried By the Sanhedrin at Night

The trial of Jesus was held in the judgment hall of Caiaphas' palace. As Sister Emmerich saw the proceeding in her visions, the members of the Sanhedrin were on a raised semicircular platform, with the seat of the High Priest being further elevated. They looked down on the prisoner standing amidst His guards in front of them. The witnesses were to His sides and behind Him. Underground there were prison cells, where Peter and John were imprisoned after the Resurrection, when Peter cured a lame man.[3] In addition to many lamps and torches, an open pit of fire, fueled by peat, provided illumination. According to Sister Emmerich, there was a carnival atmosphere due to the disorder and merriment of the rabble of soldiers, accusers, false witnesses, and women of ill repute who crowded around the fire.

Bravely seeking a way to get into Caiaphas' judgment hall, John and Peter had previously gone to John's acquaintances among messengers attached to the court of the High Priests. The messengers, who were charged with summoning the members of the Sanhedrin, lent the two of them mantles such as they themselves wore; in that way John and Peter were able to gain admittance after they had summoned Nicodemus and Joseph of Arimathea. Jesus saw Peter and John in the crowd there, but refrained from giving them a sign of recognition.

In the interrogation of Jesus, described in the Gospels of Matthew and Mark, He would not respond to the questions of Caiaphas, despite being beaten and goaded with prods. Next came the witnesses against Him, making all the charges which had been raised repeatedly during His ministry, for example His violation of the Sabbath and failure to wash His hands before eating. Surprisingly, His accusers argued among themselves, contradicting one another on points such as whether He had called Himself a king, whether He claimed to be the Son of God, and whether He was illegitimate. Caiaphas and some of the Sanhedrin members continued to taunt Him and demand answers, while their servants struck Him. Finally, Caiaphas took over the interrogation:

"Caiaphas, infuriated by the wrangling of the last two witnesses, rose from his seat, went down a couple of steps to Jesus, and said: 'Answerest Thou nothing to this testimony against Thee?' He was vexed that Jesus would not look at him. At this the archers pulled Our Lord's head back by the hair, and with their fist gave Him blows under His chin. But His glance was still downcast. Caiaphas angrily raised his hands and said in a tone full of rage: 'I adjure Thee by the living God that Thou tell us whether Thou be Christ, the Messiah, the Son of the Most Blessed God.'

"*A solemn silence fell upon the clamoring crowd. Jesus, strengthened by God, said in a voice inexpressibly majestic, a voice that struck awe into all hearts, the voice of the Eternal Word: 'I am! Thou sayest it! And I say to you, soon you shall see the Son of Man sitting on the right hand of the power of God, and coming in the clouds of heaven!'*

"*While Jesus was pronouncing these words, I saw Him shining with light. The heavens were open above Him and, in an inexpressible manner, I saw God, the Father Almighty. I saw the angels and the prayers of the just crying as it were and pleading for Jesus. I saw, besides, the Divinity as if speaking from the Father and from Jesus at the same time: 'If it were possible for Me to suffer, I would do so, but because I am merciful, I have taken flesh in the Person of My Son, in order that the Son of Man may suffer. I am just—but behold! He is carrying the sins of these men, the sins of the whole world!'*

"Caiaphas, as if inspired by hell, seized the hem of his magnificent mantle, clipped it with a knife and, with a whizzing noise, tore it as he exclaimed in a loud voice: 'He has blasphemed! What need have we of further witnesses? Behold now ye have heard the blasphemy, what think ye?' At these words, the whole assembly rose and cried out in a horrid voice: 'He is guilty of death! He is guilty of death!' . . . The High Priest, addressing the executioners, said: 'I deliver this King to you. Render to the Blasphemer the honors due Him!'"

John, with a glance at Jesus, hurried from the scene to bring the terrible news to Jesus' Mother, lest she hear it first from an enemy. And now, the executioners and the rabble resumed their torture of

Jesus. They pulled tufts of His hair out of His head and beard, spit upon Him, struck Him with fists and cudgels, and put on Him various mock crowns which they then proceeded to knock off His head while they railed at Him as a pretend king. By this time, He had been stripped of His long robe, woolen shirt, and scapular, and He stood before them with only His loins covered. They hung around His neck a long iron chain ending in rings studded with sharp points, which dug into His knees as He was forced to walk. Blindfolding Him, they called upon Him to prophesy who was striking Him, and they covered Him with filth, while jeeringly referring to Magdalene's anointment of Him.

### Peter Denies Knowing Jesus

Peter could not bring himself to go with John on his sorrowful errand, and so he remained, weeping, but trying to hide it. Then began his own time of trial, described in all four Gospels. While he was sitting by the fire, his silence and evident distress made him a marked man. First one servant girl and then another accosted him, asking if he were not one of Jesus' disciples, which he vehemently denied out of fear of the consequences. The cock crowed for the first time. Peter then went outside where, according to Sister Emmerich, he came into contact with many disciples, who had not been able to gain entrance to the judgment hall. He tearfully advised them to flee for their safety, which they did. Being totally distraught, Peter could not rest anywhere, and so went back inside again, by the open fire. Once more he attracted attention by his demeanor, leading to the third and final challenge and denial that he knew Jesus.

Running out into the court that surrounding the house, Peter heard the cock crow again. Sister Emmerich saw that, "just at that moment, Jesus was being led from the circular hall and across this court down into a prison under it. He turned toward Peter and cast upon him a glance of mingled pity and sadness. Forcibly and with a terrifying power, the word of Jesus fell upon his heart: 'Before the cock crows twice, thou wilt deny Me thrice!' Worn out with grief and anxiety, Peter had entirely forgotten his presumptuous protestation on the Mount of Olives, rather to die with his Master than to deny Him, as also the warning he had then received from Jesus. But at that glance, the enormity of his fault rose up before him and well-nigh broke his heart. He had sinned. He had sinned against his ill-treated, unjustly condemned Savior, who was silently enduring the most horrible outrages, who had so truly warned him to be on his guard. Filled with remorse and sorrow he covered his head with his mantle and hurried into the other court weeping bitterly. He no longer feared being accosted. To every one he met he would willingly have proclaimed who he was, and how great was the crime that rested on him."

### New Pains Are Inflicted on Jesus' Mother

It was not enough for the Mother of Jesus to suffer through an interior awareness of the tortures of her Son, in the relative safety of the house of Mary Marcus. She was drawn to be close to Him physically, and so John led her and the Holy Women to Caiaphas' palace. Because the women were lamenting as they walked, bystanders noticed them, and, identifying her as Jesus' mother, subjected her to abuse. Her distress was greatly augmented by passing the scene in a courtyard across from the palace, where workmen were constructing the cross for Jesus, and cursing at being forced to do this unexpected additional work at night.

As the women reached the outer court of the palace, Peter happened to rush out, weeping. "It seemed to him that conscience, which the glance of the Son had roused and terrified, stood before Him in the person of the Mother. Oh, how the soul of poor Peter quivered when Mary accosted him with: 'Oh, Simon, what about my Son, what about Jesus?' Unable to speak or to support the glance of Mary's eyes, Peter turned away wringing his hands. But Mary would not desist. . . . In the deepest woe, Peter exclaimed: 'Oh Mother, speak not to me! Thy Son is suffering cruelly. Speak not to me! They have condemned Him to death, and I have shamefully denied Him thrice!' And when John drew near to speak to him, Peter like one crazed by grief hurried out of the court and fled from the city."

### Some Sanhedrin Members Protest the Morning Trial

For the few remaining hours of that night, Jesus was kept in an underground cell, where He prayed for His executioners. At dawn, when the guards were dozing, a ray of light entered the cell and Jesus uttered a prayer—*not of deliverance but of thanksgiving*—thanksgiving that this day essential for our salvation had finally arrived.

The next stage of the Passion was His return to the judgment hall of Caiaphas for a formal trial and condemnation. St. Matthew and St. John do not mention the morning trial, and St. Mark mentions it only in passing; only St. Luke reports the dialogue between Jesus and Caiaphas. The visions of Sister Emmerich provide the explanation for this strange event: under Jewish law, a nighttime trial was *illegal.* Thus, a valid sentence could not have been passed at the proceeding which took place in the middle of the night.

Most of the Sanhedrin members had slept in Caiaphas' palace, and they prepared to act very rapidly when Jesus was brought before them again. According to St. John, "There were many, even among the Sanhedrin, who believed in Him; but they refused to admit it because of the Pharisees, for fear that they might be ejected from the synagogue. They preferred the praise of men to the glory of God." As it was, according to Sister Emmerich, *Nicodemus, Joseph of Arimathea and a few others opposed the overwhelming majority, arguing that further consideration should be postponed until after the feast and that no verdict could be reached on the basis of the contradictory testimony. They failed to derail the conviction,* as she recounted:

"The High Priests and their large party became exasperated by this opposition, and they told their opponents in plain terms that they understood clearly why this trial was so repugnant to them since, perhaps, they themselves were not quite innocent of having taken part in the doctrines of the Galilean. *The High Priests even went so far as to exclude from the Council all those that were in any way well disposed toward Jesus. These members protested against taking any part in its proceedings, left the judgment-hall, and betook themselves to the Temple. From that time forward they never sat in the Council.*"

### Jesus is Condemned by the Sanhedrin Under Caiaphas

"Caiaphas now ordered poor, abused Jesus, who was consumed from want of rest, to be brought from the prison and presented before the Council, so that after the sentence He might without delay be taken to Pilate. . . . Like a poor animal for sacrifice, with blows and mockery, Jesus was dragged by the executioners into the judgment-hall through the rows of soldiers assembled in front of the house. And as through ill-treatment and exhaustion He presented so unsightly an appearance, His only covering being His torn and soiled undergarment, the disgust of His enemies filled them with still greater rage."

Since the proceeding held at night had shown that Jesus was ready to claim that He was the Son of God, Caiaphas was able to establish the apparent blasphemy immediately. He demanded: "'If Thou be the Anointed of the Lord, the Messiah, tell us!'

"Then Jesus raised His head and, with divine forbearance and solemn dignity, said: 'If I shall tell you, you will not believe Me. And if I shall also ask you, you will not answer Me, nor let Me go. But hereafter the Son of Man shall be sitting on the right hand of the power of God.' The members of the Council glanced from one to another and, smiling scornfully, said to Jesus with disdain: 'So then, Thou! Thou art the Son of God?' With the voice of Eternal Truth, Jesus answered: 'Yes, it is as ye say. I am He!'

"At this word of the Lord all looked at one another, saying: 'What need we any further testimony? For we ourselves have heard it from His own mouth.' Then all rose up with abusive words against Jesus, 'the poor, wandering, miserable, destitute creature of low degree, who was their Messiah, and who would one day sit upon the right hand of God!' They ordered the executioners to bind Him anew, to place the chain around His neck, and to lead Him as a condemned criminal to Pilate."

### Was the Sanhedrin's Verdict Justified?

Let us set aside all consideration of evil motives which individual members of the Sanhedrin may have had in putting Jesus on trial. Let us also lay aside the illegality of the nighttime proceedings, for a morning trial was held as well. Finally, let us lay aside the Gospel accounts, and the visions of Sister Emmerich, insofar as they allege that false testimony was procured against Him with bribes—for it does not appear that such testimony had any effect on the outcome. Instead, let us consider only the charge on which He was convicted and the evidence for it.

That charge was that He was blaspheming in claiming to be God's Son,[4] and the evidence was that, in open court, He admitted to making that claim. The only matter left to decide was whether His claim was valid or not.

This point was put forcefully by the esteemed Catholic apologist Father R.L. Bruckberger: "Jesus in fact greatly simplified the problem for the Sanhedrin. No one could have dared hope for a more cooperative accused. His personal claims went far beyond the original accusation. In fact, he left his judges no choice but to condemn him to death for blasphemy or to kneel down before him and adore him."[5]

As for the option of kneeling down and adoring Him, while Nicodemus and Joseph of Arimathea had already done so in private with Him, that would have been anathema to many other pious Jews. Think of Saul of Tarsus—a "Pharisee of Pharisees," and so zealous for the Law that he thought it righteous to persecute the early Christians even unto death. Given what Jesus had openly said and done, Saul and others like him had in good faith (albeit mistakenly) concluded that Jesus was a false prophet, an imposter who was seriously misleading people about God and the Law. As they understood the word of God declared to the Prophet Moses, Jesus had

*made Himself liable to the judgment of death prescribed by God in*
*the Book of Leviticus: "Take the blasphemer outside the camp . . . and*
*let the whole community stone him."*[6]

### The Devil Drives Judas to a Horrible End

Judas had roamed that night through the Valley of Hinnom, the
city dump for all sorts of filth including animal carcasses and ordure,
where fires continually fed upon the refuse. In the morning, he
emerged to hear what was transpiring with Jesus. He learned of the
sentence passed, and also the popular revulsion at his own treachery.
Becoming still more anguished and despairing, he ran to the Temple,
all the while holding the bag of silver pieces so that they would not
jangle as he went. There he found some of the officials in charge, and
sought to undue what could not be undone. Throwing the blood
money away, he rushed out of the city and hanged himself, driven mad
by the Devil, who was whispering curses in his ear. Perhaps also, Judas
remembered what, according to the Gospel of Matthew, Jesus Himself
said at the Last Supper: "Woe to that man by whom the Son of Man
is betrayed. Better for him if he had never been born."

---

[1] Psalm 110, v.7.

[2] Historians know that it was Caiaphas, not Annas, who was the High Priest
at the time Jesus was tried, but St. John's references to Annas (as well as
Caiaphas) being a "High Priest" are understandable in that Annas had been
the High Priest circa 6 A.D.–15 A.D., and had sufficient continuing influence
to have five of his sons appointed to the same position. Caiaphas was his son-
in-law.

[3] Acts 3:1–4:4.

[4] *See* Raymond E. Brown, *The Death of the Messiah* 1:391–97, 534–47.

[5] *See* R.L. Bruckberger, *The History of Jesus Christ* (New York: Viking Press
1965) 306–07 (emphasis added).

[6] Lv 24:10–16 (emphasis added).

# CHAPTER NINETEEN

*Pilate's Prior Intelligence Concerning Jesus*

It is inconceivable that Pilate had heard nothing of Jesus until the day the Jewish leaders turned Him over for trial. We know that the Roman forces were always on alert for an insurrection, and we can be confident that news of the emergence of a possible Messiah, working miracles and speaking of *His* kingdom, would have come to the attention of Pilate early on.

Indeed, Sister Emmerich had a vision of Roman soldiers attending one of Jesus' instructions for the express purpose of reporting on His doctrines. In another vision, she saw Pilate question his officers about Jesus before leaving on a trip to Rome. Pilate's questions were exactly what one would have expected from a man in his position concerned about possible trouble in his absence:

"Pilate asked: 'Is He followed by a crowd? Are they armed?' 'No,' was the answer. 'He goes about with only a few disciples and people of no account whatever, people from the very lowest classes, and sometimes He goes alone. He teaches on the mountains and in the synagogues, cures the sick and gives alms. To hear His instructions, people gather from all quarters often to the number of several thousands.' 'Does He not speak against the Emperor?' asked Pilate. 'No. His teachings are all on the improvement of morals. He inculcates the practice of mercy, and impresses upon His hearers to render to the Emperor that which belongs to him, and to God that which is His. But He often makes mention of a Kingdom that He calls His own, and says that it is near at hand.'

"Thereupon Pilate replied: 'So long as He does not go around working His miracles with soldiers or an armed crowd, there is nothing to be feared from Him. As soon as He leaves a place in which He has performed miracles and goes to another, He will be forgotten and calumniated. Indeed I hear that the Jewish priests themselves are against Him. No danger is to be apprehended from Him. But if He is once seen going about with armed followers, His roving must come to an end!'"

## *Jesus is Brought Before Pilate for the First Time*

As the four Gospels and Sister Emmerich's visions make clear, almost all of the members of the Sanhedrin ultimately concluded that Jesus deserved to die. Then why did they not have Him executed themselves? One scholar's analysis of why they turned Him over to Pilate can be summarized as follows: *first*, Jesus was not convicted of one of the few offenses for which the Jews clearly had the right to execute a criminal without reference to the Roman authorities; *second*, although in some cases the Jewish leaders might expect to get away with stretching their punitive authority, the execution of Jesus by them in Jerusalem at the height of the religious festival would not have escaped Pilate's notice nor been politically wise; *third*, the Jewish leaders had reasons to fear a backlash among the people, and thus found it expedient to let the Romans do their dirty work; and *fourth*, by hanging Jesus on a tree, the Romans would be bringing Jesus under the curse of the Law,[1] further discrediting Him in Jewish eyes.[2]

Caiaphas and Annas led a procession to Pilate's palace, followed by the witnesses, scribes and Pharisees, and then by the soldiers and executioners with Jesus. By this time, He was totally disfigured, clothed in filthy undergarments, and wearing a heavy chain around His neck. It was a reverse image of His triumphal entry into Jerusalem, for this time people jeered Him and put dirty rags, stones and branches in His path, so that He would stumble when He was dragged over them.

Jesus was brought into the praetorium, the part of Pilate's palace used for judgment, very early in the morning. According to Sister Emmerich, Pilate sat on a chair, surrounded by soldiers, on a projecting terrace at the top of a flight of marble steps. Opposite the terrace were stone benches, on which the Jewish leaders seated themselves. The first audience that day began with Pilate addressing them in a haughty manner, sarcastically noting that they had already begun to execute their prisoner. Jesus was then dragged up the steps of the terrace to Pilate, who demanded to know what accusations were brought against Him and suggested that His accusers judge Him according to their own law, which they refused to do.

## *Were the Charges Against Jesus Valid?*

Sister Emmerich heard them bring three charges against Jesus, the first of which was itself a collection of several different points. All were worded to make it appear that Jesus was acting against the Emperor. "The first charge they alleged was: 'Jesus is a seducer of the people, a disturber of the peace, an agitator,' and then they brought forth some witnesses to substantiate that point. Next they said: 'He goes about holding great meetings, breaking the Sabbath, and healing on the Sabbath.' Here Pilate interrupted them scornfully: 'It is easily seen that none of you were sick, else you would not be scandalized at healing on the Sabbath.' They continued: 'He seduces the people by horrible teaching, for He says that to have eternal life, they must eat His Flesh and Blood.' Pilate was provoked at the furious hate with which they uttered this charge. He glanced at his officers and with a smile said sharply to the Jews: 'It would almost appear that you yourselves are following His teaching and are aiming at eternal life, since you, too, seem so desirous of eating His Flesh and His Blood.'"

*This first omnibus charge was not an unreasonable one. Jesus did heal on the Sabbath and teach things which agitated the populace, ranging from His denunciations of the pillars of the religious establishment, to prophecies of the coming destruction of the Temple and Jerusalem, to the doctrine that—as His accusers correctly said— in order to have eternal life, it was necessary to eat His flesh and blood. If Jesus did not have a divine mission to say and do what He did, His accusers were right to brand Him as a disturber of the peace and a seducer, propagating false doctrines and leading people away from their religion.*

"Their second accusation was: 'Jesus stirs up the people not to pay tribute to the Emperor.'" *This was clearly a false charge, for Jesus was well known for counseling the people to "render unto Caesar what is Caesar's" and pay their taxes. But, it caused no harm, for, according to Sister Emmerich, "Pilate interrupted them angrily. As one whose office it was to know about such things, he retorted with emphasis: 'That is a great lie! I know better than that!'*

"Then the Jews shouted out their third accusation: 'Let it be so! This Man of low, obscure and doubtful origin, puts Himself at the head of a large party and cries woe to Jerusalem. He scatters also among the people parables of double meaning of a king who is preparing a wedding feast for his son. The people gathered in great crowds around Him on a mountain, and once they wanted to make Him king; but it was sooner than He wished, and so He hid Himself. During the last few days He came forward more boldly. He made a tumultuous entrance into Jerusalem, causing regal honors to be shown Him while the people by His order cried 'Hosanna to the Son of David! Blessed be the reign of our Father David which is now come!' — Besides this, He teaches that He is the Christ, the Anointed of the Lord, the Messiah, the promised King of the Jews, and allows Himself so to be called.'"

*That charge was true!*

Pilate decided to have Jesus brought inside, where he could interrogate Him privately: was He indeed the King of the Jews? According to the Gospel of John, Jesus did not deny it, though He answered in somewhat elliptical fashion—but He said expressly that His kingdom was not of this world, as set forth in the Gospel of John. And He also told Pilate: *"You would have no power over me whatever unless it were given you from above. That is why he who handed me over to you is guilty of the greater sin."*

Sister Emmerich then saw events taking place as reported by St. Luke. Pilate, perceiving no threat to the Emperor from this wretched prisoner, went out and announced that he had found no case against Jesus. That threw His accusers into a frenzy, and they poured out accusations against Him, but He did not deign to answer. When, in their tirade, His accusers mentioned that He had spread His doctrine from Galilee to Jerusalem, Pilate saw an opportunity to get rid of the whole matter conveniently. He asked them whether Jesus was from Galilee—and thus a subject of Herod. As that was the case, Pilate ordered that He be taken to Herod for judgment. Pilate thought that this would make it unnecessary for himself to pass judgment, and also would please Herod, with whom he had strained relations.

## Pontius Pilate's Superstitions

While Jesus was being delivered to Herod, Pilate met with his wife, Claudia Procla. She was greatly agitated by dreams which she had had of the life of Jesus the night before. She begged him to do no harm to Jesus, and he agreed, giving her a pledge of his word. As Sister Emmerich saw, Pilate had serious character flaws, which ultimately led him to disregard his wife's entreaties and break his promise:

"I saw Pilate as a crack-brained, covetous, proud, vacillating man, with a great fund of meanness in his character. He was deterred by no high fear of God from working out his own ends, could give himself to the meanest actions, and at the same time practiced the lowest, the most dastardly kind of superstitious idolatry and divination when he found himself in any difficulty. So now, off he hurried to his gods, before whom in a retired apartment of his house he burned incense and demanded of them all kinds of signs. He afterward watched the sacred chickens eating, and Satan whispered to him sometimes one thing, sometimes another."

*"At one time he thought that Jesus ought to be released as innocent; again, he feared that his own gods would take vengeance on him if he saved the life of a man who exercised so singular an*

*influence upon him that he believed him some kind of a demigod, for Jesus might do much harm to his divinities. 'Perhaps,' thought he, 'He is indeed a kind of Jewish god. There are so many Prophecies that point to a king of the Jews who shall conquer all things. Kings from the star worshippers of the East have already been here seeking such a king in this country. He might, perhaps, elevate Himself above my gods and my Emperor, and so I should have much to answer for, if He does not die. Perhaps His death would be a triumph for my gods.'"[3]*

### Herod Refuses to Judge Jesus

At last, Herod had the opportunity he desired to see Jesus, of whom He had heard so much. But, Jesus presented such a wretched appearance that He hardly looked like a wonder worker. Herod had Jesus cleaned up somewhat, and referred to Jesus' captors as butchers who had begun their work before time.

Herod began by feigning good nature, and posing all sorts of questions to Jesus about the accusations and His background—including asking whether He was the one whom the Three Kings had come to see. Jesus remained silent, looking at the ground.

Then, Herod tried sarcasm, to no avail. Jesus' accusers renewed their charges, and brought up that Jesus had called Herod a "fox." *To their consternation, Herod did not want to condemn Jesus. This was so for a number of reasons: his own guilt at murdering John the Baptist; his dislike of the High Priests, who had refused to condone his adultery; and, primarily, his perception that it would not be politically astute to condemn Jesus in view of Pilate's declaration that he could not find a case against Him.*

Ultimately Herod commanded: "Take this fool away, and show the honor due to so ridiculous a king. He is more fool than malefactor." Thereupon, Jesus was led outside and again severely maltreated, as Sister Emmerich saw:

"When they led Him out into the court, a soldier brought from the lodge at the gate a large white sack in which cotton had been packed. They cut a hole in the bottom of the sack and, amid shouts of derisive laughter from all present, threw it over Jesus' head. It hung in wide folds over His feet. Another soldier laid a red rag like a collar around His neck. And now they bowed before Him, pushed Him here and there, insulted Him, spat upon Him, struck Him in the face, because He had refused to answer their king, and rendered Him a thousand acts of mock homage.

"They threw filth upon Him, pulled Him about as if He were dancing, forced Him in the wide, trailing mantle of derision, to fall to the earth, and dragged Him through a gutter which ran around the court the whole length of the buildings, so that His sacred head struck against the pillars and stones at the corners." The vicious sport had to be ended, as the enemies of Jesus wanted Him executed before the Passover began. They led Jesus back to Pilate by a different route, to expose His degradation to still more bystanders, whom they encouraged to vilify Him as He passed.

### What Turned the Crowd Against Jesus?

"When the High Priests and enemies of Jesus saw that Herod would in no way comply with their wishes, they dispatched some of their number with money to Acre, a section of the city where at present many Pharisees were stopping. The messengers were directed to summon them to be in attendance at once with all their people in the vicinity of Pilate's palace. A large sum of money was put into the hands of these Pharisees for distribution among the people as bribes, that with furious and vehement clamoring they might demand Jesus' death." "*Other messengers were sent to spread among the people threats of God's vengeance if they did not insist upon the death of this blasphemer. They gave out the report also that if Jesus were not put to death, He would go over to the Romans, that this was what He meant by that kingdom of which He had so constantly spoken. Then, indeed, would the Jews be utterly ruined. On other sides, they spread the report that Herod had condemned Jesus, but that the people must express their will on the subject, that His followers were to be feared, for if Jesus were freed in any way, the feast would be altogether upset, and then would the Romans and His followers unite in taking vengeance. Thus were scattered abroad confused and alarming rumors in order to rouse and exasperate the populace.*"

### The Crowd Chooses Barrabas

Back from Herod's palace, Jesus was again dragged and kicked up the marble steps of the praetorium, striking His head several times and staining the steps with His blood. According to St. Luke, Pilate spoke: "You have brought this Man before me as one who subverts the people. I have examined Him in your presence and have no charge against Him arising from your allegations. Neither has Herod, who therefore has sent Him back to us; obviously this man has done nothing that calls for death. Therefore I mean to release him, once I have taught him a lesson."

*Note that Pilate came to the same conclusion on the merits of the case as the Roman procurator Albinus did thirty years later, when he had to deal with Jesus the Son of Ananus, a disturber of the peace at that time—Jesus should be scourged to teach Him a lesson, but then let go.*

The crowd shouted loudly its disapproval. In the face of that opposition, Pilate backed off and tried a slightly different tack: he offered to release either Barrabas or Jesus as a traditional act of clemency, hoping that the crowd would choose Jesus. According to Sister Emmerich, Barrabas had committed murder in an insurrection, and was given to sorcery, which had involved his cutting open the womb of a pregnant woman. Before the crowd could answer, Pilate was momentarily called aside by one of his wife's servants, who had been sent to remind him of the pledge he had made to her earlier that morning. Pilate refused to give any assurance, and turned back to hear the crowd's answer: a thunderous acclamation in favor of Barrabas.

Not wanting to accept that decision, Pilate tried to reason with them, as described in the Synoptic Gospels, but they loudly demanded that he crucify Jesus. Pilate ordered Jesus to be scourged—but only as a temporizing step, for he was not yet prepared to have Him crucified.

## Jesus is Inhumanly Scourged

The executioners were the vilest dregs of mankind, criminals themselves, who were used for this purpose because of their depravity. Sister Emmerich recounted in great detail the ghastly procedure as Jesus stood stretched against the whipping post, bound hand and foot:

"The first rods, or scourges, that they used looked as if made of flexible white wood or they might have been bunches of ox sinews, or strips of hard, white leather. Our Lord and Savior, the Son of God, true God and true Man, quivered and writhed like a poor worm under the strokes of the criminals' rods. He cried in a suppressed voice, and a clear, sweet sounding wailing, like a loving prayer under excruciating torture, formed a touching accompaniment to the hissing strokes of His tormentors.

"Now and then the cries of the populace and the Pharisees mingled with those pitiful, holy, blessed, plaintive tones like frightful peals of thunder from an angry storm cloud. Many voices cried out together: 'Away with Him! Crucify Him!'—for Pilate was still negotiating with the people. The uproar was so great that, when he wanted to utter a few words, silence had to be enforced by the flourish of a trumpet. At such moments could be heard the strokes of the rods, the moans of Jesus, the blasphemy of the executioners, and the bleating of the Paschal lambs, which were being washed in the pool near the sheep-gate to the east.

"Some executioners of the High Priests went up to the scourgers and slipped them money, and a large jug of thick, red juice was brought to them, from which they guzzled until they became perfectly furious from intoxication. They had been at work about a quarter of an hour, when they ceased to strike, and joined two of the others in drinking. Jesus' body was livid, brown, blue, and red, and entirely covered with swollen cuts. His sacred blood was running down on the ground. He trembled and shuddered. Derision and mockery assailed Him on all sides.

"The second pair of scourgers now fell upon Jesus with fresh fury. They made use of different rods, rough, as if set with thorns, and here and there provided with knots and splinters. Under their furious blows, the swollen welts on Jesus' sacred body were torn and rent, His blood spurted around so that the arms of His tormentors were sprinkled with it. Jesus moaned and prayed and shuddered in His agony.

"The last two scourgers struck Jesus with whips consisting of small chains, or straps, fastened to an iron handle, the ends furnished with iron points, or hooks. They tore off whole pieces of skin and flesh from His ribs. Oh, who can describe the awful barbarity of that spectacle!" This last instrument of torture was the *flagrum taxolatum*—a dreaded whip, which had dumbbell shaped metal tips attached to short, broad lashes, in order to rip into the victim's flesh. *Those who regard the Shroud of Turin as authentic, or at least as a miraculously created, authentic depiction of the scourging Jesus suffered, believe that He was lashed with more than a hundred strokes of this whip—enough to cause death all by itself.*

According to Sister Emmerich, the executioners unbound Him, turned Him face out, and rebound Him to the pillar, so that they could work over His front side. Even after three quarters of an hour, they were continuing to beat Him, when a well disposed man ran out of the crowd and, brandishing a knife, cut Him down. Jesus sank down unconscious on the ground wet with His own blood.

## Jesus is Crowned With Thorns

Sister Emmerich saw the crowning with thorns take place next in the inner court of the guardhouse: "The mob at first crowded in eagerly, but was soon displaced by the thousand Roman soldiers who surrounded the building. They stood in rank and order, jeering and laughing, thereby giving to Jesus' tormentors new inducement to multiply His sufferings. . . . There was a hole in the middle of the court, and to this they had rolled the base of an old column. . . . On that base they placed a low, round stool with an upright at the back by which to raise it, and maliciously covered it with sharp stones and potsherds.

"Once more they tore Jesus' clothing from His wounded body, and threw over Him instead an old, red, military cloak tattered and so short that it did not reach to the knees. Shreds of yellow tassels hung on it here and there. It was kept in a corner of the executioners' room and used to throw around criminals after their scourging, either to dry the blood or to turn them into derision. Now they dragged Jesus to the stool covered with stones and potsherds, and violently forced His wounded, naked body down upon them. Then they put upon Him the crown of thorns.

"It was two hands high, thick, skillfully plaited with a projecting edge on top. They laid it like a binder round His brow and fastened it tightly in the back; thus forming it into a crown. It was skillfully woven from thorn branches three fingers thick, the thorns of which grew straight out. In plaiting the crown, as many of them as possible had been designedly pressed inward. There were three kinds of thorns, such as with us are called buckthorn, blackthorn, and hawthorn. The projecting edge on top was formed of one kind, which we call blackberry, and it was by this the torturer fastened it on and moved it in order to produce new sufferings.

"Next they placed in Jesus' hand a thick reed with a tufted top. All this was done with mock solemnity, as if they were really crowning Him king. Then they snatched the reed from His hand and with it struck the crown violently, until His eyes filled with blood. They bent the knee before Him, stuck out their tongue at Him, struck and spat in His face, and cried out: 'Hail, King of the Jews!' With shouts of mocking laughter, they upset Him along with the stool, in order to force him violently down upon it again.

"Ah! His thirst was horrible, for He was consumed with the fever of His wounds, the laceration caused by the inhuman scourging. He quivered. The flesh on His sides was in many places torn even to the ribs. His tongue contracted convulsively. Only the sacred blood trickling down from His head laved, as it were in pity, His parched lips which hung languishingly open. Those horrible monsters seeing this, turned His mouth into a receptacle for their own disgusting filth. Jesus underwent this maltreatment for about half an hour, during which time the cohort surrounding the praetorium in rank and order, kept up an uninterrupted jeering and laughing."

### Ecce Homo!

Jesus was dragged back to where Pilate, the High Priests, and the mob had been waiting. Once more, Pilate sought to release Jesus:

"And now they again led Jesus, the crown of thorns upon His head, the mock-scepter in His fettered hands, the purple mantle thrown around Him, into Pilate's palace. He was unrecognizable, on account of the blood that filled His eyes and ran down into His mouth and beard. His body, covered with swollen welts and wounds, resembled a cloth dipped in blood, and His gait was bowed down and tottering. The mantle was so short that He had to stoop in order to cover Himself with it, for at the crowning, they had again torn off all His clothing. . . . Up the steps they dragged Him again, and Pilate stepped to the front of the balcony.

"The trumpet sounded to command attention, for Pilate was going to speak. Addressing the High Priests and the people, he said: 'Behold! I bring Him forth to you, that you may know that I find no cause in Him!' Then Jesus was led forward by the executioners to the front of the balcony where Pilate was standing, so that He could be seen by all the people in the forum. Oh, what a terrible, heart rending spectacle! Silence, awful and gloomy, fell upon the multitude as the inhumanly treated Jesus, the sacred, martyrized figure of the Son of God, covered with blood and wounds, wearing the frightful crown of thorns, appeared and, from His eyes swimming in blood, cast a glance upon the surging crowd! Near by stood Pilate, pointing to Him with his finger and crying to the Jews: 'Behold the Man!'"

### Did Pilate Know "the Truth?"

Pilate once more declared that he found no fault with Jesus, and once more His accusers and the inflamed crowd demanded His death—this time arousing Pilate's superstitious anxiety by calling out that Jesus had "made Himself a Son of God." *Jesus had previously told him that "the reason why I came into the world is to testify to the truth," but Pilate snorted, "Truth—what does that mean?," and turned away without waiting for an answer.* Yet, now Pilate had Jesus brought inside for another interrogation. Jesus would not give him an answer to the question of where He had come from. At this moment, a messenger from Pilate's wife returned to remind him of the pledge he had given her, but he dismissed the messenger without any reassurance. Again Pilate went before the people to report that he found Jesus guiltless. *The crowd would not accept this judgment, for their leaders had spread yet a new falsehood, that if Jesus were set free, He would unite with the Romans and they all would be put to death.*

And so, Pilate retreated to confront Jesus. *Sister Emmerich then heard a dialogue not recorded by any of the Evangelists.* It was an important interchange, for Pilate had pointed out "I am no Jew," and thus he did not have the background which members of the Sanhedrin had in judging Jesus:

*"When alone with Him, he glanced at Him almost in fear, and thought in a confused sort of a way: 'What if this Man should indeed be a god!'—and then with an oath he at once began adjuring Jesus to say whether He was a god and not a human being, whether He was that king promised to the Jews. How far did His kingdom extend? To what rank did His divinity, belong? and ended by declaring that, if Jesus would answer his questions, he would set Him free. What Jesus said to Pilate in answer, I can repeat only in substance, not in words. The Lord spoke words of terrible import. He gave Pilate to understand what kind of a king He was, over what kind of a Kingdom He reigned, and what was the truth, for He told him the truth. He laid before him the abominable state of his own conscience, foretold the fate in store for him, exile in misery and a horrible end. He told him moreover that He would one day come to pass sentence upon him in just judgment."*

### Pilate, the Crowd, and Blood Guilt

Yet again Pilate appeared publicly and, for the last time declared his intention to release the accused. But, the leaders of the mob had finally hit upon the way to force Pilate to condemn Jesus, namely, by claiming that Pilate's failure to do so would be an act of disloyalty to Caesar: "If thou release this man, thou art not Caesar's friend, for whosoever maketh himself a king, speaketh against Caesar!" And, they threatened to denounce Pilate to Caesar as a disturber of their feast.

It was at this point that Pilate had a servant bring a vase of water and pour it over his hands into a basin, while he cried out: "I am innocent of the blood of this just Man! Look ye to it!" According to the Gospel of Matthew: "The whole people said in reply: 'Let his blood be on us and our children.'" Writing about this passage, a commentator noted "its tragic history in inflaming Christian hatred for Jews. While the whole Passion Narrative has been (mis)used in anti-Jewish ways, this text . . . has had a special role. It has been treated as if it were a self-curse by which the Jewish people brought down on themselves Jesus' blood for all times (a view correctly rejected)."[4]

To begin with, "the whole people" were not there—nor were those who were there representative of them, because only His enemies had been summoned, and people were bribed and misled with false rumors. Second, even by the standard announced in the Old Testament, God's *punishment* of future generations for the acts of their fathers was limited—it was His *mercy* that continued at length.

> "I, the Lord, am a jealous God, inflicting punishment for their fathers' wickedness on the children of those who hate me, *down to the third and fourth generation*, but bestowing mercy *down to the thousandth generation*, on the children of those who love me and keep my commandments."[5]

Consider also that, in His preaching, according to the Gospels of Matthew and Luke, Jesus charged the Pharisees of *"this generation"* with "the blood of all the prophets shed since the foundation of the world." *He did not charge them and their posterity.* Moreover, we know that Jesus, on the Cross, asked His Father to forgive the people who were persecuting Him, "for they know not what they do."

The head of His Church, Peter, brought the same message to His countrymen in Jerusalem after the Resurrection, and St. Paul confirmed that grace was indeed being bestowed to wipe out sin, confessing that: "I was once a blasphemer and a persecutor and an arrogant man, but I have been mercifully treated because I acted out of ignorance in my unbelief."[6] Consequently, as noted in the first chapter, the Catholic Church is clearly right in at last declaring unequivocally that responsibility for the execution of Jesus did not extend to other Jews of different times and places.

### "I also condemn Jesus of Nazareth"

Sister Emmerich next saw the preparations for the formal sentencing of Jesus. Pilate donned his ceremonial robes and crown, and, surrounded by soldiers and scribes, left his palace to walk to the forum, where, according to Sister Emmerich, "opposite the scourging place, there was a high, beautifully constructed judgment seat. Only when delivered from that seat had the sentence full weight. It was called Gabbatha. It consisted of a circular balcony, and up to it there were several flights of steps. It contained a seat for Pilate and behind it a bench for others connected with the tribunal.

"The balcony was surrounded and the steps occupied by soldiers. Many of the Pharisees had already left the palace and gone to the Temple. Only Annas, Caiaphas, and about twenty-eight others went at once to the judgment seat in the forum, while Pilate was putting on his robes of ceremony. . . . And now Jesus in the scarlet cloak, the crown of thorns upon His head, His hands bound, was led by the soldiers and executioners through the mocking crowd and placed between the two murderers in front of the judgment seat.

"From this seat of state Pilate once more said aloud to the enemies of Jesus: 'Behold there your King!' But they yelled: 'Away, away with this Man! Crucify Him!'—'Shall I crucify your King?' said Pilate. 'We have no king but Caesar!' responded the High Priests. From that moment Pilate spoke no word for nor with Jesus. He began the sentence of condemnation. The two thieves had been already sentenced to the cross, but their execution, at the request of the High Priests, had been postponed till today. They thought to outrage Jesus the more, by having Him crucified with two infamous murderers."

Sister Emmerich described the sentencing as follows: "Pilate first spoke some words in which with high sounding titles he named the Emperor Claudius Tiberius. Then he set forth the accusation against Jesus; that, as a seditious character, a disturber and violator of the Jewish laws, who had allowed Himself to be called the Son of God and the King of the Jews, He had been sentenced to death by the High Priests, and by the unanimous voice of the people given over to be crucified. Furthermore Pilate, that iniquitous judge, who had in these last hours so frequently and publicly asserted the innocence of Jesus, now proclaimed that he found the sentence of the High Priests just, and ended with the words: 'I also condemn Jesus of Nazareth, King of the Jews, to be nailed to the cross.' Then he ordered the executioners to bring the cross."

Sister Emmerich saw Pilate writing out the sentence of death—but in doing so, materially changing the words he had spoken, so that the writing better accorded with his previous failure to find guilt: "'Urged by the High Priests, and the Sanhedrin, and fearing an insurrection of the people who accuse Jesus of Nazareth of sedition, blasphemy, and infraction of the laws, and who demand that He should be put to death, I have (though indeed without being able to substantiate their accusations) delivered Him to be crucified along with two other condemned criminals whose execution was postponed through the influence of the High Priests because they wanted Jesus to suffer with them. I have condemned Jesus because I do not wish to be accused to the Emperor as an unjust judge of the Jews and as an abettor of insurrections; and I have condemned Him as a criminal who has acted against the laws, and whose death has been violently demanded by the Jews.'"[7]

The sentence, as written, infuriated the High Priests, and they were still more incensed at what Pilate wrote in varnish on a little board, to be placed over Jesus' head, the inscription identifying Him as "King of the Jews." They protested that it should read instead, "This man *claimed* to be King of the Jews," but Pilate had had enough of them and dismissed them.

[1] Dt 21:23.
[2] *See* Raymond E. Brown, *The Death of the Messiah* 1:371–72. Brown speculated that offenses which the Jews could punish by death were certain offenses committed inside the Temple and, perhaps, adultery. *Ibid.*
[3] A survey of hundreds of Pilate legends, and the factual setting of his times, was presented in an especially engaging manner by Ann Wroe in her book, *Pontius Pilate* (New York: Random House 1999); however, she apparently was not acquainted with the visions of Anne Catherine Emmerich.
[4] *See* Raymond E. Brown, *The Death of the Messiah* 1:831.
[5] Ex 20:5–6.
[6] 1 Tm 1:12–14.
[7] This text differs in substance from the text of an apocryphal letter from Pilate to the Emperor [wrongly identified in it as Claudius] about Jesus, except that in both, Pilate attributes his decision to the request of the Jewish leaders. *See* Edgar Hennecke, *New Testament Apocrypha* 1:477–78.

# CHAPTER TWENTY

*Devotion to the Way of the Cross*

The oldest Christian devotion, begun by the Blessed Virgin Mary while Jesus' blood was still fresh on the ground, consists of walking the "Way of the Cross"—the route traversed by Jesus from the place where He was judged, to the site of His crucifixion, and on to the tomb where He was buried. According to Sister Emmerich's visions, immediately after His death it was such a popular devotion that the religious authorities undertook vigorous measures to suppress it by making the route impassable at points. Of course, when Jerusalem was destroyed thirty-odd years later, it became impossible to retrace His steps exactly.

After Constantine became Emperor, and pilgrimages to the Holy Land became common, pilgrims on the night of Holy Thursday would walk from Gesthemane to Calvary. Changes in the route were made from time to time over the centuries thereafter, and the "stations," where pilgrims would stop to meditate on particular events such as His falls, were varied in number and what they represented. Replicas of the Way of the Cross were created in Europe, and in the 16th century, a meditational book with 12 stations was published, so that it was possible to undertake this devotion wherever one was. The number of Stations of the Cross was standardized at 14 by Pope Clement XII. In the 19th century it became customary for parish churches to have a set of these stations, although some now have a fifteenth station, marking Jesus' Resurrection.[1]

Many of the foremost religious figures of our time, such as Pope John Paul II, St. Pio (Padre Pio), St. Escrivá, Mother Teresa of Calcutta, and Bishop Fulton Sheen, have written booklets on this devotion.[2] The stations which they cover are as follows:

I    Jesus is Condemned to Death
II   Jesus Takes Up His Cross
III  Jesus Falls the First Time
IV  Jesus Meets His Blessed Mother
V    Simon of Cyrene Helps Jesus to Carry the Cross

The Gospels speak of the events commemorated in only some of these stations—I, II, V, VIII, X, XI, XII, and XIV—but the other events are in themselves highly probable, and were seen by Sister Emmerich in her mystical visions.

### Jesus Embraces His Cross

According to Sister Emmerich, after Pilate pronounced judgment, the executioners tore the crown of thorns off Jesus' head and the red cloak from His back, and gave Him back His own clothing. A girdle with ropes was fastened around Him, so that He could be dragged to Calvary. Each thief was made to carry the cross piece (*patibulum*)—not the trunk (*stipes*)—of his own cross, across his back, as was customary in executions, while Jesus was uniquely given a crushing burden: the long trunk itself, with two arms bound to it.[3] Jesus immediately knelt down and embraced the Cross, kissing it, and saying a prayer of thanksgiving for the coming Redemption. The Cross was then put on His right shoulder, but He was so weak He could not have lifted the weight and stood up were it not for angelic help.

### The Heartbreaking Procession Begins

Sister Emmerich gave the following description of the heartbreaking procession, headed by Pilate himself, surrounded by a troop of cavalry and 300 foot soldiers. "A trumpeter sounded his trumpet at every street corner and proclaimed the execution. Some paces behind him came a crowd of boys and other rude fellows, carrying drink, cords, nails, wedges, and baskets of tools of all kinds, while sturdy servant men bore poles, ladders, and the trunks belonging to the crosses of the thieves. Then followed some of the mounted Pharisees, after whom came a lad bearing on his breast the inscription Pilate had written for the cross. The crown of thorns . . . was taken from Christ's head and placed on the end of a pole, which this lad now carried over his shoulder.

"And next came Our Lord and Redeemer bowed down under the heavy weight of the cross, bruised, torn with scourges, exhausted, and tottering. Since the Last Supper of the preceding evening without food, drink, and sleep, under continual ill-treatment that might of itself have ended in death, consumed by loss of blood, wounds, fever, thirst, and unutterable interior pain and horror, Jesus walked with tottering steps, His back bent low, His feet naked and bleeding. With His right hand He grasped the heavy load on His right shoulder, and with the left He wearily tried to raise the flowing garment constantly impeding His uncertain steps. The four executioners held at some distance the cords fastened to His fetter-girdle. The two in front dragged Him forward, while the two behind urged Him on. In this way He was not sure of one step, and the tugging cords constantly prevented His lifting His robe."

### Jesus Falls for the First Time

The first street through which the procession went was a narrow alley, filled with refuse and filth from the adjoining houses. As Jesus passed, the residents hurled still more garbage on Him, and little children, encouraged by the adults, threw stones. At the end of the alley, where it turned, Jesus collapsed. Sister Emmerich described His continuing agony:

"The drivers with curses, pulled Him and kicked Him. This brought the procession to a halt, and a tumult arose around Jesus. In vain, did He stretch out His hand for some one to help Him. 'Ah! it will soon be over!' He exclaimed, and continued to pray. The Pharisees yelled: 'Up! Raise Him up! otherwise He'll die in our hands.' Here and there on the wayside weeping women might be seen and children whimpering from fear. With the aid of supernatural help, Jesus raised His head, and the terrible, the diabolical wretches, instead of alleviating His sufferings, put the crown of thorns again upon Him. When at last with all kinds of ill-treatment, they dragged Him up again, they laid the cross once more upon His shoulder. And now with the greatest difficulty He had to hang His poor head, racked with thorns, to one side in order to be able to carry His heavy load on His shoulder, for the crown was broad. Thus Jesus tottered with increased torture up the steep and gradually widening street."

### The Mother of the Redeemer is Jeered

Jesus' Mother was in the forum to hear the awful sentence pronounced on her Son. Desiring to get closer to Him, she begged John to take her to where the procession would pass. They went through an outer court of Caiaphas' palace, to a vantage point. But, hearing the trumpet and other approaching tumult, she asked John whether she should stay. He replied in words which explain his own steadfastness at the foot of the Cross: "If thou does not remain, it will always be to thee a cruel regret." Sister Emmerich saw the meeting of Jesus and His Mother, which was not described by any of the Evangelists, and the taunting she endured:

*"And now came on the executioner's servants, insolent and triumphant, with their instruments of torture, at sight of which the Blessed Mother trembled, sobbed, and wrung her hands. One of the men said to the bystanders: 'Who is that woman in such distress?'— and someone answered: 'She is the Mother of the Galilean.' When the miscreants heard this, they jeered at the sorrowing Mother in words of scorn, pointed at her with their fingers; and one of the base wretches, snatching up the nails intended for the crucifixion, held them up mockingly, before her face.* Wringing her hands, she gazed upon Jesus and, in her anguish, leaned for support against one of the pillars of the gate. She was pale as a corpse, her lips livid. The Pharisees came riding forward, then came the boy with the inscription—and oh! the Son of God, her own Son, the Holy One, the Redeemer!"

### Jesus Falls a Second Time

"Tottering, bowed down, His thorn-crowned head painfully bent over to one shoulder on account of the heavy cross He was carrying, Jesus staggered on. The executioners pulled Him forward with the ropes. His face was pale, wounded, and blood-stained, His beard pointed and matted with blood. From His sunken eyes full of blood He cast from under the tangled and twisted thorns of His crown, frightful to behold, a look full of earnest tenderness upon His afflicted Mother, and for the second time tottered under the weight of the cross and sank on His hands and knees to the ground."

### "My Son!"— "My Mother!"

"The most sorrowful Mother, in the vehemence of her love and anguish, saw neither soldiers nor executioners, saw only her beloved, suffering, maltreated Son. Wringing her hands, she sprang over the couple of steps between the gateway and the executioners in advance, and rushing to Jesus, fell on her knees with her arms around Him. I heard, but I know not whether spoken with the lips, or in spirit, the words: 'My Son!'— 'My Mother!'"

### Simon the Cyrene is Forced to Help Carry the Cross

On the procession went, until Jesus tripped over a stepping stone where three streets met, and it became obvious even to the Pharisees that He lacked the strength to rise and carry on. Determined that He should not die before He was nailed to the Cross, they looked around for someone they could force to assist Him, and they spotted Simon the Cyrene. They were able to misuse Simon in this way because he was a pagan day-laborer, about 40 years old, who was in town to work on gardens at the time of the feast. They saw him approach with a bundle of shoots in his arms, followed by his three sons. He resisted being impressed, but had no choice. Walking close behind Jesus, he greatly lightened the load.

### Seraphia's Veil is Imprinted With Jesus' Face

The Gospels do not record that a woman, in the middle of Jesus' sad procession, gave Him the refreshment of wiping His face with her veil, receiving in return the imprint of His sacred face on the cloth. However, that event is celebrated with one of the stations on the Way of the Cross. There has been criticism that, if the event actually occurred, the woman's name surely was not Veronica, for that is only a symbolic name, meaning true (vera) image (icona). Sister Emmerich provided the explanation that her name was really Seraphia, but that she was thereafter known as Veronica as the result of that miraculous event. Seraphia, a majestic woman over 50 years old, was a cousin of John the Baptist, and was acquainted with the Holy Family.

She had married late in life one of the Sanhedrin members, Sirach. Initially, he was against Jesus, and forbade her from following Him. Eventually, under the influence of Nicodemus and Joseph of Arimathea, he became lenient, and finally, at the trial before Caiaphas, he had declared for Jesus and left the Sanhedrin. Their house lay right on the route of the procession, and Sister Emmerich saw the imprinting of Jesus' face take place when she pressed her way through the crowd to Jesus' side and handed Him the cloth.

Supposedly, the very same veil, which had been acquired by the Vatican, was stolen from it in the 17th century, and now is kept in the Capuchin friary in Manoppello, Italy. Its authenticity has not been established, but microscopic inspection has revealed that the fibers are not colored, nor was anything painted on them. Also, the face on the veil appears to be superimposable on the face which appears on the Shroud of Turin.[4]

*Jesus Cries "Woe!" to Jerusalem but Comforts the Sorrowing Women*
Jesus fell for the fourth time by the gate where Pilate, with most
of the soldiers, turned back. Here it was that Jesus cried "Woe! Woe,
Jerusalem! How often would I have gathered together thy children as
a hen doth gather her chickens under her wings, and thou dost cast
me so cruelly out of thy gate!"[5] Outside the gate stood a post with a
board on which the death sentence of the three condemned men had
been written. Nearby were a group of women who showed their
compassion for Him by weeping and extending their scarves. He fell
again, and addressed to them the words recounted by St. Luke,
prophesying that they would one day weep over themselves and their
children. He also said: "Your tears shall be rewarded. Henceforth ye
shall tread another path." Jesus was then forced up the rough path
outside the wall, to Calvary, falling twice more. At the top, Simon the
Cyrene, transformed in spirit, wanted to assist Him, but was driven
away; he soon joined the disciples.

*The "Place of the Skull"*
Sister Emmerich had a vision which explained how the place of
Christ's execution had come to be named the "place of the skull." She
saw, in a much earlier time, a companion of the Prophet Elijah enter
one of the caves on Mount Calvary and, finding a stone coffin, remove
a skull, with some yellow hair still on it; an angel appeared, warning
him not to remove the skull as it was that of Adam.

According to her, in the time of Jesus, Golgotha was a circular
spot surrounded by a low earthen berm, in which had been cut five
entrances. It was surrounded by mounted Pharisees who had come to
make sure that Jesus was truly crucified. Also, there were a hundred
soldiers, plus workmen and boys employed in the executions, and a
crowd of onlookers.

Just as she had previously traversed the way between Gesthemane
and Caiaphas' palace, the Blessed Virgin Mary now followed in Jesus'
footsteps from the place of judgment to Golgotha, conducted by John
and about fifteen of the Holy Women. She was interiorly guided, and
could point out all the places where He had especially suffered.
Magdalene, who was with her, was completely distraught, scarcely
able to control herself. The one moment of relief for the Holy Women
came when they stopped at the house of Seraphia, and were uplifted
by the sight of her veil with its miraculous imprint. The women
climbed to the top of the hill, and stood outside the circular berm,
awaiting the Crucifixion.

## The Holy Cross

Shortly before noon, the Cross was taken from Jesus, and He was thrown down with the mocking words: "We must take the measure of Thy throne for Thee, O King!" Jesus laid Himself on the Cross, so that they could mark the places where they would have to bore holes for the nails. They then dragged Him to a nearby cave cut in the rock, where He was again thrown down, to await their pleasure. The executioners chiseled out holes in the rocky ground for the three crosses. The cross for each thief consisted of a short trunk (*crux humilis*), to which the cross piece, with the victim on it, would be attached on top. The trunk of the Cross of Jesus was longer (*crux immissa*) and it had two separate arms, which were fitted into the trunk with mortis and tenon joints and wedges, and a top was added for the inscription. Altogether, it consisted of five pieces, with the arms at oblique angles upward, rather than being perpendicular to the trunk as it is traditionally shown. The Cross also had a foot-block (*suppedaneum*) nailed on, and the front was shaped to receive the crown of thorns and Jesus' back. The intent was to have Jesus stand, rather than hang by His hands—thus preventing the hands from being torn free by His weight, precipitating His death.[6]

## The Special Barbarity of Jesus' Crucifixion

Crucifixion is inherently barbarous, but what happened to Jesus was unimaginably horrible. The executioners dragged Jesus from the little holding-cave and began to strip Him. They had to tear the crown of thorns off Him once again, to get off the brown, seamless robe which His Mother had knitted for Him. He was bleeding all over, as the fabric had stuck to His open wounds. They even stripped Him of the scapular over His chest and back, and His loincloth. The crown of thorns was thrust back on His head, and He was offered a drink of vinegar and gall, which He refused. They were about to throw Him down and nail Him to the Cross, when Jonadab, a nephew of St. Joseph, ran up out of the crowd, and handed Him a strip of linen, to clothe His loins.

In 14th to 16th century England, a cycle of mystery plays was performed on the feast of Corpus Christi in the town of York, from pageant wagons which would stop at designated sites where the players would put on their particular drama. One of these performances was a depiction of the Crucifixion of Christ, ending with His burial. A significant part of the play dealt with the process of nailing Him to the Cross—for while the workmen talked about the need to do a good job, they actually performed incompetently, with the result that the holes for the hands and feet were bored too far apart. Rather than bore new holes, they racked Jesus' poor body by pulling it almost apart with ropes, stretching Him to accommodate their shoddy handiwork. Once they had Him nailed down, they emplaced the heavy Cross in such a way as to intensify His sufferings, by dropping it into its hole in the ground.[7]

*It may well be that the racking depicted in the mystery play was the remnant of an oral tradition of the Crucifixion, for Sister Emmerich described just such a torture in her visions of the actual event.* Her words make a powerful Lenten meditation:

"Jesus was now stretched on the cross by the executioners. He had lain Himself upon it; but they pushed Him lower down into the hollow places, rudely drew His right hand to the hole for the nail in the right arm of the cross and tied His wrist fast. One knelt on His sacred breast and held the closing hand flat; another placed the long, thick nail, which had been filed to a sharp point, upon the palm of His sacred hand, and struck furious blows with the iron hammer. A sweet, clear, spasmodic cry of anguish broke from the Lord's lips, and His blood spurted out upon the arms of the executioners. The muscles and ligaments of the hand had been torn and, by the three-edged nail, driven into the narrow hole. . . . The Blessed Virgin sobbed in a low voice, but Magdalene was perfectly crazed.

"The nails, at the sight of which Jesus shuddered, were so long that, when the executioners grasped them in their fists, they projected about an inch at either end. The head consisted of a little plate with a knob, and it covered as much of the palm of the hand as a crown-piece would do. They were three-edged, thick near the head as a moderate sized thumb, then tapered to the thickness of a little finger, and lastly were filed to a point. When hammered in, the point could be seen projecting a little on the opposite side of the cross.

*"After nailing Our Lord's right hand, the crucifiers found that His left, which also was fastened to the cross-piece, did not reach to the hole made for the nail, for they had bored a good two inches from the finger tips. They consequently unbound Jesus' arm from the cross, wound cords around it and, with their feet supported firmly against the cross, pulled it forward until the hand reached the hole. Now, kneeling on the arm and breast of the Lord, they fastened the arm again on the beam, and hammered the second nail through the left hand. The blood spurted up and Jesus' sweet, clear cry of agony sounded above the strokes of the heavy hammer."* "Both arms had been torn from their sockets, the shoulders were distended and hollow

and, at the elbows, one could see the disjointed bones. Jesus' breast
heaved, and His legs were drawn up doubled to His body. His arms
were stretched out in so straight a line that they no longer covered
the obliquely rising cross-pieces. One could see through the space thus
made between them and His armpits.

"The whole body of our Blessed Redeemer had been contracted
by the violent stretching of the arms to the holes for the nails, and
His knees were forcibly drawn up. The executioners now fell
furiously upon them and, winding ropes around them, fastened them
down to the cross; but on account of the mistake made in the holes
in the cross-piece, the sacred feet of Jesus did not reach even to the
block.

"When the executioners saw this, they gave vent to curses and
insults. Some thought they would have to bore new holes in the
transverse arm, for that would be far less difficult than moving the
foot block. Others with horrible scoffing cried out: 'He will not stretch
Himself out, but we will help Him!' Then they tied ropes around the
right leg and, with horrible violence and terrible torture to Jesus,
pulled the foot down to the block, and tied the leg fast with cords.
Jesus' body was thus most horribly distended. His chest gave way
with a cracking sound, and He moaned aloud. 'Oh God! Oh God!'
They had tied down His arms and His breast also that His hands
might not be torn away from the nails. The abdomen was entirely
displaced, and it seemed as if the ribs broke away from the breastbone.
The suffering was horrible.

"With similar violence the left foot was drawn and fastened
tightly with cords over the right; and because it did not rest firmly
enough over the right one for nailing, the instep was bored with a fine,
flathead piercer, much finer than the one used for the hands. It was
like an auger with a puncher attached. Then seizing the most frightful
looking nail of all, which was much longer than the others, they drove
it with great effort through the wounded instep of the left foot and
that of the right foot resting below. With a cracking sound, it passed
through Jesus' feet into the hole prepared for it in the foot block, and
through that again back into the trunk of the cross. . . . The nailing
of the feet was the most horrible of all, on account of the distension
of the whole body."

The Cross, with Jesus nailed to it, was raised by ropes over a
derrick until it was upright, and then it was guided to its hole. When
released, the Cross dropped heavily, opening His wounds further. His
Mother was there to hear the terrible sounds of Him being racked and
nailed, and His cries of pain. She was physically borne up by the Holy

Women, as she was jeered by the Pharisees. She, John and the Holy Women stretched forth their hands to Jesus, conveying by that gesture their support, as they stood by the Cross.

### Two Criminals Are Crucified Beside Him

The executioners then attended to the two criminals who had been left lying on the ground. Sister Emmerich referred to them as Dismas and Gesmas, but could not recall their true names. In her visions, they both were in a band of robbers that waylaid travelers on the road near the border with Egypt. Dismas, the so-called "good" thief, was a very young boy when the Holy Family was temporarily held captive by the gang, and he was cured of leprosy by being washed in the bathwater of Jesus. Throughout the whole crucifixion, Dismas was affected by the plight of Jesus, whereas his companion was full of curses and mockery.

The thieves were untied and the cross pieces which they had carried to Golgotha were affixed to the tops of the trunks. The men were then stripped and, by ropes under their arms, they were hoisted up and their arms were twisted over the cross pieces. They were not nailed to their crosses; rather their wrists, elbows, knees and ankles were bound so tightly to the wood that they shrieked in pain. There was enough distance between their crosses and that of Jesus, which was in the center, for a man on horseback to ride between them.

All of Jesus' garments—the mantle, the long, white garment, linen scarf, breast scapular—with the exception of His brown, woven robe—were torn into strips and divided among the executioners, despite being soaked with His blood. As to the robe, they threw stones with markings on them onto a board with numbers in order to decide who would receive it. Joseph of Arimathea and Nicodemus sent a messenger with an offer to buy His garments, which they readily accepted.

### Jesus is Left to Suffer on His Cross

After the Cross was dropped into its hole, the executioners mounted their ladders and loosened the ropes binding Him, thereby allowing the blood to flow freely from His wounds:

"For seven minutes He hung in silence as if dead, sunk in an abyss of untold pain, and for some moments unbroken stillness reigned around the cross. Under the weight of the thorny crown, the sacred head had sunk upon the breast and, from its countless wounds the trickling blood had filled the eyes, the hair, the beard, and the mouth open, parched, and languishing.

"*The sacred face, on account of the immense crown, could be uplifted only with unspeakable pain. The breast was widely distended and violently torn upward; the shoulders were hollow and frightfully stretched; the elbows and wrists, dislocated; and the blood was streaming down the arms from the now enlarged wounds of the hands. Below the contracted breast, there was a deep hollow place, and the entire abdomen was sunken and collapsed, as if shrunken away from the frame.*

"*Like the arms, the loins and legs were most horribly disjointed. Jesus' limbs had been so violently distended, His muscles and the torn skin so pitifully stretched that His bones could be counted one by one. The blood trickled down the cross from under the terrible nail that pierced His sacred feet. The whole of the sacred body was covered with wounds, red swellings and scars, with bruises and boils, blue, brown and yellow, and with bloody places from which the skin had been peeled. All these wounds had been reopened by the violent tension of the cords, and were again pouring forth red blood. Later the stream became whitish and watery, and the sacred body paler. When the crusts fell off, the wounds looked like flesh drained of blood. In spite of its frightful disfigurement, Our Lord's sacred body presented upon the cross an appearance at once noble and touching. Yes, the Son of God, the Eternal sacrificing Himself in time, was beautiful, holy, and pure in the shattered body of the dying Paschal Lamb laden with the sins of the whole human race.*"

---

[1] *See generally*, Jerome M. O'Connor, "The Geography of Faith—Tracing the Via Dolorosa," *Bible Review* (December 1996) 32; "The Stations of the Cross," *God's Word Today* (March 1989) 38; Maria S. Ceplecha, "The Artists' Way and the Way of the Cross," *Crisis* (June 2003) 38. According to the *Catechism of the Catholic Church*, at § 2669: "Christian prayer loves to follow *the way of the cross* in the Savior's steps." Despite the horrible physical and mental anguish of Jesus carrying His Cross, one scholar concluded that St. Mark portrayed it in a way that his first century audience would have recognized as the *triumphal march* of a Roman emperor. *See* Thomas Schmidt, "Jesus' Triumphal March to Crucifixion," *Bible Review* (February 1997) 30.
[2] *See* Pope John Paul II, *Way of the Cross—Meditations of Pope John Paul II* (New York: Catholic Near East Welfare Association 1982); *The Way of the Cross* (San Giovanni Rotondo, Italy: Our Lady of Grace Capuchin Friary 1979); Josemaría Escrivá, *The Way of the Cross* (New York: Scepter 1983); Mother Teresa of Calcutta & Brother Roger of Taizé, *Meditations on the Way of the Cross* (New York: Pilgrim Press 1987); Fulton J. Sheen, *The Way of the Cross*

(Huntington, IN: Our Sunday Visitor 1982). An extremely popular modern booklet is *Everyone's Way of the Cross*, by Clarence Enzler (Notre Dame, IN: Ave Maria Press 1986). There are also meditation booklets for special purposes, *e.g.*: Richard G. Furey, *Mary's Way of the Cross* (Mystic, CT: Twenty-Third Pub. 1984); Susan Tassone, The Way of the Cross for the Holy Souls in Purgatory (Huntington, IN: Our Sunday Visitor 2000); and Cletus Healy, "Stations of the Cross for the Victims of Abortion," *The Wanderer* (March 16, 1995) 6.

[3] Thus, depictions of Jesus as carrying only the cross-piece as was traditional, *e.g.*, by William D. Edwards, Wesley J. Gabel, and Floyd E. Hosmer, "On the Physical Death of Jesus Christ," *J. Am. Med. Ass'n* (March 21, 1986) 1455, 1458, are incorrect; however, it seems from Sister Emmerich's description that the two arms (rather than a single cross piece) were tied to the trunk, and thus the burden Jesus carried was not in the form of a cross.

[4] *See* Antonio Gaspari, "Has Veronica's Veil Been Found?," *Inside the Vatican* (November 1999) 42. http://www.catholic-forum.com.

[5] The Gospels of Matthew and Luke report Him uttering this lament on an earlier occasion.

[6] The scientific observation that the weight of a crucified man would pull his hands free unless the nails were expertly placed through a bony area was first made a century after Sister Emmerich's visions. *See* Pierre Barbet, *A Doctor at Calvary* (New York: Doubleday Image 1963), 103 et seq. While Barbet's anatomical commentary, and his deduction of the placement of the nails in Christ's hands, were convincingly challenged by a well known medical examiner, the latter agreed that the hands would have pulled free if they had been nailed in the center of the palms. *See* Frederick T. Zugibe, "Two Questions About Crucifixion," *Bible Review* (April 1989) 35, and "Pierre Barbet Revisited." http://www.shroud.com/zugibe.htm. The point to be noted is that Sister Emmerich's visions solved a scientific problem which no one even raised until a hundred years after her death—namely, how could the nails have been hammered through Jesus' hands without His body pulling free of the Cross?

[7] *See The Corpus Christi Cycle—The Crucifixion of Christ* (from York—the Pinneres and Painters).

# CHAPTER TWENTY-ONE

## The Seven Last Words of Christ

For three hours, Jesus—whom we Christians believe to be *one in being* with the Father—hung on a Cross, suffering in His human state unimaginable agonies, agonies beyond even those of other crucifixion victims, because of the diabolically cruel way in which He was racked as He was pinioned to the wood of the tree. St. John, the only Evangelist who was actually there, and his fellow Evangelists chose to emphasize different aspects of that holy period, which we traditionally commemorate on "Good Friday." In trying to understand as best as we can precisely what happened, commentators as far back as the early centuries attempted to weave the four accounts together, using as building blocks what Jesus is recorded to have said. A pastiche has been formed, consisting of the "Seven Last Words" of Jesus, which are used as the basis for meditations on His sacrifice.[1] The visions of Sister Emmerich change in small ways the traditional composite.

## The First Word

Having completed their work, the executioners left, and a new troop of soldiers arrived to relieve the ones who had been on duty. According to Sister Emmerich, the head of the detachment was Abenadar, and his second in command was Cassius, later renamed Longinus. A new troop of Pharisees, Sadducees, and scribes rode up to the crosses. They reviled the Blessed Virgin Mary, calling her a dissolute woman, and they taunted Jesus:

"They wagged their heads contemptuously, saying: 'Fie upon Thee, liar! How dost Thou destroy the Temple, and buildest it again in three days?'— 'He always wanted to help others, and He can not help Himself!'— 'Art Thou the Son of God? Then, come down from the cross!'— 'Is He the King of Israel? Then let Him come down from the cross, and we will believe in Him.'— 'He trusted in God. Let Him help Him now!'

"The soldiers, in like manner, mocked and said: 'If Thou art the King of the Jews, help Thyself now!' And now Jesus, raising His head a little, exclaimed: *'Father, forgive them, for they know not what they do!,'* and then He prayed in a low tone."[2]

## The Second Word

Sister Emmerich saw that the "good" thief was aided by special graces: "He raised his voice and cried in a clear and commanding tone. 'How is it possible that ye can revile Him when He is praying for you! He has kept silence and patience, He prays for you, and you outrage Him! He is a Prophet! He is our King! He is the Son of God!' At this unexpected reproof out of the mouth of the murderer hanging there in misery, a tumult arose among the scoffers. They picked up stones to stone him on the cross. The Centurion Abenadar however repulsed their attack, caused them to be dispersed, and restored order and quiet."

When the "bad" thief cried to Jesus: "'If Thou be the Christ, help Thyself and us!', the other one answered him: 'Neither dost thou fear God, seeing thou art under the same condemnation. And we indeed justly, for we receive the due reward of our deeds, but this man had done no evil. Oh, bethink thee of thy sins, and change thy sentiments!' Thoroughly enlightened and touched, he then confessed his crime to Jesus, saying: 'Lord, if Thou dost condemn me, it will be just. But have mercy on me!' *Jesus replied: 'Thou shalt experience My mercy.'*

"At these words Dismas received the grace of deep contrition, which he indulged for the next quarter of an hour. . . . Dismas, in deepest contrition and humble hope, raised his head to Jesus and said: 'Lord, let me go to some place whence Thou mayest rescue me! Remember me when Thou shalt come into Thy kingdom!' Jesus replied to him: *'Amen, I say to thee, this day thou shalt be with Me in Paradise!'*"

## Darkness Covers the Land

The Synoptic Gospels all report that darkness fell over the land from noon till three o'clock. Sister Emmerich saw that the ominous happening in Jerusalem frightened the inhabitants including Pilate, Herod and the religious leaders: "Anxiety and terror reached their height in the Temple. The slaughtering of the Paschal lamb had just begun when the darkness of night suddenly fell upon Jerusalem. All were filled with consternation, while here and there broke forth loud cries of woe. The High Priests did all they could to maintain peace and order. The lamps were lighted, making the sacred precincts as bright as day, but the consternation became only the greater."

Sister Emmerich described the darkness as a sort of red fog. Despite St. Luke's mention of an eclipse, astronomers do not calculate one as being possible then.[3] The experience, thus, was like nothing so much as the great miracle which took place at Fatima, Portugal on October 13, 1917. There, 70,000 people gathered outside an obscure Portuguese village, trusting the word of three children that the Blessed Virgin Mary had promised a great miracle. It was just as they had foretold: the crowd saw the sun dim, whirl around, plunge toward the earth, engage in gyrations, and spin out multicolored streams of light. This was not an instance of group hypnosis, as even people 20 miles away saw the miraculous show, which lasted for ten minutes—yet nothing untoward was reported by astronomers to have happened in the heavens. To this day, no scientist knows how the sun "danced" at Fatima, but the newspaper reports of the time leave no doubt that that is just what the multitudes saw happen.[4]

### The Third Word

The Blessed Virgin Mary and John, together with Mary Cleophas and Mary Magdalene, were standing by the Cross, which rose above them so that their heads were at about the level of His feet, when Jesus joined His Mother and the Beloved Disciple in a special way: *"The Blessed Virgin, overcome by maternal love, was in her heart fervently imploring Jesus to let her die with Him. At that moment, the Lord cast an earnest and compassionate glance down upon His Mother and, turning His eyes toward John, said to her: 'Woman, behold, this is thy son! He will be thy son more truly than if thou hadst given him birth.' Then He praised John, and said: 'He has always been innocent and full of simple faith. He was never scandalized, excepting when His Mother wanted to have him elevated to a high position.' To John, He said: 'Behold, this is thy Mother!' and John reverently and like a filial son embraced beneath the cross of the dying Redeemer Jesus' mother, who had now become his mother also."*

### The Fourth Word

Sister Emmerich described these moments as being ones of gloomy silence, when many of the crowd drifted away and the Pharisees who remained ceased to revile Jesus, who was experiencing extreme abandonment in His own soul: *"Jesus, more keenly than any human being can conceive, endured this pain of utter abandonment. . . . Being in His sacred humanity wholly abandoned by the Father, He felt most perfectly that bereavement. He drained to the dregs the bitter cup of dereliction, He experienced for the time what a soul* endures that has lost its God forever. *Toward the third hour, Jesus cried in a loud voice: 'Eli, Eli, lamma sabacthani!' which means: 'My God! My God! Why hast Thou forsaken Me!'"* Christians believe that even those words of apparent despair actually signified trust in God, for they came from the 22nd Psalm, which is about the passion and triumph of the Messiah.[5]

### The Fifth Word

Sister Emmerich related that, as it grew light again, the body of Jesus could be seen on the Cross, "weak, perfectly exhausted, and becoming whiter from the great loss of blood. He said, I know not whether praying in voice audible to me alone, or half-aloud: *'I am pressed like the wine which was once trodden here in the wine-press. I must pour out all My blood until water cometh, and the shell becometh white, but wine shall here be made no more.'"* This "Fifth Word," does *not* appear in the Gospels, and it requires an explanation, one which Sister Emmerich received in a separate vision: at an earlier time, on the same mount where Jesus was later crucified, grapes were grown and made into wine.[6]

### The Sixth Word

The Gospels tell that Jesus exclaimed about His thirst, which must have been agonizing due to His loss of blood and body fluids beginning the night before. Sister Emmerich's account is fuller: *"Jesus was now completely exhausted. With His parched tongue, He uttered the words: 'I thirst!' And when His friends looked up at Him sadly, He said to them: 'Could you not have given Me a drink of water?'* He meant that during the darkness no one would have prevented their doing so. John was troubled at Jesus' words, and he replied: 'O Lord, we forgot it!' Jesus continued to speak in words such as these: *'My nearest friends must forget Me and offer Me no drink, that the Scriptures may be fulfilled.'"*

### With His Last Words, Jesus Dies

Sister Emmerich saw the death of Jesus, and its immediate aftermath, as follows: "Of some of the words that I heard the Lord speaking in admonition to the people, I remember only that He said: *'And when I shall no longer have voice, the mouth of the dead shall speak.'"* (These words, not reported in the Gospels, were a prophecy of the appearance of the dead in Jerusalem immediately following Jesus' own demise.) Continuing with Sister Emmerich's account: "some of the bystanders cried out: 'He still blasphemes!' But Abenadar commanded peace. The hour of the Lord was now come. He was struggling with death, and a cold sweat burst out on every limb. John was standing by the cross and wiping Jesus' feet with His handkerchief. Magdalene, utterly crushed with grief, was leaning at the back of the cross. The Blessed Virgin, supported in the arms of Mary Cleophas and Salome, was standing between Jesus and the cross of the good thief, her gaze fixed upon her dying son.

"*Jesus spoke: 'It is consummated!' — and raising His head He cried with a loud voice: 'Father, into Thy hands I commend My Spirit!' The sweet, loud cry rang through heaven and earth. Then He bowed His head and gave up the ghost. I saw His soul like a luminous phantom descending through the earth near the cross down to the sphere of limbo. John and the Holy Women sank, face downward, prostrate on the earth.*

"Abenadar the Centurion, an Arab by birth, had . . . remained seated on his horse close to the eminence upon which the Cross was raised, the forefeet of the animal planted near it and, consequently, higher than the hindfeet. Deeply affected, he gazed long, earnestly and fixedly into the thorn-crowned countenance of Jesus. The horse hung his head as if in fear, and Abenadar, whose pride was humbled, let the reins hang loose. When the Lord, in a clear strong voice uttered those last words, when He died with that loud cry that rang through heaven, earth, and hell, the earth quaked and the rock between Him and the thief on His left was rent asunder with a crashing sound. That loud cry, that witness of God, resounded like a warning arousing terror and shuddering in mourning nature.

"Then it was that grace penetrated the soul of Abenadar. The horse trembled under his rider, who was reeling with emotion; then it was that grace conquered that proud mind, hard as the rock of Calvary. He threw his lance to the ground and, with his great clenched fist, struck his breast vigorous blows, crying aloud in the voice of a changed man: 'Blessed be God the Almighty, the God of Abraham and Jacob! This was a just Man! Truly, He is the Son of God!' And many of the soldiers deeply affected by his words, followed his example."

### Death's Pallid Hue Lay Over Him

Sister Emmerich gave the following description of how Jesus' body looked in death, still hanging on the Cross: "*It became perfectly white, and the streams of blood running down from the numerous wounds grew darker and more perceptible. His face was elongated, His cheeks sunken, His nose sharp and pinched. His underjaw fell, and His eyes, which had been closed and full of blood, opened halfway. For a few instants He raised His thorn-crowned head for the last time and then let it sink on His breast under the burden of pain. His lips, blue and parted, disclosed the bloody tongue in His open mouth. His fingers, which had been contracted around the heads of the nails, now relaxed and fell a little forward while the arms stretched out to their natural size. His back straightened itself against the cross, and the whole weight of His sacred body fell upon the feet. His knees bent and fell to one side, and His feet twisted a little around the nail that pierced them."*[7]

### Frightful Events Follow Jesus' Death

The earthquake which split off the cross of the bad thief from the other two crosses initially frightened the onlookers, but soon the Pharisees grew bolder and went over to examine the gap. What they found was an abyss which they could not reach the bottom of with their ropes, and so they went off. The city was even more upset, as the earthquake felt on Mount Calvary also knocked down buildings. More terrifying, the corpses of dead persons rose from their graves and were seen in the streets, giving warnings in hollow voices.

It was in the Temple itself that the greatest turmoil occurred: "The High Priests in the Temple had recommenced the slaughtering of the lambs, which had been interrupted by the frightful darkness. They were rejoicing triumphantly over the returning light when suddenly the ground began to quake, a hollow rumbling was heard, and the crash of toppling walls, accompanied by the hissing noise made by the rending of the veil, produced for the moment in the vast assemblage speechless terror broken only by an occasional cry of woe. But . . . it was not till the dead made their appearance in different parts of the Temple that the ceremonies were entirely interrupted and the sacrifices discontinued, as if the Temple had become polluted.

"I remember the following striking incidents: The two great columns at the entrance of the Holy of Holies in the Temple, between which hung a magnificent curtain, fell in opposite directions, the left-hand one to the south, the right-hand to the north. The beam which they supported gave way and the great curtain was, with a hissing noise, rent from top to bottom, so that opening on either side it fell. This curtain was red, blue, white, and yellow. Many celestial spheres were described upon it, also figures like the brazen serpent. The people could now see into the Holy of Holies. . . . *In the Holy of Holies, between the porch and the altar, an apparition of the murdered High Priest Zachary was seen. He uttered threatening words, spoke of the*

*death of the other Zachary, also that of John, denominating the High
Priests the murderers of the Prophets.*

"*Jeremiah appeared at the altar and uttered words of denunciation. The sacrifice of the Old Law was ended, he said, and a new one
had begun. . . . And now there arose a great clamor, the doors of the
sanctuary sprang open, a voice cried out: 'Let us go hence!' and I saw
the angels departing from the Temple.*"

Consider: (1) the comparison between God's rending of the
heavens at the Jordan, at the beginning of Jesus' ministry, and God's
rending of the Temple veil at the end of His ministry; (2) the
comparison between the High Priest's rending of his garment to
protest Jesus' alleged blasphemy, and God's rending of the Temple veil
to protest the blasphemy of executing Jesus; and (3) God's *spiritual*
destruction of the Temple sanctuary in answer to the mockery of
Jesus' alleged claim that He would "destroy the Temple."[8]

The apocryphal Gospel of Peter recounted that at the signs following Jesus' death, the elders, priests and Pharisees beat their breasts
and confessed that Jesus had been a just man. Similarly, at the end of
the lengthy, apocryphal Acts of Pilate (Gospel of Nicodemus), after
many post-Resurrection miracles, the Jewish leaders were supposed
to have confessed to Pilate that Jesus was indeed the Christ. Contrary
to such unbelievable conversion accounts, according to the visions of
Sister Emmerich, while some Pharisees were indeed shocked enough
by the events at Mount Calvary and the Temple to be converted to
belief in Jesus, they were the exception. Annas and Caiaphas in particular refused to acknowledge the divine intervention. Although
Annas, who had been Jesus' chief persecutor, was driven insane with
fear, Caiaphas successfully commanded the worshippers to carry on,
and frightened into silence with the threat of excommunication any
who spoke of the signs as a punishment by God for their treatment
of Jesus. Those signs which he could not attribute to the working of
Jesus' human followers, Caiaphas ascribed to deviltry.

According to Sister Emmerich's visions, many tombs were broken
open, and about a hundred of the dead emerged to testify to Jesus, as
Sister Emmerich heard Him predict would happen just before He
expired. "On the crossways upon which Jesus' punishment was
trumpeted as the procession moved on to Golgotha, they stood still
and proclaimed glory to Jesus and woe to His murderers. The people
standing afar hearkened, shuddered, and fled, as the dead floated
toward them. I heard them on the forum in front of Pilate's palace
crying aloud in threatening terms. I remember the words: 'Cruel
judge!' The people fled into the most secret corners of their houses

and hid. Intense fear pervaded the whole city. About four o'clock, the
dead returned to their graves."

### Damage in Capernaum and Elsewhere from the Earthquake

Sister Emmerich saw in her visions damage from the earthquake
in many parts of Israel and even in other countries, for example, the
cities of the Decapolis. In Nazareth, half of the synagogue fell, and
the mountain from which the Pharisees sought to hurl Jesus down
was altered. The damage was extensive in Capernaum, especially to
the homes of those Pharisees who had been most zealous in
persecuting Jesus. *The course of the Jordan and the bed of the Sea of
Galilee were substantially changed, and the Sea flooded the valley
which had lain between it and Capernaum, whose ruins are now on
the shore.*

### The Wound in Jesus' Side Brings Grace to Cassius

Joseph of Arimathea and Nicodemus determined to bury the body
of Jesus in the former's own sepulcher, and to that end Joseph asked
Pilate for an order turning the corpse over to him. Pilate was surprised
that Jesus was already dead; to verify this, he summoned Abenadar,
who reported to him the circumstances surrounding Jesus' death.
Pilate was glad to grant Joseph's request, in part because he knew it
would greatly annoy the Jewish religious leaders, who would have had
Jesus buried in disgrace with the two thieves. It was then four o'clock
in the afternoon. Nicodemus purchased the needed cloths, spices,
which were kept in little kegs, and aromatic herbs, in bags of
parchment or leather. Joseph bought the long winding sheet, and had
his servants gather the necessary supplies and tools, from water bottles
and sponges, to ladders.

While this was happening, the executioners returned to Mount
Calvary. With heavy, triangular iron bars, they struck savagely,
breaking the two thieves' arms above and below the elbows, and also
their legs above the knees and the ankles. The "bad thief" was then
dispatched with blows to his chest, while the "good thief" simply
expired. The cords binding them to their crosses were untied, and then
retied around their fallen corpses, which were dragged down into the
valley and buried. Sister Emmerich mentioned that the three crosses
also were buried.[9]

She described how the body of Jesus came to be spared further
indignity by the executioners, while receiving a final wound: "The
executioners appeared still to have some doubts as to the death of

the Lord, and His friends, after witnessing the terrible scene just described, were more anxious than ever for them to withdraw. Cassius, the subaltern officer, afterward known as Longinus, a somewhat hasty, impetuous man of twenty-five, whose airs of importance and officiousness joined to his weak, squinting eyes often exposed him to the ridicule of his inferiors, was suddenly seized by wonderful ardor.

"The barbarity, the base fury of the executioners, the anguish of the Blessed Virgin, and the grace accorded him in that sudden and supernatural impulse of zeal, all combined to make of him the fulfiller of a prophecy. His lance, which was shortened by having one section run into another, he drew out to its full length, stuck the point upon it, turned his horse's head, and drove him boldly up to the narrow space on top of the eminence upon which the cross was planted. There was scarcely room for the animal to turn, and I saw Cassius reining him up in front of the chasm made by the cleft rock.

"He halted between Jesus' Cross and that of the good thief, on the right of Our Savior's body, grasped the lance with both hands, and drove it upward with such violence into the hollow, distended right side of the sacred body, through the entrails and the heart, that its point opened a little wound in the left breast. When with all his force he drew the blessed lance from the wide wound it had made in the right side of Jesus, a copious stream of blood and water rushed forth and flowed over his upraised face, bedewing him with grace and salvation. He sprang quickly from his horse, fell upon his knees, struck his breast, and before all present proclaimed aloud his belief in Jesus.

"The Blessed Virgin, John, and the holy women, whose eyes were riveted upon Jesus, witnessed with terror the sudden action, accompanied the thrust of the lance with a cry of woe, and rushed up to the Cross. *Mary, as if the thrust had transfixed her own heart, felt the sharp point piercing her through and through.* She sank into the arms of her friends, while Cassius, still on his knees, was loudly confessing the Lord and joyfully praising God. He was enlightened; he now saw plainly and distinctly. The eyes of his body like those of his soul were healed and opened.

"All were seized with a sentiment of the deepest reverence at sight of the Redeemer's blood which, mixed with water, fell in a foamy stream into a hollow in the rock at the foot of the cross. Mary, Cassius, the Holy Women, and John scooped it up in the drinking cups they had with them, poured it into flasks, and dried the hollow with linen cloths."

*The Descent from the Cross*

Sister Emmerich described the deportment from the Cross as taking place in the presence of the Blessed Virgin Mary, several of the other Holy Women, John, Joseph of Arimathea, Nicodemus, and the Roman guard, headed again by Abenadar, assisted by Cassius. On ladders, Nicodemus and Joseph bound the body of Jesus to the Cross with a linen cloth and straps, while they hammered the backs of the arms of the Cross to knock out the nails through His hands. The Centurion did likewise with the long nail through His feet. The nails were reverently laid beside Mary, and they proceeded to lower the body to the ground, where they wrapped it in linen from the knees to the waist.

"The Blessed Virgin was seated upon a large cover spread upon the ground, her right knee raised a little, and her back supported by a kind of cushion made, perhaps, of mantles rolled together. There sat the poor Mother, exhausted by grief and fatigue, in the position best suited for rendering love's last, sad duties to the remains of her murdered son. The men laid the sacred body on a sheet spread upon the mother's lap. The adorable head of Jesus rested upon her slightly raised knee, and His body lay outstretched upon the sheet. Love and grief in equal degrees struggled in the breast of the Blessed Mother. She held in her arms the body of her beloved son, whose long martyrdom she had been able to soothe by no loving ministrations; and at the same time she beheld the frightful maltreatment exercised upon it, she gazed upon its wounds now close under her eyes. She pressed her lips to His bloodstained cheeks, while Magdalene knelt with her face bowed upon His feet."

---

[1] *See, e.g.,* Morton T. Kelsey, *The Cross: Meditations on the Seven Last Words of Christ,* (New York: Paulist Press 1980).

[2] As to *whom* Jesus was praying for, *see* the analysis of Raymond E. Brown in *The Death of the Messiah* 2:972–75.

[3] *See* Raymond E. Brown, *The Death of the Messiah* 2:1034–43 (debunking attempts to provide a "natural" explanation for the darkness, and citing to the many Old Testament references to unusual darknesses sent by God).

[4] Among the many accounts of the miracle at Fatima are Joseph A. Pelletier, *The Sun Danced at Fatima* (Garden City, NY: Doubleday Image Books 1983), and William T. Walsh, *Our Lady of Fatima* (Garden City, NY: Doubleday Image Books 1954). For documentation, including newspaper accounts at the

time, *see* Antonio M. Martins, *Documents on Fatima & the Memoirs of Sister Lucia* (Alexandria, SD: Fatima Family Apostolate 1992).

[5] Joseph Ratzinger, *Behold the Pierced One* (San Francisco: Ignatius 1986)22–23.

[6] Sister Emmerich's vision was of the Patriarch Japheth (a son of Noah) camped on Mount Calvary with his flocks, after the Deluge. (Gen 9:18)

[7] Various theories have been expressed as to the exact cause of Jesus' death. *See, e.g.*, William D. Edwards, et al., "On the Physical Death of Jesus Christ," *J. Am. Med. Ass'n* (March 21, 1986) 1455 (death from hypovolemic shock and exhaustion asphyxia); Frederick T. Zugibe, "Pierre Barbet Revisited" (1995), http://www.shroud.com (death from shock); Robert Bucklin, "The Legal and Medical Aspects of the Trial and Death of Christ" (1970), http://www.shroud.com (death from congestive heart failure).

[8] These comparisons were made by a biblical scholar, albeit he viewed the reported events at the Temple upon the death of Jesus as being only *symbolic* and not historical. *See* Raymond E. Brown, *The Death of the Messiah* 1:451, 2: 1133–35, and nn. 94 &95.

[9] *See* Jan W. Drijvers, "The True Cross—Separating Myth from History," *Bible Review* (Aug. 2003) 24 (accounts that the Church of the Holy Sepulchre had pieces of the True Cross date back to the fourth century).

# CHAPTER TWENTY-TWO

*Jesus' Body is Lovingly Prepared for Burial*

There were no enemies to disturb the preparation of Jesus' body for His burial—even the Roman soldiers, following the lead of Cassius, were respectful and rendered help when asked. Sister Emmerich described the process in detail. The Blessed Virgin Mary carefully opened the crown of thorns in the back where it had been tied together, and then cut off the thorns that were embedded and would not come free when the crown was loosed from His head. Using pincers, she removed those thorns and laid them with the crown. Then, she washed the sacred head and face, and soaked the dried blood off His hair, much of which had been torn out. The water was brought from the well at Gihon in leather bottles, and the sponges were periodically squeezed into other bottles, so that none of His blood was lost in the washing.

Finally, His Mother began the process of embalming Him, rubbing ointment into His wounds, and filling His ears, nostrils, and side wound with sweet spices. Attending to His head, she closed His eyes and mouth. Her face pressed to His, she watered it with her tears. Magdalene performed a like service for His feet.

Joseph of Arimathea and Nicodemus used two very large sheets in the process of washing His body, which they did in a cave down from the top of Mount Calvary. The lower sheet was pierced in places to allow water to run through it, while the top one modestly covered Him as they worked under it, first to loosen the covering for His loins provided by Jonadab, and then to wash the whole body. His back was washed without turning the body over. When the body was clean, they poured water of myrrh over it, and then embalmed it with aromatic herbs and spices, wrapped next to Him by linen strips.

*The Shroud*

Possibly the most famous piece of cloth in the world is the so-called "Shroud of Turin," which many believe to have been the actual shroud wrapping Jesus in the tomb. It bears a remarkable *negative* image of a heavily scourged and crucified man, conformable to the Gospels' description of Jesus and His crucifixion. Carbon-14 tests initially seemed to prove that the Shroud dates back only to the Middle Ages, but various theories have been put forth arguing why the testing was invalid.[1] Perhaps the most significant challenge is the assertion that the miniscule piece of material used for sampling had been repaired in the 16th century, and, thus, the reported approximate date of 1300 A.D. was a weighted average derived from a composite of 1st century and 16th century threads.[2] Also, microscopic analysis has shown that the Shroud is contaminated by bacteria and fungi from later centuries (presumably the sample was too).[3] In any event, there are many books detailing scientific tests which prove that the markings were not painted on, or otherwise made by any process known to modern science—much less one known in the Middle Ages—and no one has yet been able to explain how, in keeping with the results of many scientific tests, the image of the crucified man was produced on the Shroud.[4]

In light of the crowds which come to venerate the Shroud whenever it is publicly displayed in Turin, and the continuing scientific debate over its authenticity, it is important to note that, although Sister Emmerich saw His image appearing on the outside of His shroud, her description of the winding sheet and the image do not match the Shroud of Turin. But, that is not the end of the matter, for according to her visions, three impressions were supernaturally made at a later date and consecrated by contact with the original; she further related that the three copies had effected great miracles. If her account is correct, it may be that the Shroud of Turin is one of those three supernaturally made "impressions"—in which case it would faithfully depict for us the appearance and wounds of Christ, even though it would not date back to 29 A.D.

## The Burial

Sister Emmerich described the burial place of Jesus as being a grotto in a garden a few minutes away from Mount Calvary, near the Bethlehem gate.[5] The body of Jesus, lying on a leather litter, was carried there by four men on their shoulders: Nicodemus and Joseph in front, and Abenadar and John in the rear. After them came the Blessed Virgin Mary, the Holy Women, and Cassius with his troop of soldiers. Light was provided in the grotto by two soldiers carrying torches in front. The mourners sang psalms until they reached the garden.

"The Holy Women sat down upon a seat opposite the entrance of the grotto. The four men carried the Lord's body down into it, set it down, strewed the stone couch with sweet spices, spread over it a linen cloth and deposited the sacred remains upon it. The cloth hung down over the couch. Then, having with tears and embraces given expression to their love for Jesus, they left the cave. The Blessed Virgin now went in, and I saw her sitting on the head of the tomb, which was about two feet from the ground. She was bending low over the corpse of her child and weeping. When she left the cave, Magdalene hurried in with flowers and branches which she had gathered in the garden and which she now scattered over the sacred body. She wrung her hands, and with tears and sighs embraced the feet of Jesus."

Night was falling, and the time came to close the tomb. The metal doors were shut and sealed with a large stone. Sister Emmerich described it as being "in shape almost like a chest or tomb, and was large enough for a man to lie at full length upon it."[6] The men rolled it into place with the aid of poles from the garden.

### Holy Saturday

The Holy Women who stayed in the Cenacle that night got only a few hours sleep, before they arose at midnight and assembled in the women's hall around the Blessed Virgin Mary for nocturnal prayers. John and the men did likewise separately, and when they were finished, the two groups joined together to go to the Temple at about three in the morning. Sister Emmerich explained what this surprising visit was about:

"It was customary among many of the Jews to visit the Temple at daybreak the morning after the eating of the Paschal Lamb. It was in consequence opened about midnight, because the sacrifices on that morning began very early. But today, on account of the disturbance of the feast and the defilement of the Temple, everything had been neglected, and it seemed to me as if the Blessed Virgin with her friends wanted to take leave of it. It was there that she had been reared,[7] there she had adored the Holy Mystery, until she herself bore in her womb that same Holy Mystery, that Holy One who, as the true Paschal Lamb, had been so barbarously immolated the day before. . . . The sacred edifice, with the exception of a few guards and servants, was quite deserted; marks of yesterday's disorder and confusion lay everywhere around. It had been defiled by the presence of the dead."

The day following the Crucifixion was the Sabbath, and Jesus' closest followers spent it in sorrowful prayer in the Cenacle. Sister Emmerich noted that: "all experienced an inward reverence for John and a feeling of confusion in his presence, since he had been at the death of the Lord. But John was full of love and sympathy toward them, and, simple and ingenuous as a child, he gave place to every one."

### The Miraculous Escape of Joseph of Arimathea

A miracle occurred on Holy Saturday. Friday night, leaving the Cenacle, Joseph of Arimathea had been arrested by an armed band of pagan soldiers, under orders from Caiaphas, who intended to imprison and starve him to death in a tower cell of an unused building. But, the next night, Joseph saw the roof miraculously raised, and a shining figure letting down a strip of linen. He used it to clamber up the wall and escape back to his home town.[8]

### The Guard at the Tomb

After Jesus was buried, Cassius reported to Pilate what had taken place, including his verifying the death of Jesus with a lance thrust. Caiaphas led a delegation to Pilate's palace, as recounted by St. Matthew, seeking a guard at the tomb so that Jesus' followers could not steal the body and pretend that He had risen from the dead. Pilate told them to post their own guard, which they did with twelve Temple soldiers, who verified that the body was there and then sealed the sepulchre with string and seals. Pilate also appointed Cassius to observe what happened at the scene; doing so, he became still more spiritually enlightened.

### Christ's Descent Into Hell

*Christians believe—as is set forth in the Apostle's Creed—that after Jesus died, "He descended into hell," before arising on "the third day." The Catholic Church teaches this, explaining what is, and isn't meant by "hell," and denying the hypothesis of universal salvation, as follows:*

> Scripture calls the abode of the dead, to which the dead Christ went down, "hell"—*Sheol* in Hebrew or *Hades* in Greek—because those who are there are deprived of the vision of God. Such is the case for all the dead, whether evil or righteous, while they await the redeemer: which does not mean that their lot is identical, as Jesus showed through the parable of the beggar Lazarus who was received into "Abraham's bosom"; "It is precisely these holy souls, who awaited their Savior in Abraham's bosom, whom Christ the Lord delivered when he descended into hell." Jesus did not descend into hell to deliver

the damned, nor to destroy the hell of damnation, but to free the just who had gone before him.

The gospel was preached even to the dead. The descent into hell brings the Gospel message of salvation to complete fulfillment.[9] Obviously, no human being accompanied Jesus to "hell." While it is possible that the Church could have deduced His descent there from the salvific nature of His mission, it is likely that the Church's knowledge of that journey came from the risen Christ Himself, as taught to His disciples, and from His Mother, who was the first to know of the Resurrection. Sister Emmerich had visions and was instructed regarding many of the mysteries of Christ's descent into "hell," which area she saw as three distinct spheres: the first holding Adam and Eve, the Patriarchs, Prophets, Judges, Kings, relatives of Jesus, and other holy people; the second holding pious pagans; and the third holding the damned. As to the later, she had this vision:

"At last I saw Him, His countenance grave and severe, approaching the center of the abyss, namely, hell itself. In shape it looked to me like an immeasurably vast, frightful, black stone building that shone with a metallic luster. Its entrance was guarded by immense, awful looking doors, black like the rest of the building, and furnished with bolts and locks that inspired feelings of terror. Rearing and yelling most horrible could plainly be heard, and when the doors were pushed open, a frightful, gloomy world was disclosed to view .. . all was pain and torment. As in the sojourns of the blessed all appears formed upon motives and conditions of infinite peace, eternal harmony and satisfaction, so here are the disorder, the malformation of eternal wrath, disunion, and despair.

"As in heaven there are innumerable abodes of joy and worship, unspeakably beautiful in their glittering transparency, so here in hell, are gloomy prisons without number, caves of torment, of cursing, and despair. As in heaven there are gardens most wonderful to behold, filled with fruits that afford divine nourishment, so here in hell, there are horrible wildernesses and swamps full of torture and pain and of all that can give birth to feelings of detestation, of loathing, and of horror.

"When the gates were swung open by the angels, one beheld before him a struggling, blaspheming, mocking, howling, and lamenting throng. I saw that Jesus spoke some words to the soul of Judas. Some of the angels forced that multitude of evil spirits to prostrate before Jesus, for all had to acknowledge and adore Him.[10]

This was for them the most terrible torment. A great number were chained in a circle around others who were in turn bound down by them. In the center was an abyss of darkness. Lucifer was cast into it, chained, and thick black vapor mounted up around him. This took place by the Divine Decree. I heard that Lucifer (if I do not mistake) will be freed again for awhile fifty or sixty years before the year 2000 A.D."

### His Mother Sees the Souls of Christ and the Prophets

The followers of Jesus stayed hidden on Holy Saturday, but performed their Sabbath obligations. That night, preceding the Resurrection, many supernatural events took place. One seen by Sister Emmerich in her visions was the visit of the soul of Jesus to the tomb under Golgotha, where He conversed with the souls of Adam and Eve, and then took them to visit the tombs of the Prophets, adding their souls to His procession. He showed the souls all places which had been significant to His own life and Passion, and explained to them the events which had occurred there. At the place of His baptism, He permitted the grace thus imparted to flow over them too.

Sister Emmerich also had a vision of an angel coming to the Blessed Virgin Mary that evening, to summon Mary to go out to the special gate in the city wall cut for Joseph and Nicodemus, there to meet her Son: "I saw the Blessed Virgin suddenly halt in her hurried walk. She glazed as if ravished with joyous longing up at the top of the wall. Floating down toward her in the midst of a great multitude of the souls of the ancient Patriarchs, I saw the most holy soul of Jesus resplendent with light and without trace of wound. Turning to the Patriarchs and pointing to the Blessed Virgin, He uttered the words: 'Mary, My Mother!' and appeared to embrace her. Then He vanished. The Blessed Virgin sank on her knees and kissed the ground upon which He had stood."

A few hours after the Blessed Virgin Mary had returned to the Cenacle, she felt moved by compassion to retrace the Way of the Cross, beginning this time at Caiaphas' palace. She would kneel and kiss the ground at places where she sensed the blood of her Son. Reaching Calvary at last, the soul of her Son appeared once again to her:

"It was as if the apparition of Jesus with His sacred, martyred body stepped before her. One angel preceded Him, the two adoring angels of the tomb were at His side, and a multitude of released souls followed Him. He seemed not to walk, but looked like a corpse floating along environed with light. I heard a voice proceeding from Him, which related to His Mother what He had done in limbo. Now, He continued, He was about to come forth from the tomb alive, in a glorified body, and He bade her await Him near Mount Calvary, on the stone upon which He had fallen. Then I saw the apparition going to the city, and the Blessed Virgin kneeling and praying on the spot indicated by the Lord. It may now have been past twelve o'clock, for Mary had spent a considerable time in the Way of the Cross.

"Then I saw the Lord's procession going over the whole of the same dolorous way. In a mysterious manner, the angels gathered up all the sacred substance, the flesh and the blood, that had been torn from Jesus during His Passion. I saw that the nailing to the cross, the raising of the same, the opening of the sacred side, the taking down from the cross, and the preparing of the holy body for burial, were shown to the souls in Jesus' train. The Blessed Virgin also saw it all in spirit. She loved and adored. Afterward it was as if the Lord's body rested again in the holy sepulchre. With it was all that had been torn from it during the Passion and replaced in an incomprehensible manner by the angels."

## The Resurrection, and How It Became Known

St. Paul expressed the centrality of the Resurrection in these words: "if Christ has not been raised, our preaching is void of content and your faith is empty too."[11] In that vein, the Catholic Church teaches that:

> The Resurrection of Jesus is the crowning truth of our faith in Christ, a faith believed and lived as the central truth by the first Christian community; handed on as fundamental by Tradition; established by the documents of the New Testament; and preached as an essential part of the Paschal mystery along with the cross. . . . The mystery of Christ's resurrection is a real event, with manifestations that were historically verified, as the New Testament bears witness.[12]

While the stories of who was the first to discover the empty tomb may seem mutually contradictory,[13] Sister Emmerich's visions provide the framework for reconciling the Gospel accounts—and also support the ancient tradition of the Church that the risen Christ showed Himself first to His Mother.[14] In summary, the sequence on the first morning was: (1) Jesus appeared to His Mother on Mount Calvary away from the tomb; (2) Mary Magdalene approached the tomb, saw that it was empty, and left temporarily; (3) the other Holy Women came and saw the angels, but not Jesus, at the tomb; (4) Mary Magdalene spoke to Peter and John, and ran back to the tomb before them, at which time she saw the angels and then Jesus; (5) John and Peter arrived at the tomb, and John, at least, saw an angel; (6) Jesus appeared to James the Lesser and Jude Thaddeus; and (7) Jesus appeared to the Holy Women. Here is how Sister Emmerich described the Resurrection itself, and then the appearance of Jesus to His Mother:

"The blessed soul of Jesus in dazzling splendor, between two warrior angels and surrounded by a multitude of resplendent figures, came floating down through the rocky roof of the tomb upon the sacred body. It seemed to incline over it and melt, as it were, into one with it. I saw the sacred limbs moving beneath the swathing-bands, and the dazzling, living body of the Lord with His soul and His Divinity coming forth from the side of the winding-sheet as if from the wounded side. The sight reminded me of Eve coming forth from Adam's side. The whole place was resplendent with light and glory.

"Now I saw the Lord floating in glory up through the rock. The earth trembled, and an angel in warrior garb shot like lightning from heaven down to the tomb, rolled the stone to one side, and seated himself upon it. The trembling of the earth was so great that the lanterns swung from side to side, and the flames flashed around. The guards fell stunned to the ground and lay there stiff and contorted, as if dead. Cassius saw indeed the glory that environed the holy sepulchre, the rolling away of the stone by the angel, and his seating himself upon it, but he did not see the risen Savior Himself. He recovered himself quickly, stepped to the stone couch, felt among the empty linens, and left the sepulchre, outside of which, full of eager desire, he tarried awhile to become the witness of a new and wonderful apparition.

"*At the instant the angel shot down to the tomb and the earth quaked, I saw the risen Lord appearing to His Blessed Mother, on Mount Calvary. He was transcendently beautiful and glorious, His manner full of earnestness. His garment, which was like a white mantle thrown about His limbs, floated in the breeze behind Him as He walked. It glistened blue and white, like smoke curling in the sunshine.*

"*His wounds were very large and sparkling; in those of His hands, one could easily insert a finger. The lips of the wounds formed*

*the sides of an equilateral triangle which met, as it were, in the center
of a circle, and from the palm of the hand shot rays of light toward
the fingers.* The souls of the early Patriarchs bowed low before the
Blessed Mother, to whom Jesus said something about seeing her again.
He showed her His wounds and, when she fell on her knees to kiss
His feet, He grasped her hand, raised her up, and disappeared.

It was shortly thereafter that the Holy Women came to the tomb,
bearing aromatic shrubs, nard water, fresh flowers, and various oils.
They were frightened when they saw the soldiers lying around the
tomb and so, with the exception of Mary Magdalene and Salome, they
walked a bit past it. The latter two passed through the stunned
soldiers, and Magdalene looked into the tomb, seeing the empty
linens. Magdalene then ran off in haste to tell the Apostles, while
Salome told the other Holy Women. The latter took courage when
Cassius recounted to them what he had seen and urged them to go
right into the sepulcher. When they did so, they beheld the two angels,
who instructed them as described in the Synoptic Gospels.

Meanwhile, Magdalene had gone to the Cenacle and told Peter
and John that Jesus' body had been taken away. Then, she hurried back
to the tomb, and arrived before they did. It was at this point that she
had the experience with the risen Christ, mistaking Him at first for
the gardener, as described by St. John. After this sighting, Peter and
John appeared to examine the tomb. They saw and believed, and, on
their way back, they encountered James the Lesser and Jude Thaddeus,
who reported that the Lord had just appeared to them. The other
sighting of Jesus which Sister Emmerich recounted came at about the
same time. After her second visit to the tomb, Mary Magdalene found
the Holy Women and told them what she had seen. They went to
the garden, where they were treated to a brief appearance of Jesus
Himself.

### The Lie About the Empty Tomb

Pilate was very frightened, first by the report he received from
Cassius, beginning with the appearance of the angel who rolled away
the stone, and then by what the guards related about the empty tomb.
He tried to persuade them to say nothing, but instead, they went to
the Temple and started telling the bystanders what had occurred. The
authorities quickly cracked down: those guards who would not keep
quiet were imprisoned. As reported in Matthew's Gospel, the
authorities propagated the lie that Jesus' body had been stolen by His
disciples.[15]

[1] *See, e.g.,* Thomas W. Case, *The Shroud of Turin and the C-14 Dating Fiasco* (Cincinnati: White Horse Press 1997); Rodney Hoare, *The Turin Shroud is Genuine* (London: Souvenir Press 1994) 95; Stefano M. Paci, "All Those Carbon 14 Errors," *30 Days* (1993–No. 9) 60.

[2] *See* Joseph G. Marino and M. Sue Benford, "Evidence For the Skewing of the C-14 Dating of the Shroud of Turin Due to Repairs" (2000), and Historical Support of a 16th Century Restoration in the Shroud C-14 Sample Area (2002). http://www.shroud.com. This thesis may be supported by a statistical analysis challenging the Carbon-14 dating: Remi Van Haelst, "Radiocarbon Dating the Shroud" (1997). http://www.shroud.com.

[3] *See* Jim Barrett, "Science & the Shroud." http://www.shroud.com. Supporters and debunkers argue over many other issues, such as whether grains of pollen found on the Shroud prove its origin in Jerusalem. *Compare* Mary & Alan Whanger, *The Shroud of Turin: An Adventure of Discovery* (Franklin, TN: Providence House Publishers 1998), at ch. 7, *and* Avinoam Danim, "Pressed Flowers: Where Did the Shroud of Turin Originate?—A Botanical Quest" (1997), http://www.shroud.com, *with* Vaughn M. Bryant, Jr., "Does Pollen Prove the Shroud Authentic?," *Biblical Archaeology Review* (Nov/Dec 2000).

[4] *See, e.g.,* Gilbert R. Lavoie, *Resurrected* (Allen, TX: Thomas More 2000), and *Unlocking the Secrets of the Shroud* (Allen, TX: Thomas More 1998); Ian Wilson, *The Blood and the Shroud* (New York: The Free Press 1998); Mary and Alan Whanger, *The Shroud of Turin*; Gino Moretto, *The Shroud: A Guide* (London: St. Pauls 1998); Kenneth E. Stevenson and Gary R. Habermas, *Verdict on the Shroud* (Ann Arbor, MI: Servant Books 1981); Jack Kilmon, "The Shroud of Turin." http:// www.shroud.com.

[5] For the location of the tomb, *see* Dan Bahat, "Does the Holy Sepulchre Church Mark the Burial of Jesus?," *Biblical Archaeology Review* (May/June 1986).

[6] The description which Sister Emmerich gave of the blocking stone was clearly not of a disk-shaped one that rolled easily into place, in contradiction to the image which can be formed from reading the Gospel accounts. However, one scholar suggests that the Gospel accounts in Greek do not necessarily imply that a round stone was used, and he furthermore asserts that, in that time period, a square or rectangular blocking stone, which is what Sister Emmerich saw, was the shape normally used. *See* Amos Kloner, "Did A Rolling Stone Close Jesus' Tomb?," *Biblical Archaeology Review* (Sept/Oct 1999).

[7] Sister Emmerich had visions of the Blessed Virgin Mary entering Temple service at the age of three and leaving at the age of fourteen to wed Joseph. Contrary to Sister Emmerich's visions and various apocrypha mentioning the practice, most modern biblical scholars do not believe that there were Temple virgins—an opinion which is usually expressed in their commentaries on the apocryphal Protevangelium of James. *See, e.g.,* Edgar Hennecke, *New Testament Apocrypha* 1:372; Mary Clayton, *The Apocryphal Gospels of Mary in Anglo-Saxon England* (Cambridge: Cambridge U. Press 1998) 12; Charles L. Quarles, *Midrash Criticism* (New York: University Press of America 1998)

126–27. However, it must be kept in mind that the visions of Sister Emmerich did not correspond in many ways with the Protevangelium of James, and thus the scholarly criticisms of the latter are inapplicable to the former on many points.

For more than four centuries, the Catholic Church has celebrated the Feast of the Presentation of the Blessed Virgin Mary, without explicitly specifying when she was presented in the Temple, or whether she lived there. See the entry for the "Blessed Virgin Mary" in The Catholic Encyclopedia. http:// www.newadvent.org/cathen. There are a number of authorities in opposition to the scholars who opine that Temple virgins existed only in pagan religions. See especially 2 Baruch 10:19, a verse in the Book of the Apocalypse of Baruch, the Son of Neriah, probably composed around the end of the first century A.D., which strongly implies the existence of Temple virgins, albeit prior to the destruction of the First Temple. See similar indication of Temple virgins making Temple veils in Louis Ginzberg, Legends of the Jews 3:303–04 (Philadelphia: Jewish Pub. Soc. of America 1911). Other authorities suggestive of such a group are cited in the TAN Books edition of the Life of the Blessed Virgin Mary, in the footnote at 128.

[8] The story of Joseph of Arimathea's imprisonment and escape is not found in any of the Gospels. The apocryphal Acts of Pilate (Gospel of Nicodemus) includes a fanciful tale of his imprisonment, but the major details of this lengthy story are otherwise very different from what Sister Emmerich related, and thus her visions were not based on that apocrypha. In the latter, Jesus Himself frees Joseph, whose escape is immediately noted because he is sent for by the Sanhedrin, which intends to kill him. Later, Joseph is found in Arimathea and all rejoice, confess that they have sinned against him, welcome him back, and, most unbelievable of all, listen to him lecture them about Jesus. See Edgar Hennecke, New Testament Apocrypha 1:449.

For a discussion of the bizarre legends which grew up about Joseph of Arimathea, including that he was the guardian of the young Jesus and took Him to England for a number of years (a conceit which formed the basis for William Blake's poem "Jerusalem"), see Raymond E. Brown, The Death of the Messiah 2:1233–34; C.C. Dobson, Did Our Lord Visit Britain as They Say in Cornwall and Somerset? (Glastonbury: Avalon Press 1936).

[9] Catechism of the Catholic Church §§ 633–34, citing to 1 P 4:6. To the same effect see 1 P 3:18–19; Ep 4:7–10; Rm 10:6–7. Christ's descent into hell was described in Ode 42 of the Odes of Solomon, a first century Christian work. See James H. Charlesworth (ed.), The Old Testament Pseudepigrapha 2:770–71 (New York: Doubleday & Co. 1985). It is also imagined at length in the apocryphal Acts of Pilate (Gospel of Nicodemus), and in other apocrypha. For a survey of writings on the descent, see Heidi J. Hornik & Mikeal C. Parsons, "The Harrowing of Hell," Bible Review (June 2003) 18. There is a Calvinist doctrine, picked up by the Catholic theologian Hans Urs von Balthasar, that the soul of Christ actually descended into the Hell of the damned as a damned

soul in order to endure fully the Father's wrath for the purpose of our salvation. This doctrine is denied by the Catholic Church. *See* "Anne Barbeau Gardiner Answers Jacques Servais," *New Oxford Review* (September 2002) 42–45.

¹⁰ Ph 2:9–10.

¹¹ 1 Co 15:14.

¹² *See Catechism of the Catholic Church* §§ 638–39.

¹³ *See, e.g.,* Malcolm L. Peel, "The Resurrection in Recent Scholarly Research," *Bible Review* (August 1989) 14.

¹⁴ *See* Lucio Brunelli, "And Jesus Appeared to Mary," *30 Days* (1994–No. 4) (citing an address by Pope John Paul II and other sources).

¹⁵ In our own times, a similar fiction became the best-selling novel, *The Passover Plot*, by Hugh J. Schonfield (New York: Bantam Books 1967).

# CHAPTER TWENTY-THREE

*The Risen Christ Appears to His Disciples and Apostles*

The Gospels of Mark and Luke are the source of the famous account of the appearance of the Risen Christ to two disciples traveling along the road to Emmaus immediately after His Resurrection. Although the Gospels do not identify the disciples, according to Sister Emmerich, one was Luke, the future Evangelist; the other was Cleophas, whom she identified as a grandson of Mary Cleophas' paternal uncle. Neither one had been a disciple for long, and their faith was shaken by Jesus' execution. The Gospels report their encounter with Jesus (although they were supernaturally prevented from recognizing Him) as they were traveling away from Jerusalem, with the result that their minds were opened to the passages of Scripture which showed why the Messiah had to die. The three then stopped to eat at a public-house, where Luke and Cleophas finally were enabled to recognize Him as He broke the bread for them, as set forth in the Gospels.

Instantly, Jesus vanished from their sight, and so Luke and Cleophas went back at once to the Cenacle in Jerusalem. There, they found all the Apostles, except Thomas, plus Joseph of Arimathea, Nicodemus and other disciples, in prayer. In the open hall were the Blessed Virgin Mary, Mary Cleophas and Magdalene. While the group was still rejoicing at the news from the two returned disciples, Jesus appeared to the group:

"Jesus was come in through the closed doors. He was robed in a long, white garment simply girded. They did not appear to be really conscious of His approach, until He passed through the circles and stood in their midst under the lamp. Then they became very much amazed and agitated. He showed them His hands and feet and, opening His garment, disclosed the Wound in His side. He spoke to them and, seeing that they were very much terrified, He asked for something to eat. I saw rays of light proceeding from His mouth. The Apostles and disciples were as if completely ravished.

"After that I saw Him teaching and imparting strength. The circles around Him were still triple, the ten Apostles forming the inmost. Thomas was not there. It appeared wonderful to me that part of Jesus' words and instructions was heard by the ten Apostles only, though I ought not to say heard, for I did not see Jesus moving His lips. He was resplendent. Light streamed over them from His hands, His feet, His side, His mouth, as He breathed upon them. It flowed in upon them. They became interiorly recollected, and felt themselves endued with power to forgive sins, to baptize and heal and impose hands; and I saw that, if they drank any poisonous thing, it would be without receiving harm from it.

"But here I saw no talking with the mouth, no hearing with the ears. I knew not how it was, but I felt that Jesus did not impart these gifts with words, that He spoke not in words, and that all did not hear what He said; but that He infused these gifts substantially, with a substance as it were, with a flashing of light in upon their soul. . . . *Jesus explained to the Apostles several points of Holy Scripture relative to Himself and the Blessed Sacrament, and ordered the latter to be venerated at the close of the Sabbath solemnities.*"

Two thousand years later, veneration of the Blessed Sacrament is a practice still alive and treasured within the Catholic Church:

> "The Catholic Church has always offered and still offers to the sacrament of the Eucharist the cult of adoration, not only during Mass, but also outside of it, reserving the consecrated hosts with the utmost care, exposing them to the solemn veneration of the faithful, and carrying them in procession."[1]

### Proselytizing and Persecution

No sooner had the Apostles, other than Thomas, been strengthened by the Risen Christ, than they began to speak out and to perform cures in His name. Peter spoke fearlessly and honestly about the events of Christ's Passion, including his own denial of the Lord. According to Sister Emmerich, who related a talk Peter gave at the school in Thaanach, when Peter told of "His rising again on the third day, of His appearing first to the women, then to some of the others, and lastly to all in general, and he called upon all present that had seen Him to witness to His words, upwards of a hundred hands were raised in answer to his call. . . . Peter then called upon the people to leave all things, to join the new Community, and to follow Jesus. He invited the less courageous to go to Jerusalem where the Faithful would share all they had with them."

Peter specifically reached out with a message of forgiveness to those who had acted against Jesus out of a wrong understanding. He was inspired to instruct his countrymen from Solomon's Portico, shortly after the Resurrection, in these words: *"You disowned the Holy and Just One and preferred instead to be granted the release of a murderer. You put to death the Author of life. . . . Yet I know, my brothers, that you acted out of ignorance, just as your leaders did."*[2]

At the same time, Sister Emmerich saw that the High Priests were vigorously attempting to stamp out the New Way. They sent out deputies, inquiring who was in contact with the disciples, and discharging such persons from any public employment they had. Some followers of Jesus were arrested. In addition, the authorities were at pains to attempt to block access to the Holy Sepulchre, by planting hedges and digging ditches.

### Doubting Thomas Sees and Believes

Although Jesus appeared in many places and to many people, He did not appear for some time to Thomas, who was firm in his doubts and virtually cut himself off from his fellow Apostles. As St. John reported, Thomas even told them: "Unless I . . . put my finger into the place of the nails, and put my hand into His side, I will not believe!" The day came when Thomas attended a ceremonial meal of the Apostles and disciples, at which occurred the never-to-be-forgotten encounter between Jesus and Thomas, as reported by St. John, and as described in more detail by Sister Emmerich:

"Jesus did not enter walking properly so called, that is, in the usual way of mortals, and yet it was not a floating along, or hovering as I have seen spirits doing. It reminded me, as I saw them all falling back, of a priest in his alb passing through a crowded congregation. Everything in the hall appeared to become suddenly large and bright. Jesus was environed with light. The Apostles had fallen back from the radiant circle, otherwise they would not have been able to see Him.

"Jesus' first words were: 'Peace be to you!' . . . Jesus now slipped under the lamp, and the Apostles closed around Him. Thomas, very much frightened at the sight of the Lord, timidly drew back. But Jesus, grasping his right hand in His own right hand, took the forefinger and laid the tip of it in the wound of His left hand; then taking the left hand in His own left, He placed the forefinger in the wound of His right hand, lastly, taking again Thomas's right hand in His own right, He put it, without uncovering His breast, under His garment, and laid the fore and middle fingers in the wound of His right side. He spoke some words as He did this. With the exclamation: 'My Lord, and my God!' Thomas sank down like one unconscious, Jesus still holding his hand. The nearest of the Apostles supported him, and Jesus raised him up by the hand. . . . When Jesus grasped Thomas's hand, I saw that His wounds were not like bloody marks, but like little radiant suns."

### Peter is Invested as Chief Shepherd

*Sister Emmerich saw that on this same occasion, after Jesus dealt with doubting Thomas, He invested Peter in his office as chief shepherd, with special symbols and rites:*

"John brought . . . the large, colored, embroidered mantle, which James had received from Mary and on which, in those last days, the holy women had worked at Bethania. Besides that, he brought also a hollow, slender staff, high and bent at the top like a shepherd's crook. It was shining and looked like a long pipe. The mantle was white with broad red stripes, and on it were embroidered in colors wheat, grapes, a lamb, and other symbols. It was wide and long enough to reach to the feet. It was fastened over the breast with a little four cornered metal shield and bordered down the front with red stripes which were crossed by shorter ones on which were letters. It had a collar and a kind of hood, of a sky-blue color, which could be drawn up over the neck and head.

"Peter next knelt down before Jesus, who gave him to eat a round morsel, like a little cake. I do not remember seeing any plate, nor do I know where Jesus got the morsel, but I do know that it shone with light. I felt that Peter received with it some special power, and I saw also strength and vigor poured into his soul when Jesus breathed upon him. This action of Jesus was not a simple, ordinary breathing. It was words, a power, something substantial that Peter received, but no merely spoken words. Jesus put His mouth to Peter's mouth, then to his ears, and poured that strength into each of the three, It was not the Holy Spirit Himself, but something that the Holy Spirit was to quicken and vivify in Peter at Pentecost. Jesus laid His hands on him, gave him a special kind of strength, and invested him with chief power over the others. Then He placed upon him the mantle that John, who was standing next to Him, was holding on his arm, and put the staff into his hand. While performing this action, Jesus said that the mantle would preserve in him all the strength and virtue that He had just imparted to him, and that he should wear it whenever he had to make use of the power with which he had been endued."

### Jesus Appears to Five Hundred Brothers

St. Paul mentioned in passing that the Risen Christ once appeared to five hundred brothers at once.[3] Sister Emmerich's visions locate the occurrence as being on a plateau above the Sea of Galilee, where a

crowd was spread out on a hill, and Peter was teaching them from a
pillar. Jesus approached, shining with light, and took over the
instruction from Peter:

"He spoke of abandoning one's relatives, of following Him, and
of the persecution that they would have to endure. About two hundred
of His hearers withdrew when they heard Him talking of such things.
All these were gone away, said Jesus. He had spoken to them mildly
in order not to scandalize the weak. *He uttered some very grave words
upon the sufferings and persecution of those that would follow Him
upon earth, and He alluded to their eternal reward. He addressed these
remarks to the Apostles and disciples, as He had once before done in
His last instruction in the Temple. He told them that they should at
first remain in Jerusalem. When He should have sent them the Spirit,
they should baptize in the name of the Father, and of the Son, and of
the Holy Ghost, and should at once establish a Community. Then He
told them how they should disperse, form distant Communities, meet
together once more, again separate for far-off countries, and receive
at last the baptism of blood. . . .* While Jesus was speaking, the spirits
of the ancient Patriarchs encircled the whole assembly, though
invisibly. Jesus vanished. His disappearance was like a light suddenly
extinguished in their midst. Many fell prostrate on their face. Peter
again taught and prayed. This was Jesus' principal apparition in
Galilee, where He taught and gave proof to all of His Resurrection.
The other apparitions were more secret."

### The New Community Increases Greatly

The growth of a cohesive community of believers in Jesus as the
Christ was spurred by the breaking of ties with non-believers, forced
by the authorities headed by the High Priests. Perhaps the most
striking aspect of the new community, which came together first in
Jerusalem, and then relocated to areas near Bethania after Pentecost,
was that, as noted in the Acts of the Apostles, all things were held in
common.[4] Newcomers came with their possessions to donate—money,
sheep, goats, birds, all manner of woven stuffs, etc. There were a
number of wealthy and important men and women, including
Lazarus, Joseph of Arimathea, and Nicodemus, who contributed their
own fortunes, lands and houses, and who personally served in
organizing and distributing welfare, which included food and clothing
for the poor. The Apostles did similar work, until the appointment
of deacons.[5]

In her visions, Sister Emmerich saw the Blessed Virgin Mary,
Peter's wife and stepdaughter, Mark's wife, and many other leading

women at work with their hands. In this regard, Sister Emmerich had this rather significant vision of a piece of embroidery: "Once they embroidered a representation of the Most Holy Trinity. It was like God the Father handing the cross to the Son, who looked like a High Priest. *From both proceeded the Holy Ghost, though not in the form of a dove, for instead of wings there were arms. The figures were arranged more in a triangular form than one below the other.*" Note that this embroidery was consistent with the Church's later formulation in the Nicene Creed, that the Holy Spirit, "the Lord, the giver of life . . . proceeds from the Father and the Son."

## Jesus Specially Empowers the Blessed Virgin Mary

One of the mystical visions of Sister Emmerich concerned the special empowering of the Blessed Virgin Mary by Jesus, prior to Pentecost. The setting was the Cenacle, where the inner circle had gathered:

"When midnight had sounded, the Blessed Virgin kneeling received the Blessed Sacrament from Peter. He carried the Bread that had been consecrated and broken by Jesus on the little plate belonging to the chalice. At that instant I saw Jesus appear to her, though not visible to the others. Mary was penetrated with light and splendor. She was still in prayer. I saw that the Holy Apostles were very reverent in their manner toward her. Mary next went to the little dwelling on the right of the entrance into the court of the Cenacle, in which she now had her apartment. Here standing she recited the Magnificat, the Canticle of the three youths in the fiery furnace, and the 131st Psalm [Humble Trust in God].

"*The day was beginning to dawn when I saw Jesus entering through the closed doors. He spoke long to her, telling her that she was to help the Apostles, and explaining what she was to be to them. He gave her power over the whole Church, endued her with His strength, His protecting influence, and it was as if His light flowed in upon her, as if He penetrated her through and through. I can not express it. . . . When Jesus appeared to Mary in her cell, I saw her head encircled by a crown of stars as it had been at her Communion.*"

## Mary—Mediatrix of All Graces

*The Catholic Church has always understood the words "Woman, behold, this is thy son," spoken by Jesus on the Cross, to be a commission to Mary to act as the Mother of the Church which He had just established. While not in any way contradicting St. Paul, who spoke of Jesus Christ as the one mediator between man and God,*[6] *the*

*Church has proclaimed that Mary's maternal role includes acting— in a subordinate way to Jesus—as "Mediatrix" of all graces.* According to the Council Fathers at Vatican II:

> This maternity of Mary in the order of grace began with the consent which she gave in faith at the Annunciation and which she sustained without wavering beneath the cross, and lasts until the eternal fulfillment of all the elect. Taken up to heaven she did not lay aside this salvific duty, but by her constant intercession continued to bring us the gifts of eternal salvation. By her maternal charity, she cares for the brethren of her Son, who still journey on earth surrounded by dangers and difficulties, until they are led into the happiness of their true home. Therefore the Blessed Virgin is invoked by the Church under the titles of Advocate, Auxiliatrix, Adjutrix, and Mediatrix.[7]

*According to Sister Emmerich's visions, this role for the Blessed Virgin Mary was established by the Risen Christ on the morning of His Ascension.* The day began early, at the Cenacle, where Jesus again confirmed Peter's authority over the others. He presented His Mother to them as their mother, their Mediatrix and their Advocate, and she blessed them. Sister Emmerich's further visions confirm the Blessed Virgin Mary acting as Mediatrix of Graces:

"I saw Jesus on a throne, shining like the sun; by Him were Mary, Joseph and John, and before Him knelt poor repentant sinners, supplicating Mary to intercede for them. I saw then that Mary is a true refuge for sinners. All that fly to her find favor, if they only have a little faith. . . . Above the dome lay a still higher world in which I saw the Most Blessed Trinity represented by three figures . . . Around them sat the twenty-four ancients in a circle. The cherubim and seraphim with many other spirits stood around the throne of God hymning incessant praise. *In the center above Michael, stood Mary surrounded by innumerable circles of luminous souls, angels, and virgins. The grace of Jesus flows through Mary to the three archangels, each of whom radiates three kinds of gifts upon three of the nine inferior choirs. These in turn pour them forth upon all nature and the whole human race.*"[8]

## The Ascension—Jesus Disappears in Light

Sister Emmerich's visions add to the accounts of the Ascension of Jesus found in the Gospel of Luke and the Acts of the Apostles.[9] As she saw it, Jesus went out at dawn, followed by the Blessed Virgin Mary, the Apostles, and disciples, in a procession which covered some of the same paths as He had taken on Palm Sunday and on the Way of the Cross. Where passage had been blocked by the authorities, disciples raced ahead and, using implements from adjacent gardens, made the way passable again. Jesus led the way to the Mount of Olives. There, a crowd gathered, and He proceeded to teach them before continuing His ascent.

"Jesus at each instant shone more brightly and His motions became more rapid. The disciples hastened after Him, but it was impossible to overtake Him. When He reached the top of the mountain, He was resplendent as a beam of white sunlight. A shining circle, glancing in all the colors of the rainbow fell from heaven around Him. The pressing crowd stood in a wide circle outside, as if blending with it. Jesus Himself shone still more brightly than the glory about Him. He laid the left hand on His breast and, raising the right turned slowly around, blessing the whole world. The crowd stood motionless. I saw all receive the benediction. Jesus did not impart it with the flat, open hand, like the rabbis, but like the Christian Bishops. With great joy I felt His blessing of the whole world.

"And now the rays of light from above united with the glory emanating from Jesus, and I saw Him disappearing, dissolving as it were in the light from heaven, vanishing as He rose. I lost sight of His head first. It appeared as if one sun was lost in another, as if one flame entered another, as if a spark floated into a flame. It was as if one were gazing into the full midday splendors of the sun, though this light was whiter and clearer. Full day compared with this would be dark. First, I lost sight of Jesus' head, then His whole person, and lastly His feet radiant with light disappeared in the celestial glory. I saw innumerable souls from all sides going into that light and vanishing on high with the Lord. I can not say that I saw Him becoming apparently smaller and smaller like something flying up in the air, for He disappeared as it were in a cloud of light."

## The Ecstasy of Pentecost

On the eve of the feast of Pentecost (the Greek name for the Jewish agricultural Feast of Weeks, which came seven weeks after Passover), the Apostles, disciples and Holy Women were gathered for prayer in the Cenacle. Sister Emmerich saw a cloud of light descend over the house, with a noise as of rushing wind. She described the scene inside as follows:

"The Apostles, the disciples, and the women became more and more silent, more deeply recollected. Afterward there shot from the rushing cloud streams of white light down upon the house and its surroundings. The streams intersected one another in sevenfold rays, and below each intersection resolved into fine threads of light and fiery drops. The point at which the seven streams intersected was surrounded by a rainbow light, in which floated a luminous figure with outstretched wings, or rays of light that looked like wings, attached to the shoulders. In that same instant, the whole house and its surroundings were penetrated through and through with light. The five-branched lamp no longer shone.

"The assembled faithful were ravished in ecstasy. Each involuntarily threw back his head, and raised his eyes eagerly on high, while into the mouth of everyone there flowed a stream of light like a burning tongue of fire. It looked as if they were breathing, as if they were eagerly drinking in the fire, and as if their ardent desire flamed forth from their mouth to meet the entering flame. The sacred fire was poured forth also upon the disciples, and the women present in the antechamber, and thus the resplendent cloud gradually dissolved as if in a rain of light. The flames descended on each in different colors and in different degrees of intensity.

"After that effusion of heavenly light, a joyous courage pervaded the assembly. All were full of emotion, and as if intoxicated with joy and confidence. They gathered around the Blessed Virgin who was, I saw, the only one perfectly calm, the only one that retained a quiet, holy self-possession. The Apostles embraced one another and, urged by joyous confidence, exclaimed: 'What were we? What are we now?' The Holy Women too embraced. The disciples in the side halls were similarly affected, and the Apostles hastened out to them. A new life full of joy, of confidence, and of courage had been infused into all. Their joy found vent in thanksgiving. They ranged for prayer, gave thanks and praised God with great emotion."

### The Apostles Carry Out Directions Given by Jesus

It may be wondered how the Apostles and disciples decided upon their missions after Jesus had ascended to His Father. The answer, according to Sister Emmerich, is that shortly before His Passion, Jesus gave the Apostles many instructions regarding the development of the Church after He was no longer on earth, and asked them to write down His words:

"He touched upon many things that would take place after His return to the Father. To Peter He said that He would have much to suffer, but he should not fear, he should stand firm at the head of the

Community *(the Church)*, which would increase wonderfully. For three years he should with John and James the Lesser remain with the Faithful in Jerusalem. . . . Zacchaeus was to go to the region of Galaad; Philip and Bartholomew, to Gessur on the confines of Syria. . . . James the Greater and one of the disciples were sent to the pagan regions north of Capernaum. Thomas and Matthew were dispatched to Ephesus, in order to prepare the country where at a future day Jesus' mother and many of those that believed in Him were to dwell. They wondered greatly at the fact of Mary's going to live there. Thaddeus and Simon were to go first to Samaria, though none cared to go there. All preferred cities entirely pagan.

"Jesus told them that they would all meet twice in Jerusalem before going to preach the Gospel in distant pagan lands. He spoke of a man between Samaria and Jericho, who would like Himself perform many miracles, though by the power of the devil. He would manifest a desire of conversion, and they must kindly receive him, for even the devil should contribute to His glory. Simon Magus was meant by these words of Jesus."[10]

### How Was the Early Church Organized?

The visions of Sister Emmerich previously recounted make it clear that, in institutionalizing His Church, Jesus went far beyond merely appointing Peter as the chief shepherd, for example by expressly putting the Apostles hierarchically over the disciples. The Apostles then continued this work to transform groups of individual believers into communities whose faith would be safeguarded by the Apostles and their successors. In her visions, she saw all the Apostles meeting in Jerusalem three years after the Resurrection. At that time, Peter and John took the Blessed Virgin Mary, who had been baptized by John, to Ephesus, to keep her safe from the persecution of the followers of Christ.

Three years later, again according to Sister Emmerich, the Apostles held a final, and highly significant assembly in Jerusalem: "They drew up the Creed, made rules,[11] relinquished all that they possessed, distributed it to the poor, and divided the Church into dioceses, after which they separated and went into far off heathen countries." Thus, Sister Emmerich's visions support the Church's teaching that the first bishops appeared at the beginning of the Church's history—being the Apostles themselves or persons appointed by them[12]—and they identify the Church's first attempt to formulate a creed as also being the work of the Apostles.[13]

## The Death of the Blessed Virgin Mary

Near Ephesus, John built the Blessed Virgin Mary a small stone house, divided into rooms by movable wicker screens. She lived there alone with a maid, and was visited by the Holy Women, John, and, from time to time, various Apostles and disciples. She spent a great deal of time in devotions, especially a Way of the Cross which she marked out near her home. Twice, the Blessed Virgin Mary visited Jerusalem. The second time she evidenced such weakness that a tomb was prepared for her in a cave on the Mount of Olives (later giving rise to an incorrect account that she had been buried in Jerusalem), but she recovered sufficiently to return to Ephesus.

Sister Emmerich's visions agree with the apocryphal tales that the Blessed Virgin Mary, knowing she was dying, bade a formal farewell to the assembled Apostles, except for Thomas, who had not yet arrived for the ceremony, and James the Greater, who had by then been executed. Each knelt in turn at her side, while she laid her hands crosswise over him and blessed him. She did likewise with the disciples and Holy Women. Mass was then celebrated by Peter, vested in white and red, at an altar in the Blessed Virgin's oratory. Peter took the Blessed Sacrament to Mary, and then anointed her with Holy Oil. Then, John bore her the chalice of the Most Sacred Blood:

"After Communion, Mary spoke no more. Her countenance, blooming and smiling as in youth, was raised above. I no longer saw the roof of her chamber, and the lamp appeared to be suspended in the open air. A pathway of light arose from Mary up to the heavenly Jerusalem, up to the throne of the Most Holy Trinity. On either side of this pathway, I saw clouds of light, out of which gazed angelic faces. Mary raised her arms to the Heavenly Jerusalem. Her body with all its wrappings was floating so high above the couch that I could see under it. A figure of light, also with upraised arms, appeared to issue from Mary. The two choirs of angels united under this figure and soared up with it, as if separating it from the body, which now sank back upon the couch, the hands crossed upon the breast."

According to Sister Emmerich's visions, the Blessed Virgin Mary truly died, and did not merely fall asleep. A burial place was prepared by the men in the grotto which had been designated to represent the Holy Sepulchre at the end of Mary's Way of the Cross. The women, including John Mark's mother, washed and embalmed the body. When they were finished, Peter anointed the forehead, hands and feet. A wreath of white, red and blue flowers was placed on her head, and a transparent veil over the face. Her light body, wrapped in linen, was lowered into a wooden coffin, which was carried on a litter by the Apostles to the gravesite. After depositing the coffin in the grotto, the tomb was shut by a wicker screen, in front of which blooming flowers and bushes were immediately planted."

### The Assumption into Heaven of the Blessed Virgin Mary

Sister Emmerich had this mystical vision of the assent of Mary's soul to heaven directly following her death: "Many holy souls, among whom I recognized Joseph, Anne, Joachim, John the Baptist, Zachary, and Elizabeth, came to meet her. But up she soared, followed by them, to her Son, whose wounds were flashing light far more brilliant than that which surrounded Him. He received her and placed in her hand a scepter, pointing at the same time over the whole circumference of the earth. At last I saw, and the sight filled me with joy, a multitude of souls released from purgatory and soaring up to heaven, and I received the surety that every year, on the feast of Mary's assumption, many of her devout clients are freed from purgatory."

Catholics believe that not only the soul, but also the physical body, of the Blessed Virgin Mary did not long remain in the tomb; rather, it was "assumed" into Heaven:

"The Immaculate Virgin, preserved free from all stain of original sin, when the course of her earthly life was finished, was taken up body and soul into heavenly glory, and exalted by the Lord as Queen over all things, so that she might be the more fully conformed to her Son, the Lord of lords and conqueror of sin and death." The Assumption of the Blessed Virgin is a singular participation in her Son's Resurrection and an anticipation of the resurrection of other Christians.[14]

Fanciful accounts of the Assumption appeared in fourth century apocrypha, though they may have been circulating orally earlier.[15] Belief in it has been widely held since at least the middle of the seventh century, when a feast was established, to be celebrated on August 15th. The dogma of the Assumption, defined in the Apostolic Constitution *Munificentissimus Deus*, by Pope Pius XII in 1950, was arrived at by a slow process of reflection, on the part of the laity as well as the clergy, involving reasoning such as the following:

Her leaving the world ought to answer to her entering the world. Immaculate in her Conception and spotless in her life, it is becoming that the Virgin be preserved, not from death, but from the decomposition of the tomb which is properly the punishment for sin. United as she was during her life to her divine Son by the closest union and associated with all the mysteries of His life, how would she be separated from Him after death? Her virginity, confirmed by her admirable Motherhood, calls for the same privilege. For this body which has given birth without corruption to the body of Christ cannot become the prey of worms.[16]

Sister Emmerich had a mystical vision of the assumption of the body of the Blessed Virgin Mary taking place after her soul came down from heaven and was reunited with her body—just such a reunion as had happened in the case of her Son: "On the night following the burial, took place the bodily assumption of the Blessed Virgin into heaven. I saw on this night several of the Apostles and holy women in the little garden, praying and singing Psalms before the grotto. I saw a broad pathway of light descend from heaven and rest upon the tomb. In it were circles of glory full of angels, in the midst of whom the Resplendent soul of the Blessed Virgin came floating down. Before her went her Divine Son, the marks of His wounds flashing with light. . . . The blessed soul of Mary, floating before Jesus, penetrated through the rock and into the tomb, out of which she again arose radiant with light in her glorified body and, escorted by the entire multitude of celestial spirits, returned in triumph to the heavenly Jerusalem."

*The most interesting aspect of Sister Emmerich's visions is that they provide a rationale as to why belief in the Assumption may have begun among the early Christians.*

She saw the Apostle Thomas appearing at Mary's house the day after burial, wanting to pay his last respects: "The Apostles, who had not interrupted their choir-chanting on account of his coming, now gathered around him, raised him up, embraced him, and set before him and his companions bread, honey, and some kind of beverage in little jugs. After that they accompanied him with lights to the tomb. Two disciples bent the shrubbery to one side. Thomas, Eleasar, and John went in and prayed before the coffin. Then John loosened the three straps that bound it, for it rose high enough above the troughlike couch to admit of being opened. *They stood the lid of the coffin on one side and, to their intense astonishment, beheld only the empty winding sheets lying like a husk, or shell, and in perfect order. Only over the face was it drawn apart, and over the breast slightly opened. The swathing bands of the arms and hands lay separate, as if gently drawn off, but in perfect order. The Apostles gazed in amazement, their hands raised. John cried out: 'She is no longer here!' The others came in quickly, wept, prayed, looking upward with raised arms, and finally cast themselves on the ground, remembering the radiant cloud of the preceding night.* Then, rising, they took the winding sheet just as it was, all the grave linens, and the coffin to keep as relics, and returned to the house by the Holy Way, praying and singing Psalms."[17]

*As the empty tomb of Christ proved to His followers that He had conquered death, so the empty tomb of His Mother gave proof to them of her own resurrection and assumption into heaven, body and soul—initiating her eternal role as Mother to the Church. Deo gratias!*

---

[1] See *Catechism of the Catholic Church* § 1378.
[2] Acts 3:14–15, 17 (emphasis added).
[3] 1 Cor 15:6.
[4] Acts 2:44, 4:32.
[5] Acts 6:1–6.
[6] 1 Tm 2:5–6.
[7] See *Dogmatic Constitution on the Church* (*Lumen Gentium*) § 62 (Boston: St. Paul Books & Media 1965) http://www.vatican.va/archive/hist_councils/ii_vatican_council/documents.
[8] Consider also the following prophecy by Pope John Paul II of a role for the Blessed Virgin Mary at the end of time:
In the mystery of the Assumption is expressed the faith of the Church, according to which Mary is "united by a close and indissoluble bond" to Christ, for if as Virgin and Mother she was singularly united with Him *in His first coming*, so through her continued collaboration with Him she will also be united with Him in expectation of the second: "redeemed in an especially sublime manner by reason of the merits of her Son," she also has that specifically maternal role of mediatrix of mercy *at His final coming*, when all those that belong to Christ "shall be made alive," when "the last enemy to be destroyed is death" (1 Cor 15:26).
See Pope John Paul II, *Redemptoris Mater* § 41, Encyclical (March 25, 1987). http://www.vatican.va/holy_father/john_paul_ii/encyclicals/documents.
[9] Lk 16:15–19; Acts 1:6–13.
[10] Acts 8:9–13.
[11] *Cf.* "The Didache."
[12] See *Catechism of the Catholic Church* § 77.
[13] Written evidence of a creed exists from the second century on, and there are indications that at least parts of it existed much earlier. *See* the entry for the "Apostles' Creed" in *The Catholic Encyclopedia*. http://www.newadvent.org/cathen.
[14] *Catechism of the Catholic Church* § 966 (quoting *Lumen Gentium*).

[15] *See* Montague R. James, *The Apocryphal New Testament* (New York: Oxford U. Press 1986) 194–227 (the Assumption of the Virgin). The same tales are told in the 13th century work by Jacobus de Voragine, *The Golden Legend.* 2:77.

[16] *See* Joseph Duhr, *The Glorious Assumption of the Mother of God* (New York: P.J. Kenedy & Sons 1950) 52, 65–66; *Munificentissimus Deus,* Apostolic Constitution (November 1, 1950). http://www.ewtn.com/library.

[17] A medieval legend concerning Thomas recounts not only the opening of the coffin for the benefit of Thomas, and the discovery that the body of the Blessed Virgin Mary was not there, but also the posthumous gift by her from Heaven, of her girdle to Thomas, to strengthen his weak faith in her Assumption. *See, e.g.,* "Concerning the Passing of the Blessed Virgin Mary." http://www.ccel.org/fathers2; Jacobus de Voragine, *The Golden Legend* 2:92; "Madonna della Cintola" (regarding a painting by Benozzo Gozzoli). http://www.kfki.hu/~arthp/html/g/gozzoli/1early/05cintol.html. Two churches claim possession of Mary's girdle, dating back many centuries. One is the Roman Catholic Cathedral in Prato, Italy; the other is a Syriac Orthodox church in Kerala, India. As to the latter, *see* "Manarcaud St. Mary's Jacobite Syrian Church." http://www.geocities.com/malankarav3/ManarcadChurch.htm.

# POSTSCRIPT

There are days during the year when I pay special attention at Mass to the Old Testament lesson: days when the lector intones, "a reading from the Book of Baruch." Actually, his full Hebrew name was "Berekhyahu"—"blessed of God"—according to the mark of his seal on lumps of clay which have survived unbroken for twenty-six centuries. He was a royal scribe and confidant of the major prophet Jeremiah, a man so important that four apocalypses were attributed to him.

I realize that it is highly unlikely that I am his descendant, for "Baruch" was a *given* name, not a patronymic. Still, just hearing the name we share causes me to wonder whether one of my forefathers stood in the mob before Pontius Pilate, crying out, "Crucify Him! Crucify Him!"

My father's father, born in France, was a Protestant; how far back, and for what reasons the conversion occurred, is lost in time. My mother's family, too, was Protestant, and that was the faith into which I was baptized. As a child I was a Presbyterian, a Dutch Reformed, a Congregationalist—or whatever denomination happened to have the best preaching and fellowship in the town we then resided in.

It was not until my mid-twenties, after I had finished my education and was in military service, that I felt a need for God in my life. Fortunately, at that time I was dating a young woman who was a devout Catholic, as was her family.

As part of my marriage preparation, I took a course of instruction in the Catholic faith. What persuaded me of its truth was the words of the Gospels recorded in a good, old Protestant Bible—the King James Version—about the Real Presence of the Lord in the Eucharistic meal. According to the three Synoptic Gospels, on the night of the Last Supper, Jesus specially took bread, blessed it, broke it, and gave it to His disciples, saying "Take, eat; *this is my body.*" And He took the cup, gave thanks, and gave it to them, saying "Drink ye all of it, for *this is my blood* of the new testament, which is shed for many for the remission of sins."

If Jesus had been speaking metaphorically, He would have used the words "this is *like* my body," or "this *represents* my body," or even "this is *a symbol* of my body"—*but that is not what any of the Gospel accounts state.* Similarly, St. John recorded that, after Jesus taught that "except ye eat the flesh of the Son of man, and drink his blood, ye have no life in you," "many of his disciples went back, and walked no more with him"—which obviously was because they understood that He was speaking *literally* and not *figuratively.* Now that I thought about it, I saw that the Catholic Church was the one offering eternal life in the Eucharistic celebration, which it had preserved since Apostolic times. And so, at age 26, I became a convert.

Although I then began to read books on religious topics, it was not until thirty years later that I ran across the name of Anne Catherine Emmerich, when I picked up a copy of *The Dolorous Passion of Our Lord Jesus Christ* for Lenten reading. It proved so fascinating that I sought out her visions published in other volumes, and studied them in detail, comparing them with biblical commentaries, apocryphal gospels, archaeological findings, and, most important, the explicit teachings of the Gospels and the Magisterium. For the task, I had no background in languages or training in theology; what I brought to the table was decades of experience as an attorney in attempting to uncover and present to a court the truth about extremely complex matters, through the examination of large quantities of documents and the interrogation of expert and lay witnesses. Not that there were live witnesses to question, of course, but I had thousands of pages of "testimony" just from her to assess, and thousands more pages of "testimony" in the writings of biblical scholars, including those who had considered her revelations.

My fundamental conclusion was that the visions set forth in Sister Emmerich's *Life of Jesus Christ* have the aura of authenticity. Of course, I do not give *more than* human credence to anything that is contained therein—or even *merely* human credence to every point. A few of her observations dealing with subjects other than the life of Jesus are untenably bizarre (including the "blood libel" of the Jews), and one can find a handful of infelicitously worded observations about the Jewish people (whom she pitied rather than despised), as well as trivial inconsistencies and errors. But, I am persuaded that the claimed revelations were neither fraudulent (deliberately contrived) nor false (wrongly imagined by her to be supernatural or substantively inaccurate).

Further, I believe that in the main, the visions related by Sister Emmerich give us a reasonable approximation of actual events in the life of Jesus, that they are consonant with the Magisterium of the Catholic Church, and that they can be of significant spiritual value in illuminating the words of the Gospels. Hopefully, this volume will make her unique insights readily accessible to all who are interested in the Son of Man, whom she served in her lifetime by redemptive suffering.

HURD BARUCH received degrees from Hamilton College, Yale Law School and Columbia University Graduate School of Business, and was elected to membership in Phi Beta Kappa, the Order of the Coif, and Beta Gamma Sigma. He practiced law for more than forty years, in the fields of corporate and securities law and litigation, with particular emphasis on investigating corporate wrongdoing in this country and abroad. He served as an official in the Office of the Secretary of Defense (1962-1964), and at the Securities and Exchange Commission (1969-1972), where he authored *Wall Street: Security Risk* (Washington: Acropolis Books 1971; Baltimore: Penguin Books 1972), a book about the near collapse of the brokerage industry at that time. He has also authored various articles, and a legal treatise. He is now retired in Tucson, where he lives with his wife.